Contributions to Economics

# Contributions to Econometrics and Empirical Economics

The *Contributions to Econometrics and Empirical Economics* book series is a dedicated platform for cutting-edge research and comprehensive textbooks that explore the diverse applications of econometric techniques and other empirical methods in the field of economics. The series is designed to appeal to a wide audience, including academics, advanced students, and practitioners seeking a deeper understanding of econometric and statistical tools as well as other empirical methods and their practical implementation in empirical analysis.

The series welcomes monographs, edited volumes, and textbooks that cover a wide range of topics, including but not limited to

- Development and refinement of econometric methods, including regression analysis, time series analysis, panel data analysis, experimental methods, survey methods, and simulation methods.
- Empirical studies using quantitative or qualitative empirical methods to address pressing economic issues.
- Applications of econometric techniques in macroeconomics, microeconomics, labor economics, health economics, and beyond.
- Policy evaluation using advanced econometric techniques.
- Machine learning and big data applications in econometrics.

Each volume in the series is rigorously reviewed to ensure that it provides high-quality, innovative, and accessible content. The series values works that bridge theoretical insights with empirical realities, providing tools and guidance for those seeking to solve real-world economic challenges.

Whether you are an established expert or an emerging scholar, Contributions to Econometrics and Empirical Economics provides a platform to share your work with a global audience eager to advance the frontiers of econometric and empirical research.

Sarit Maitra

# A Practical Guide to Static and Dynamic Econometric Modelling

## Examples and Analysis with Python Code Embedded

Springer

Sarit Maitra
Alliance Business School
Alliance University
Bengaluru, Karnataka, India

ISSN 1431-1933 ISSN 2197-7178 (electronic)
Contributions to Economics
ISSN 3059-4642 ISSN 3059-4650 (electronic)
Contributions to Econometrics and Empirical Economics
ISBN 978-3-031-86861-0 ISBN 978-3-031-86862-7 (eBook)
https://doi.org/10.1007/978-3-031-86862-7



This Springer imprint is published by the registered company Springer Nature Switzerland AG
The registered company address is: Gewerbestrasse 11, 6330 Cham, Switzerland

# Preface

This book is divided into seven chapters; each serves as a valuable resource for finance professionals, economists, and data scientists looking to understand and apply Econometric models in their work. This book will provide you the confidence and skills when developing the Econometric theories and subsequently models and when evaluating a model that is presented to you. The introductory chapters—particularly Chaps. 1–4—are crucial for developing a theoretical ideas around the topic. To build a solid basis that will aid in the implementation phase, I would recommend delving deeply into these chapters. Subsequent Chaps. 5, 6, and 7 are solely focused on practical implementation part.

- **Chapter 1** Introduces the foundational concepts of Econometrics and discusses about the Econometric modeling and model testing using ordinary least squares regression.
- **Chapter 2** Covers the important assumptions in linear regression, theoretical concepts, and benefits of hypotheses testing.
- **Chapter 3** Introduces the theoretical concepts and significance of dynamic modeling in Econometrics. Different dynamic modeling approaches are covered in this chapter.
- **Chapter 4** Covers a theoretical overview of major foundational models in financial economics, particularly in the field of asset pricing, portfolio management, and risk-return analysis.
- **Chapter 5** Discusses the implementation of CAPM and APT models followed by hypotheses testing procedures.
- **Chapter 6** Discusses the implementation of Auto Regressive models followed by rolling forecast approach.
- **Chapter 7** Discusses dynamic Vector Auto Regression (VAR) and Vector Error Correction (VEC) models and different testing mechanisms.

The journey begins with an introduction to Econometrics, shedding light on its historical evolution and contributions from the key people in the field. This book meticulously outlines the key components of Econometrics, detailing every step from collecting data and formulating hypotheses to specifying models, estimating parameters, making inferences, and predicting outcomes. Readers will learn how to formulate a theoretical model, collect relevant data, specify the model, estimate parameters, conduct hypotheses tests, and make inferences. The book discusses about the linear regression, as the cornerstone of Econometric analysis. It also explores various data transformations, such as log and exponential transformations, and shows how to effectively manage nonlinear relationships within a linear regression framework.

The hypothesis testing and empirical analysis by applying Ordinary Least Squares (OLS) regression is covered in this book. The book addresses assumptions and conducts diagnostic tests for linearity, normality, heteroscedasticity, autocorrelation, multicollinearity, model specification, outlier detection, and parameter stability. The book then moves to advanced topics, explains the Capital Asset Pricing Model (CAPM) and Arbitrage Pricing Theory (APT), elucidating their key components, assumptions, and significance. Practical implementation is a key focus in this book; therefore, besides static modeling, this book introduces dynamic modeling concepts and techniques such as the Distributed Lag (DL), Auto Regressive Distributed Lag (ARDL), and Vector Auto Regression (VAR) models embedded directly within the text to enhance readability and allow researchers and practitioners to easily reproduce, and experiment with the study's findings.

This book is essential for anyone looking to deepen their understanding of Econometrics modeling and its applications in finance. Whether you are a finance professional, an economist, or a data scientist, this book will equip you with the knowledge and approach needed to tackle real-world problems with confidence. Supplemental material (code examples) is available on GitHub (saritmaitra/PracticalGuideEconometrics).

Bengaluru, India Sarit Maitra

# About This Book

This book is designed for undergraduates, Master's/M.B.A. students, Ph.D. research scholars, and researchers seeking a comprehensive understanding of contemporary Econometric techniques. It is suitable for courses on financial time series analysis, Econometrics in finance, and financial economics. This book provides statistical analysis and empirical testing of theories in a clear and easy-to-understand manner.

No prior knowledge of statistics, Econometrics, or algebra is needed for this book, but any prior exposure to linear algebra and basic statistics can help to understand faster. The book emphasizes the valid application of techniques to data processing, Econometric models, and statistical inferences. It covers both static and dynamic modeling techniques, complete with practical demonstrations.

The book uses Python v3.10.12 for its source code, which relies on libraries like pandas, numpy, SciPy, and matplotlib. All source code (GitHub links) (https://github.com/saritmaitra/PracticalGuideEconometrics) provided for the relevant chapters. It is advisable to look through the given code repository to better understand the underlying logic and dependencies needed for anyone looking to fully understand and implement the code provided. References (bibliography) are available at the end of each chapter. The mathematical principles behind each data transformation (exponential, logarithmic, polynomial) can help clarify why each transformation impacts Y (dependent variable) in a specific way. The choice of plot labels, legends, gridlines, and colors enhances the visual clarity and understanding of the transformations applied.

Key features of this book include comprehensive coverage, starting from theoretical basis, focus on practical implementation, integration of theory and practice, diagnostic tests, advanced Econometric models, step-by-step hypothesis testing, and relevance to finance. A comprehensive introduction to Econometrics, covering its history, key contributors, and foundational concepts are covered in this book. Moreover, this book offers a hands-on, example-based approach that introduces fundamental concepts as needed. It covers a wide range of diagnostic tests, including linearity, normality, stationarity, heteroscedasticity, autocorrelation, multicollinearity, model specification, outlier detection, and parameter stability. The book also explores dynamic modeling techniques such as Distributed Lag (DL),

Auto Regressive Distributed Lag (ARDL), and Vector Auto Regression (VAR) models.

The author recognizes that many students or readers of this book are not majoring in quantitative areas. They are typically business majors in finance, marketing, operations management, or some other business discipline who will need to analyze data and make decisions based on quantitative analysis in their jobs. This book offers a hands-on, example-based approach and introduces fundamental concepts as they are needed. After reading this book, readers will have a clear understanding of Econometric models and relevant concepts. This book shows the complete implementation of static and dynamic models using univariate and multivariate datasets. This book has been designed to be example based and practical.

# Contents

# About the Author

**Dr. Sarit Maitra** is a seasoned business transformation leader and academic with over 25 years of experience in the industry and academia, specializing in business analytics, data science, and information technology. With a Ph.D. and M.S. in Information Technology from Universiti Teknologi PETRONAS, Malaysia, he has held pivotal roles in various global organizations in the past. Currently, affiliated with Alliance University, Bengaluru, India, as a Professor of Business Analytics with the Alliance Business School. Sarit leverages his extensive industry experience to deliver courses in business analytics. He is passionate about data-driven business, and his research interest spans the applied field of business analytics (simulation, stochastic modeling), econometric modeling, optimization approaches, and applied of quantum machine learning. Sarit's passion for data-driven business decision is evident throughout his entire career. He believes in the transformative power of data to drive strategic business decisions and operational efficiencies. His deep understanding of statistics has been a cornerstone in his approach, allowing him to analyze complex datasets, identify trends, and develop models that offer actionable insights.

# Introduction to Econometrics and Linear Regression 1

This chapter introduces a foundational concept in Econometrics. The primary focus of this chapter is to develop theoretical concepts including the different types of Econometric data, essential modeling techniques, underlying mathematical principles, and the critical role of hypothesis testing in Econometric models.

## 1 Econometrics

Econometrics integrates economic theory, mathematical modeling, and statistical inference to analyze real-world economic data. It provides a structured approach to understanding complex economic phenomena, enable the exploration of topics such as consumer behavior, economic growth, inflation, market dynamics, etc. It is a subject of quantitative analysis and by quantifying relationships between variables, Econometrics helps in making predictions and policy decisions. In Econometrics studies, researchers develop models based on theoretical relationships, define hypotheses and subsequently estimate, and test those models using statistical techniques. By doing so, they aim to validate economic theories or develop new data-driven insights that can guide decision-making in policy, finance, and business.

Key methods in Econometrics include regression analysis for exploring relationships between variables. Regression in Econometrics is generally performed by taking different data types and approaches. These involve time-dependent data for examining the trends over time, panel data analysis for handling datasets with both cross-sectional and time dimensions, and causal inference techniques for identifying cause-and-effect relationships.



S. Maitra, *A Practical Guide to Static and Dynamic Econometric Modelling*, Contributions to Economics, https://doi.org/10.1007/978-3-031-86862-7_1

The history of Econometrics started with Frisch (1926),[1] who came up with the term "Econometric" in his first economic publication. Empirical studies show that, while Tinbergen[2] popularized the Econometrics theory, Frisch was primarily responsible for its creation. Tinbergen (1936, 1937) made a significant contribution to Econometrics by developing the first aggregate-level Econometric model. Later, Klein (1969) and Simon Kuznets (1971) also contributed significantly to the Econometric research. All of them won the Nobel Prize in economics for their contributions. While Klein is popular for his work in creating models to forecast economic trends, Simon Kuznets pioneered the notion of Gross Domestic Product (GDP), which captures all economic activity in a state using a single metric.

In Econometric approach, the first step is to obtain and analyze a dataset and define hypotheses based on the existing economic theories. Let us take a simple example to better understand this:

- Assuming a hypothetical scenario where we wish to find the correlation between the monthly price change of the "Tesla" stock price and the "Unemployment Rate" in the USA. So, we would collect both the datasets and define a hypothesis that *"Hypothesis → higher unemployment leads to lower Tesla stock prices"*. Here, price is the dependent or response variable, and unemployment rate is the independent or explanatory variable.

Let us model our problem. If we can model this successfully, we can run the regression and test the hypothesis to establish the findings. A model is a simplified mathematical representation of the relationships between different variables. Modeling helps clarify the structure of the relationship.

While assessing the relationship between two variables, it is critical to understand how they are related. The relationship here can be explored with a model defining a simple equation based on linear algebra, such as $Y = \beta_0 + \beta_1 X + \epsilon$ where, $Y$ is dependent variable, $X$ is the independent variable, $\beta_0$ is the slope or gradient of the line, $\beta_1$ is the intercept, and $\epsilon$ is the error. This represents a classic Econometric model.

In statistics, a linear relationship is a straight line between two variables shown in the above equation. Usually, when we look at the trend in a time-dependent dataset (time series), we get the impression that there is a true linear relationship. A trend refers to the direction or pattern in which a variable moves over time, whether it is increasing, decreasing, or staying constant. For instance:

- If a stock price is rising over time, this indicates an upward trend. In this case, higher highs and higher lows are typically observed.
- If the stock price is consistently falling over time, it shows a downward trend, characterized by lower highs and lower lows.

[1] https://en.wikipedia.org/wiki/Ragnar_Frisch.
[2] https://en.wikipedia.org/wiki/Jan_Tinbergen.

- When there is no significant upward or downward movement, the price might fluctuate within a certain range, indicating a sideways or horizontal trend.

Detecting trends is essential because they can influence forecasting and decision-making processes. Now going back to the model; a simple regression model generates a best-fit line through the data points in a scatter plot and calculates the average distance of each data point from this line. This is known as error estimation. This line of best fit, or trend line, represents the estimated position of a linear equation within the dataset.

Several explanatory variables can be added to the analysis, such as changes to "GDP" and "inflation" in addition to "unemployment", to explain the stock prices. In the case where we use more than one explanatory variable, it is known as multiple, multivariate, or multi-factor linear regression. Multi-factor regression is the most used approach in Econometrics. The common approach to employing multi-factor regression is the Ordinary Least Squares (OLS) regression, which can be performed on several types of cross-sectional or time series data.

In the following sections, we will understand different types of data that can be used for Econometric modeling. The GitHub link of the Python notebook for this chapter is available at the footnote.[3]

## 1.1 Importance of Modeling in Econometrics

We already discussed the significance of Econometric modeling. To comprehend the importance of models, let us examine a few fundamental ideas. Models provide a structured method for testing hypotheses, quantifying relations, forecasting future trends, and making evidence-based decisions in economic policy and business strategy.

The primary reasons for learning and using Econometric models are:

- Models evaluate economic ideas and challenge assumptions. Without empirical testing, economic concepts remain hypothetical.
- Models allow for the quantification of relationships between variables. For example, models measure how changes in interest rates affect inflation or how government spending impacts GDP. This quantification is essential for making informed policy decisions or business strategies.
- A major application of models is forecasting. Businesses use them to predict future sales, demand, or market trends, while governments use them for predicting economic growth or unemployment rates. These forecasts are critical for strategic planning and policy decisions.

[3] https://github.com/saritmaitra/PracticalGuideEconometrics/blob/main/Chapter_1.ipynb.

- Models are essential to evaluate the effectiveness of the policies. For instance, a government might use an Econometric model to assess the impact of a tax policy on income inequality or employment. This helps in understanding whether the policy is meeting its intended goals.

## 1.2 Types of Data

Various types of data are normally used in an Econometrics model.

1. Time series data where data collected over time and provide information about the variables in the dataset. Table 1 shows a sample Python code snippet to generate synthetic data and a subsequent line plot with daily frequency (Fig. 1).
2. Cross-sectional data refers to data collected by observing many subjects (such as individuals, companies, or countries) at one specific point in time, without considering how things change over time. Table 2 shows a simple Python code to generate cross-sectional data and a subsequent scatter plot (Fig. 2).
3. Panel data is a subset of longitudinal data in which the same subjects are observed repeatedly. Time series and cross-sectional data are special examples of panel data with a single dimension. Table 3 shows simple Python code to generate synthetic panel data, and a subsequent plot displays the visualization.
4. When the variables are qualitative in nature, the data are recorded in the form of the indicator function. These are dummy variables. Dummy variables are typically binary in nature which means they reflect only the presence or absence of a characteristic. For example, these values can be represented as '1' being male and '0' being female.

A fundamental question may arise: **"what is the difference between economics and econometrics?"**

**Table 1** Time series line plot

```
dates = pd.date_range(start = '2023-01-01', periods = 100, freq = 'D')
values = pd.Series(range(100))
data = pd.DataFrame({'Date': dates, 'Value': values})
data.set_index('Date', inplace = True)
plt.figure(figsize = (10, 6))
plt.plot(data.index, data['Value'], marker = 'o', linestyle = '-')
plt.title('Time Series Data')
plt.xlabel('Date'); plt.ylabel('Value')
plt.grid(True)
plt.show()
```

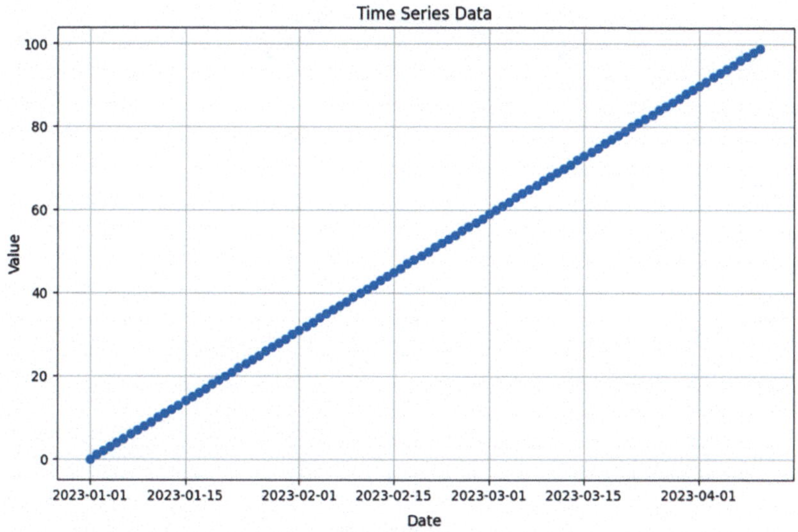


**Fig. 1** Line plot of time series data

**Table 2** Code snippet for synthetic cross-sectional data

```
data = {
    'Individual': ['A', 'B', 'C', 'D', 'E', 'F', 'G', 'H', 'I', 'J'],
    'Value': [5, 7, 8, 5, 6, 7, 8, 7, 6, 5]
}
df = pd.DataFrame(data)
plt.figure(figsize = (10, 6))
plt.scatter(df['Individual'], df['Value'], marker = 'o', color = 'b')
plt.title('Cross-Sectional Data')
plt.xlabel('Individual');
plt.ylabel('Value')
plt.grid(True)
plt.show()
```

Econometrics is the intersection of three distinct fields: economics, statistics, and mathematics, as depicted in the Venn diagram (Fig. 3).

We already have discussed that Econometrics model is a quantitative examination of economic phenomena that employs mathematical models to evaluate economic theories and hypotheses. In this context, we must note that in quantitative finance considering econometric models have traditionally been applied to smaller datasets considering many variables are available in monthly or quarterly frequency, and they are often used when researchers come up with a strong theoretical basis for the relationships being studied.

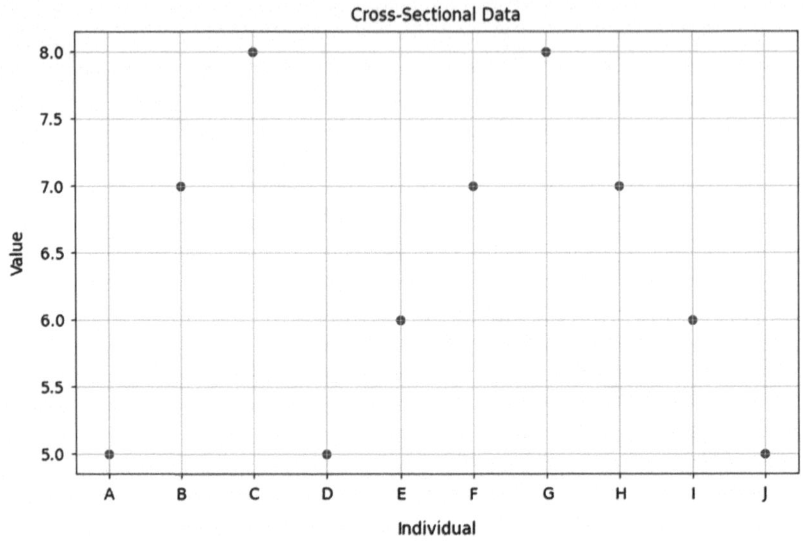


**Fig. 2** Sample scatter plot on cross-sectional data

## 1.3 Key Components

Figure 4 displays the key components of Econometric model development using a simple workflow.

Let us understand each of the steps shown in the workflow:

I. Data collection involves gathering relevant economic data, such as historical prices, consumer survey results, unemployment rates, GDP data, inflation data, etc.
II. A hypothesis proposes a solution for a specific problem or question that researchers must test. In other words, it is a testament that researchers test through research or experimentation to decide its validity.
III. Model specification involves choosing a model that is the hypothesized relationships.
IV. Estimation involves using statistical techniques to estimate the parameters of the chosen model. This often involves finding the best-fit line or curve that is the relationship between variables.
V. Inference is combining parameter estimation and hypothesis testing to make inferences about the relationships between the variables. This includes assessing the statistical significance and strength of the estimated relationships.

The final stage involves using the tested model to estimate future economic patterns and assess the possible impact of various policy interventions.

**Table 3** Code snippet for synthetic panel data

```
data = {
    'Individual': ['A', 'A', 'A', 'B', 'B', 'B', 'C', 'C', 'C'],
    'Time': ['2023-01', '2023-02', '2023-03', '2023-01', '2023-02', '2023-03', '2023-01', '2023-02', '2023-03'],
    'Value': [5, 6, 7, 7, 8, 6, 6, 5, 7]
}
df = pd.DataFrame(data)
df['Time'] = pd.to_datetime(df['Time'])

plt.figure(figsize = (10, 6))
for individual in df['Individual'].unique():
    subset = df[df['Individual'] == individual]
    plt.plot(subset['Time'], subset['Value'], marker = 'o', label = individual)
plt.title('Panel Data')
plt.xlabel('Time'); plt.ylabel('Value')
plt.legend(title = 'Individual')
plt.grid(True)
plt.show()
```

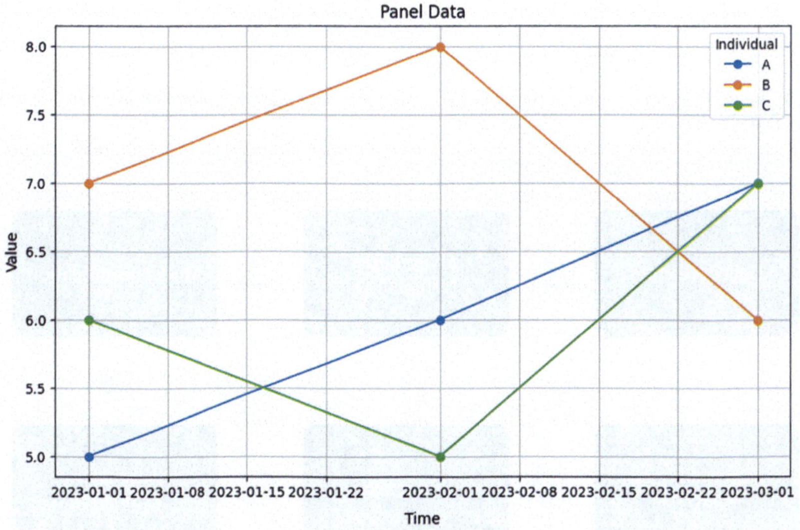


Various statistical techniques are involved in the modeling process to understand the data and subsequently process the data for robust modeling. Data cleaning and processing is a major activity for a model and reliable estimates. At a broader level, this often involves time frequency mapping, missing data handling, noise reduction, variable identification, frequency distributions, probability distributions, correlation analysis, and regression analysis.

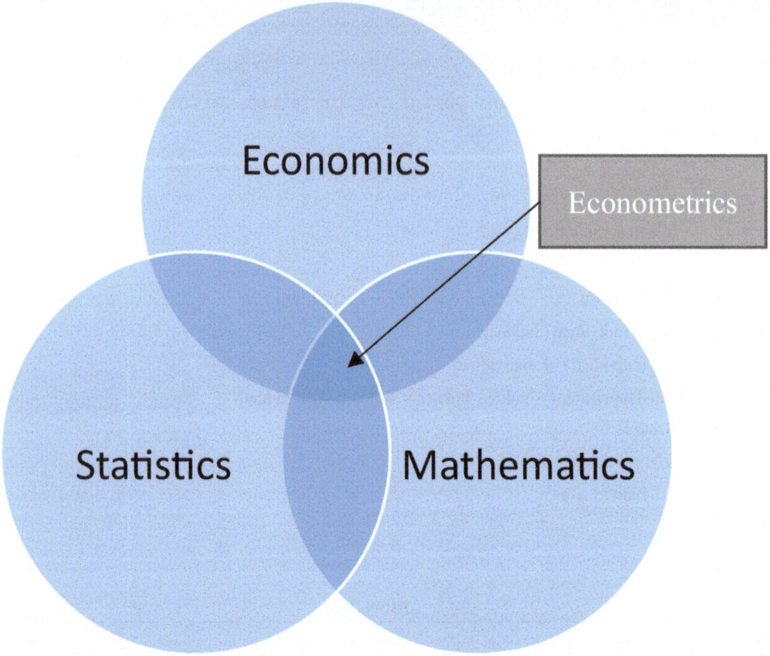


**Fig. 3** Venn diagram comprises of economics, statistics and mathematics. Econometrics is at the cross section of these three important areas

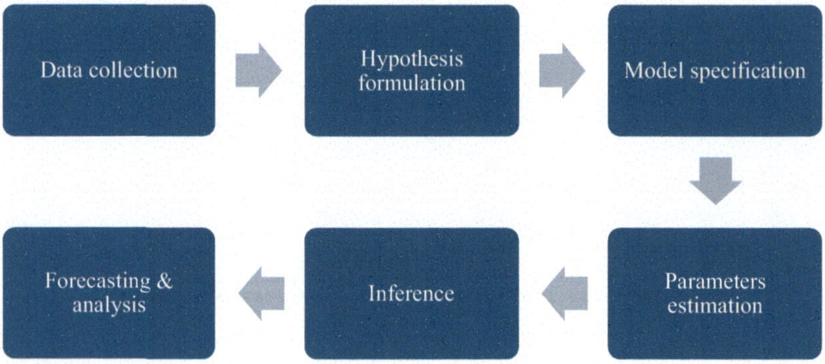


**Fig. 4** Econometric workflow

- Frequency distributions are a summary of how often different values occur within a dataset. It is generally displayed as a table or histogram showing the frequency of each value or range of values.

- Probability distributions provide the probability of the occurrence of different outcomes. The normal distribution (Gaussian distribution) is the common probability distribution which displays that data near the mean are more frequent in occurrence than data far from the mean.
- Correlation analysis measures the strength and direction of the relationship between two variables. The correlation coefficient ranges from −1 to 1, where 1 means a perfect positive correlation, −1 means a perfect negative correlation, and 0 means no correlation.
- Regression analysis is commonly used to estimate variable relationships. It is a statistical technique to examine the relationship between one dependent variable and one or more independent variables.

Figure 5 expands the Econometric workflow by outlining a conceptual framework.

The process starts with formulating a theory of the problem. We can obtain the required data from published government sources. For estimation, either a univariate or a multivariate modeling equation can be used. The model's optimal parameter estimation relies on satisfying statistical assumptions and describing the data. Multiple hypotheses and validation processes are involved at this stage. If the assumptions are violated, we need to reformulate the work, collect more data, or choose a less stringent estimation technique. The hypothesis testing is done from a theoretical perspective. Once we are satisfied with the model, then use it to test the theory. We must remember that developing a robust model is always an iterative process, and the final model may differ significantly from the original proposal.

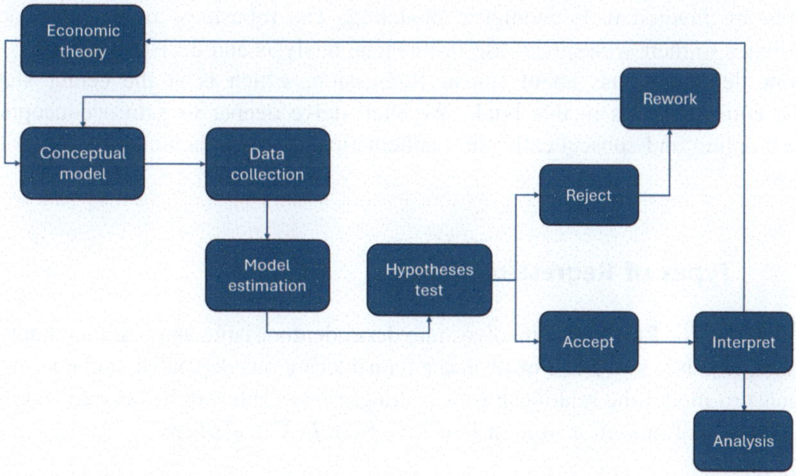


**Fig. 5** A conceptual workflow of a systematic research design showing the analysis process and feedback loop to economic theory or business process

### 1.4 Limitations

In applied economics, the biggest challenge is the lack of data for testing theories or hypotheses. Measurement errors and data revisions are also common issues. Measurement error occurs when the variables we use in our analysis do not perfectly measure the theoretical construct it is supposed to. This can lead to biased and inconsistent parameter estimates, which can compromise the validity of Econometric analyses. Measurement errors can affect both dependent and independent variables, though the effects and mitigation strategies differ.

A common criticism of Econometrics is that, it sometimes focuses too heavily on the statistical properties of data without sufficiently considering economic theory. This can lead to a model that fits the data well but lacks meaningful interpretation. Moreover, there is a risk that Econometric analysis can identify correlations without adequately addressing causation. Without a clear understanding of causal relationships, the results might be misleading or not useful for policymaking and decision-making.

Now that we have some understanding, let us look into the fundamental aspects of regression modeling in Econometrics.

## 2 Regression

We know that regression is a statistical technique used to examine the relationship between one dependent variable and one or more independent variables. In statistical terminology, the dependent variable is called endogenous or explained variable, and the independent is known as exogenous or explanatory variables (s). Linear models are favored in Econometric modeling. The robustness of linear models contributes to their widespread use in financial analysis and decision-making.

Now, let us discuss about Linear Regression, which is at the center stage of the entire analysis in this book. We shall delve deeper to gain a conceptual understanding and subsequently the mathematical intuition behind the regression process.

### 2.1 Types of Regression

A simple Linear Regression involves one dependent variable and one independent variable, which is univariate or bivariate (considering one dependent and one independent) to model the relationship as a straight line. This can be defined through an algebraic formula of a straight line $Y = \beta_0 + \beta_1 X + \epsilon$ where,

- $Y$ = dependent variable,
- $\beta_0$ = intercept,
- $\beta_1$ = slope,
- $X$ = independent variable, and

- $\epsilon$ = error term.

The above equation can be extended to a multiple linear regression which involves one dependent variable and two or more independent variables as $Y = \beta_0 + \beta_1 X_1 + \beta_2 X_2 + \cdots + \beta_n X_n + \epsilon.$ . Here multiple independent variables $(X_1, X_2, \ldots, X_n)$ and their coefficients $(\beta_1, \beta_2, \ldots, \beta_n)$ exist.

The fundamental requirement in a Linear Regression is that the relationship between the dependent variable $Y$ and the parameters ($\beta$ coefficients) is linear. This means that the model is linear in terms of the parameters, even if the explanatory variables undergo nonlinear transformations such as $X^2$ or $X^3$, etc.

From $Y = \beta_0 + \beta_1 X_1 + \beta_2 X_2 + \cdots + \beta_n X_n + \epsilon$, the relationship between $Y$ and the parameters $\beta_0, \beta_1, \ldots, \beta_n$ is linear. When the variables undergo nonlinear transformations such as polynomials, or exponentials, etc., the model can still be linear in terms of the parameters.

Let us look at a few examples:

1. **Exponential Transformation**: Suppose we have a variable $Z$ which is an exponential function of $X$ ($Z = e^X$). The standard linear regression model ($Y = \beta_0 + \beta_1 X + \epsilon$) can be written as $Y = \beta_0 + \beta_1 e^X + \epsilon$, where $e^X$ is a transformed variable, and the relationship with the parameter $\beta_1$ remains linear. This means standard Linear Regression techniques can still estimate $\beta_0$ and $\beta_1$ by minimizing the residuals, even though the relationship between $Y$ and $X$ is nonlinear. Since $e^X$ changes nonlinearly with $X$, this results in an exponential response. A one-unit increase in $X$ changes $e^X$ to $e^{X+1}$. Since $e^{X+1} = e^X * e$, the increase in $e^X$ when $X$ increases by one unit is $\Delta(e^X) = e^{X+1} - e^X = e^X * e - e^X = e^X(e-1)$.

   This shows that for a one-unit increase in $X$, the corresponding change in $Y$ is $\Delta Y = \beta_1 \Delta(e^X) = \beta_1(e^X)(e-1)$. This means that for each one-unit change in $X$, the change in $Y$ is proportional to both $\beta_1$ and $e^X$, scaled by $(e-1)$.

Table 4 displays an exponential curve for the relationship $Y = 1 + 0.5e^X$. We can see here that as $X$ increases, the growth rate of $Y$ increases exponentially. Each unit increase in $X$ results in an increasingly larger increase in $Y$ due to the exponential function.

This nonlinear effect of $X$ means, while the model is linear in its parameters (making it feasible for the Linear Regression methods), the interpretation of $\beta_1$ adapts to reflect the exponential transformation applied to $X$.

2. **Logarithmic Transformation**: In the case of logarithmic transformation, the model is $Y = \beta_0 + \beta_1 \log(X) + \epsilon$.

   The interpretation of $\beta_1$ changes here, $\beta_1$ now is the expected change in $Y$ for a one-percent change in $X$, assuming other factors remain constant. Specifically, $\beta_1$ is the change in $Y$ for a one-unit change in $\log(X)$, rather than a one-unit change in $X$ itself. A one-unit increase in $\log(X)$ corresponds approximately to a percentage change in $X$ when $X$ changes proportionally.

**Table 4** Exponential plot on synthetic data

```
X = np.linspace(1, 10, 100)
beta_0, beta_1, beta_2 = 1, 0.5, 0.05
Y_exponential = beta_0 + beta_1 * np.exp(X)
plt.figure(figsize = (8, 6))
plt.plot(X, Y_exponential, label = r"$Y = \beta_0 + \beta_1 e^X$", color = "blue")
plt.title("Exponential Transformation")
plt.xlabel("X")
plt.ylabel("Y")
plt.legend()
plt.grid(True)
plt.show()
```

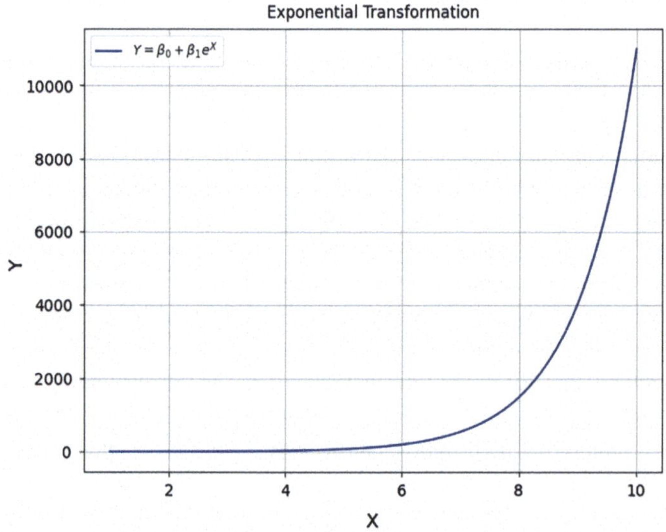


$\beta_1$ can be interpreted as the elasticity of $Y$ with respect to $X$. In economics, this elasticity measures the percentage change in one variable (in this case, $Y$) in response to a 1% change in another variable (here, $X$). When $\beta_1$ is the coefficient of $\log(X)$, it suggests that a 1% increase in $X$ results in approximately a $\beta_1$% change in $Y$.

Table 5 displays a logarithmic transformation and the relationship between $X$ and $Y$ using a model of the form $Y = \beta_0 + \beta_1 \log(X)$. The plot shows a logarithmic growth curve. As $X$ increases, the increase in $Y$ becomes smaller, meaning $Y$ grows more. Moreover, each unit increase in $X$ results in a smaller incremental change in $Y$ compared to an exponential or linear function.

**Table 5** Logarithmic transformation and visualization

```
X = np.linspace(1, 10, 100)
beta_0, beta_1, beta_2 = 1, 0.5, 0.05
Y_logarithmic = beta_0 + beta_1 * np.log(X)
plt.figure(figsize=(8, 6))
plt.plot(X, Y_logarithmic, label=r"$Y = \beta_0 + \beta_1 \log(X)$", color="green")
plt.title("Logarithmic Transformation")
plt.xlabel("X")
plt.ylabel("Y")
plt.legend()
plt.grid(True)
plt.show()
```

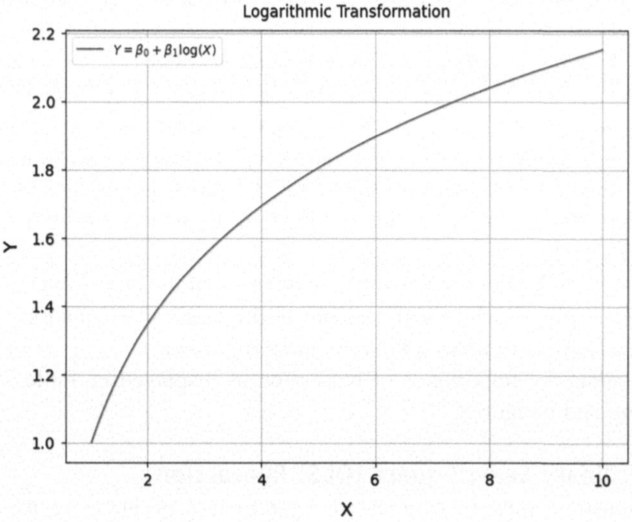


This interpretation is useful in the economic and business contexts where understanding proportional relationships, such as sensitivity or responsiveness, is valuable. A one-unit change in $\log(X)$ approximates a proportional change in $X$ when $X$ increases multiplicatively. However, the logarithmic transformation is still considered linear because the model retains the linearity in its parameters rather than the variables.

3. **Polynomial Transformation**: In the case of a polynomial transformation, the model $Y = \beta_0 + \beta_1 X + \beta_2 X^2 + \epsilon$.

   This model introduces both a linear and a quadratic component of $X$, enabling the model to capture curvature in the relationship between $X$ and $Y$. $\beta_1$ represents the linear effect of $X$ on $Y$. It shows the change in $Y$ for a one-unit change in $X$, holding the $X^2$ term constant. This linear term provides the base or initial slope of the relationship between $X$ and $Y$ and is like the slope in a simple Linear Regression.

$\beta_2$ represents the quadratic effect of $X$ on $Y$. It captures the rate at which the slope changes as $X$ changes, introducing curvature into the model. If $\beta_2$ is positive, $Y$ increases at an increasing rate as $X$ increases, resulting in an upward curve. Conversely, if $\beta_2$ is negative, $Y$ initially increases but at a decreasing rate, creating a downward curve as $X$ continues to grow.

The combination of linear and quadratic terms allows the model to better fit nonlinear relationships. In contexts where $Y$ does not change at a constant rate with $X$, this model can represent the data better than a purely linear model. Together, $\beta_1$ and $\beta_2$ capture both the direction and shape of the relationship between $X$ and $Y$. This flexibility is helpful in modeling complex relationships where $Y$ may increase or decrease in a curved fashion as $X$ changes.

Table 6 displays a polynomial transformation, where $Y$ is modeled as a quadratic function of $X$, using the equation $Y = \beta_0 + \beta_1 X + \beta_2 X^2$. The plot shows a parabolic curve, illustrating a polynomial (quadratic) transformation. The inclusion of $X^2$ introduces a curved relationship, creating a parabolic shape that either opens upward or downward based on $\beta_2$. As $X$ grows, the increase in $Y$ becomes larger due to the $X^2$ term, resulting in an accelerating effect on $Y$ for positive values of $\beta_2$.

The inclusion of $X^2$ does not change the linearity of the model in the parameters because it is simply an additional variable in the regression equation. Therefore, the polynomial model remains a type of linear regression.

Let us tabulate the importance of regression as displayed in Table 7 for better understanding and memorize.

### 2.1.1 Ordinary Least Square (OLS) Regression

Let us demonstrate how to estimate the parameters of linear regression using Ordinary Least Squares (OLS) regression works.

From $Y = \beta_0 + \beta_1 X_i + \varepsilon$, the values of $Y$ and $X$ can be easily computed from the dataset. However, that is not the case with $\beta_0$, $\beta_1$, and $\epsilon$. Here we use OLS to make an estimate based on what their values are. We will use $\widehat{\beta}_0$ and $\widehat{\beta}_1$ to denote the model estimates. OLS estimates the parameters $(\beta_0, \beta_1, \ldots, \beta_n)$ by minimizing the Residual Sum of Squares (RSS).

$$\mathrm{RSS} = \sum_{i=1}^{n} \left(Y_i - \hat{Y}_i\right)^2$$

Here, $Y_i$ is actual or observed value and $\widehat{Y}_i$ is the predicted value. By minimizing RSS, OLS finds the best-fitting line that explains the relationship between the independent and dependent variables.

We already know now that in quantitative finance, the datasets are small. Moreover, data are mostly numerical and have a low signal-to-noise ratio. Such as stock

**Table 6** Polynomial transformation and visualization

```
X = np.linspace(1, 10, 100)
beta_0, beta_1, beta_2 = 1, 0.5, 0.05
Y_polynomial = beta_0 + beta_1 * X + beta_2 * X**2
plt.figure(figsize = (8, 6))
plt.plot(X, Y_polynomial, label=r"$Y = \beta_0 + \beta_1 X + \beta_2 X^2$", color = "purple")
plt.title("Polynomial Transformation")
plt.xlabel("X")
plt.ylabel("Y")
plt.legend()
plt.grid(True)
plt.show()
```

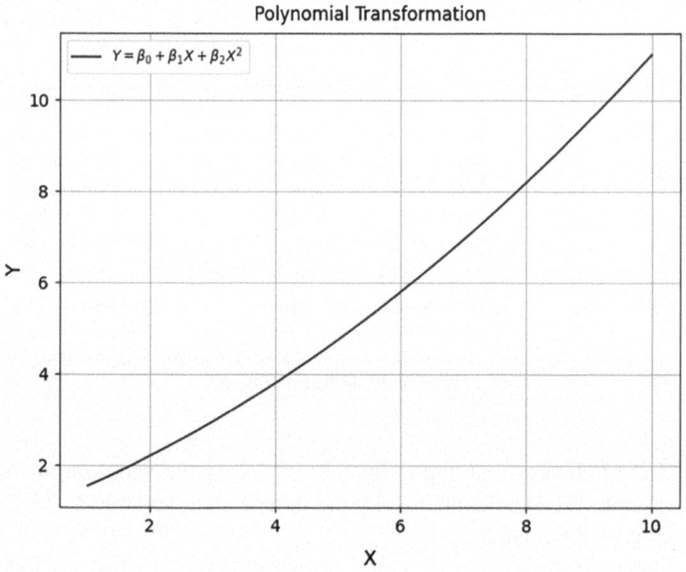


prices can be influenced by many factors, including market sentiment, macroeconomic factors, and volatility which makes it challenging to extract meaningful signals. Due to these, the statistical estimates (e.g., estimate of returns, volatility, correlations) often come with high uncertainty. This can lead to a higher margin of errors in estimates.

Before applying OLS regression, it is crucial to ensure the assumption of linearity between the independent variable ($X$) and the dependent variable ($Y$). We must check if the relationship between $X$ and $Y$ is indeed linear. Table 8 displays the spot check on linearity.

We get a bunch of output when we run OLS (Table 9). Let us understand as how to interpret the generated output.

**Table 7** Importance of regression in Econometrics

| Important factors | Description |
|---|---|
| Quantifying relationships | Regression analysis helps quantify the strength and direction of relationships between economic variables. For example, understanding how changes in interest rates affect investment levels |
| Testing economic theories | Econometricians use regression analysis to test economic theories and hypotheses |
| Forecasting | Regression models can be used to make predictions about future values of variables based on historical data. For example, predicting future GDP growth based on factors such as investment, consumption, and government spending |
| Policy evaluation | Policymakers use regression analysis to evaluate the potential impact of different policy measures. For example, assessing the impact of a tax cut on consumer spending |
| Identifying causal relationships | A correlation does not mean that the change in one variable is the cause of the change in the values of the other variable. There is a causal relationship between the two events, meaning that one event is the consequence of the other event occurring. The statistical concept of causation is often misinterpreted and applied incorrectly, leading one to assume that just because data exhibits a correlation, there must be an underlying causative relationship |
| Handling complexity | Regression analysis allows economists to handle complex relationships involving multiple variables simultaneously. This is crucial for understanding real-world economic phenomena where multiple factors interact |

I. $R^2$ (0.928) indicates that approximately 92.8% of the variation in the dependent variable $Y$ can be explained by the independent variable $X$. This suggests a good fit of the model.

II. The intercept term (const) is 0.4443, which means that when the independent variable $X$ is zero, the expected value of the dependent variable $Y$ is 0.4443. However, the $p$-value for this coefficient (0.253) > 0.05 means it is statistically not significant.

III. The slope coefficient (x1) is 2.4874, meaning that for every one unit increase in $X$, $Y$ increases by approximately 2.4874 units. This coefficient is highly significant ($p$-value = 0.000).

IV. $F$-statistic (1270) and Prob ($F$-statistic): The high $F$-statistic and its associated low $p$-value (6.76e−58) indicate that the model is statistically significant, and that the independent variable $X$ has a strong linear relationship with the dependent variable $Y$.

V. The Omnibus Test and Jarque–Bera Test suggest that there may be some deviation from normality in the residuals, though not extreme. The Durbin-Watson statistic (2.083) is close to 2, indicating that there is no significant autocorrelation in the residuals.

**Table 8** Data generation and Spot check on linearity

```
np.random.seed(0)
X = np.random.rand(100, 1) * 10
Y = 2.5 * X + np.random.randn(100, 1) * 2
data = pd.DataFrame({'X': X.flatten(), 'Y': Y.flatten()})
plt.scatter(data['X'], data['Y'])
plt.title('Scatter Plot of X vs Y')
plt.xlabel('X')
plt.ylabel('Y')
plt.grid()
plt.show()
```

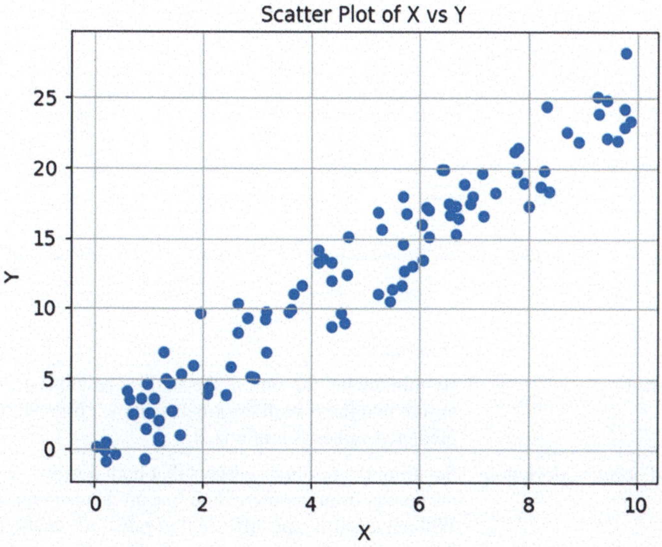


This is a simple example of the implementation and interpretation of the OLS model. We shall apply this knowledge in the subsequent sections where we explore more into the OLS regression model. Table 10 displays how to generate a line fit plot from the above model.

OLS assumes linearity, which means that the relationship between the independent variable *X* and the dependent variable *Y* can be represented by a straight line. Above plot displays the line fit plot from the OLS regression analysis. The blue dots are the data points, and the red line is the fitted line from the model. This plot visually demonstrates the relationship between the independent variable *X* and the dependent variable *Y*, along with the best-fit line being the sum of squared residuals. The process involves squaring the vertical distance between each point and the regression line and then minimizing the total sum of these squared distances (hence "least squares").

Let us now summarize and tabulate our understanding on OLS as shown below.

**Table 9** OLS regression results

```
X_with_const = sm.add_constant(X)
model = sm.OLS(Y, X_with_const).fit()
print(model.summary())
```

```
                            OLS Regression Results
==============================================================================
Dep. Variable:                      y   R-squared:                       0.928
Model:                            OLS   Adj. R-squared:                  0.928
Method:                 Least Squares   F-statistic:                     1270.
Date:                Fri, 12 Jul 2024   Prob (F-statistic):           6.76e-58
Time:                        05:52:21   Log-Likelihood:                -210.83
No. Observations:                 100   AIC:                             425.7
Df Residuals:                      98   BIC:                             430.9
Df Model:                           1
Covariance Type:            nonrobust
==============================================================================
                 coef    std err          t      P>|t|      [0.025      0.975]
------------------------------------------------------------------------------
const          0.4443      0.387      1.149      0.253      -0.323       1.211
x1             2.4874      0.070     35.630      0.000       2.349       2.626
==============================================================================
Omnibus:                       11.746   Durbin-Watson:                   2.083
Prob(Omnibus):                  0.003   Jarque-Bera (JB):                4.097
Skew:                           0.138   Prob(JB):                        0.129
Kurtosis:                       2.047   Cond. No.                         10.9
==============================================================================

Notes:
[1] Standard Errors assume that the covariance matrix of the errors is correctly specified.
```

| Reason | Description |
|---|---|
| Minimize errors | By minimizing the sum of the squared residuals (SSR), we ensure that the overall error between the observed and predicted values is minimized |
| Positive and negative deviations | Squaring the residuals ensures that both positive and negative deviations from the regression line are treated equally. Without squaring, positive, and negative residuals could cancel each other out, leading to a misleading representation of the error |
| Mathematical simplicity | The least squares method results in a quadratic optimization problem, which is easier to solve mathematically. The resulting normal equations, derived from setting the derivative of the sum of squared residuals to zero, provide a straightforward way to find the regression coefficients |
| Statistical properties | Under the assumptions of the classical linear regression model (e.g., linearity, independence, homoscedasticity, normality of errors), the least squares estimators have desirable statistical properties. They are unbiased, consistent, and efficient, meaning they have the smallest variance among all linear unbiased estimators (known as the Gauss-Markov theorem) |

**Table 10** Line fit plot

```
data['Predicted_Y'] = model.predict(X_with_const)
plt.figure(figsize = (10, 6))
plt.scatter(data['X'], data['Y'], color = 'blue', label = 'Observed Data')
plt.plot(data['X'], data['Predicted_Y'], color = 'red', label = 'Fitted Line', linewidth = 2)
plt.title('OLS Regression: Observed Data and Fitted Line')
plt.xlabel('Independent Variable (X)')
plt.ylabel('Dependent Variable (Y)')
plt.legend()
plt.grid(True)
plt.show()
```

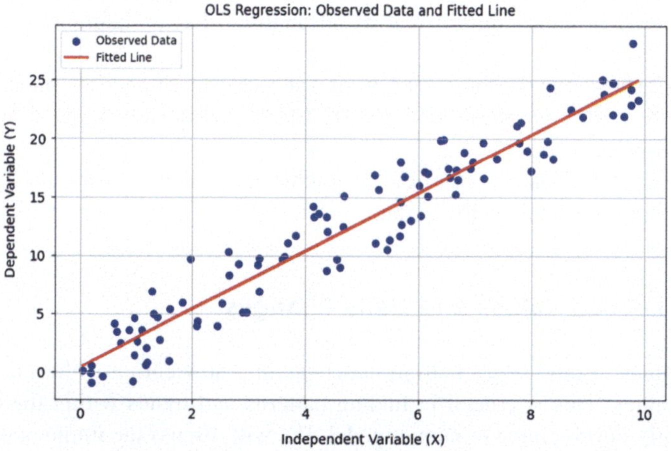


### 2.1.2 Mathematical Explanation

We are familiar with the simple linear regression formulation. Considering the formula from $Y = \beta_0 + \beta_1 X_i + \varepsilon$.

- The residual for each observation is: $e = Y - (\beta_0 + \beta_1 X_i)$.
- Our goal is to minimize the RSS: $\sum_{i=1}^{n} (Y_i - \widehat{Y}_i)^2 = \sum_{i=1}^{n} [Y_i - (\beta_0 + \beta_1 X_i)]^2$. To find the best $\beta_0$ and $\beta_1$, we solve the equations derived from setting the derivatives of the SSR to zero $\left(\frac{\partial \text{SSR}}{\partial \beta_0} = 0, \frac{\partial \text{SSR}}{\partial \beta_1} = 0\right)$.

It is important to note that while the relationship being shown as a straight line, the model needs to be linear in the parameters (e.g., $\beta_0$ and $\beta_1$). This means that the parameters $\beta_0$ (intercept) and $\beta_1$ (slope) should not be multiplied together, divided, squared, or raised to any other power. We have discussed that considering the parameters (coefficients) $\beta_0$ and $\beta_1$ are in a straight-line form, such as, $\beta_0 + \beta_1 X$, the variables $Y$ and $X$ can still be transformed in other ways (e.g., logarithms, polynomials) as long as the relationship remains linear in the parameters such as $Y = \beta_0 + \beta_1 \log(X)$ or $Y = \beta_0 + \beta_1 X^2$.

There are various terms and concepts we encounter when learning about regression and Econometrics. In Table 11 presents the relevant terminologies when explaining about Econometrics and regressions.

## 3 Time Series Data

This section addresses the fundamental aspects of handling the data. Here, we delve deeper into time series data, which is the emphasis of this book. We will learn how to ingest data and perform some basic yet significant transformations that will come in handy during real-world analysis. Let us familiarize ourselves with time series data.

Table 12 shows the data ingestion from Yahoo Finance[4] and line plots showing Tesla's daily stock price from 2018 till 2022 and, subsequently Table 13 compares each year's prices.

We can convert Tesla stock price to monthly frequency by using the following code and Table 14 displays the output.

### 3.1 Lagged Values and Daily Changes

Lagged values in time series help in understanding how current values depend on the past values. This is crucial in finding patterns and trends within the data and subsequently developing a dynamic model. We will discuss the implementation of dynamic modeling in Chapter 6.

Moreover, lagged values can be used in the stationarity tests like the Augmented Dickey-Fuller (ADF) test. Stationarity is a fundamental assumption in many time series models. ADF tests the null hypothesis showing the presence of unit root in a time series. The alternative hypothesis is that the series is stationary.

In price series, returns are estimated using daily price differences, which also helps estimate volatility. High volatility often indicates greater risk and uncertainty. Table 15 displays the necessary transformation being applied to the Tesla stock price.

### 3.2 Logarithmic Transformation

Logarithmic transformation is widely used in economics and finance because it aligns closely with how these fields conceptualize relationships between variables, stabilizes variance, reduces skewness, and provide intuitive interpretations in terms

[4] https://finance.yahoo.com/quote/TSLA/history/.

**Table 11** Regression terminologies

| Terminology | Mathematical expression | Explanation |
|---|---|---|
| Dependent variable | $Y$ | The outcome variable that the model aims to predict |
| Independent variable | $X$ | The predictor variable used to explain variations in the dependent variable |
| Coefficient | $\beta$ | Is the change in the dependent variable for a one-unit change in the independent variable |
| Intercept | $\beta_0$ | The expected value of the dependent variable when all independent variables are zero |
| Error term | $\varepsilon$ | Difference between the observed and predicted values of the dependent variable, $\varepsilon_i \sim N(0, \sigma^2)$ are i.i.d (independent and identically distributed) |
| Simple linear regression or Ordinary least Square (OLS) regression | $Y_i = \beta_0 + \beta_1 X_i + \varepsilon_i$, where where $i = 1, 2, \ldots, n$ for each of the $n$ observations | Regression model with one dependent variable and one independent variable |
| Multivariate regression | $Y_i = \beta_0 + \beta_1 X_{1i} + \beta_2 X_{2i} + \cdots + \beta_n X_n + \varepsilon_i$ | Regression model with one dependent variable and multiple independent variables |
| $R$-squared | $R^2$ | The proportion of variance in the dependent variable explained by the independent variables |
| Adjusted $R$ squared | Adj $R^2$ | Adjusted for the number of predictors in the model, providing a better measure of fit |
| Ordinary least square | $\min \sum (Y_i - \hat{y}_i)^2$ | A method for estimating the coefficients by minimizing the sum of the squared residuals |
| $F$-statistics | $F = \frac{\text{explained variance}}{\text{unexplained variance}}$ | Tests the overall significance of the regression model |
| Standard error | SE | The standard deviation of the sampling distribution of a statistic, typically a coefficient |
| $t$-statistics | $t = \frac{\beta}{\text{SE}(\beta)}$ | Tests the significance of individual coefficients |

(continued)

**Table 11** (continued)

| Terminology | Mathematical expression | Explanation |
|---|---|---|
| *p*-value | | The probability of observing the test results under the null hypothesis |
| Confidence interval | $\widehat{\beta} \pm t^* * \mathrm{SE}(\widehat{\beta})$ | The range within which the true parameter value is expected to fall with a certain probability |
| Multicollinearity | | Where independent variables are highly correlated, potentially distorting coefficient estimates |
| Homoscedasticity | | The assumption that the variance of the error terms is constant across observations |
| Heteroscedasticity | | The condition where the variance of the error terms varies across observations |
| Auto correlation | $\rho$ | The correlation of a variable with itself over successive time intervals |
| Durbin-Watson statistic | $\mathrm{DW} = \frac{\sum (e_t - e_{t-1})^2}{\sum e_t^2}$ | Used to detect the presence of autocorrelation in the residuals |
| Dummy variable | | A binary variable used to include categorical data in regression models |
| Instrumental variable | Z | A variable used to account for endogeneity, not correlated with the error term |
| Lagged variable | $X_{t-1}$ | It is the prior time period's value used in time series analysis |
| Cointegration | | Statistical property of time series variables that move together in the long run |
| Stationary | | Property of a time series where mean and variance are constant over time |

of percentages and elasticity. Many economic and financial relationships are non-linear in nature. A log transformation can linearize these relationships, making them easier to model using traditional linear regression techniques. Moreover, Heteroscedasticity (non-constant variance of errors) is common in economic and financial data, where variability increases with the size of the variable. Log transformation can stabilize the variance, improving model reliability and the validity of

**Table 12** Time series data

```
data = yf.download('TSLA', start = '2018-01-01', end = '2023-01-01')['Close']
data.plot(grid = True)
plt.show()
```

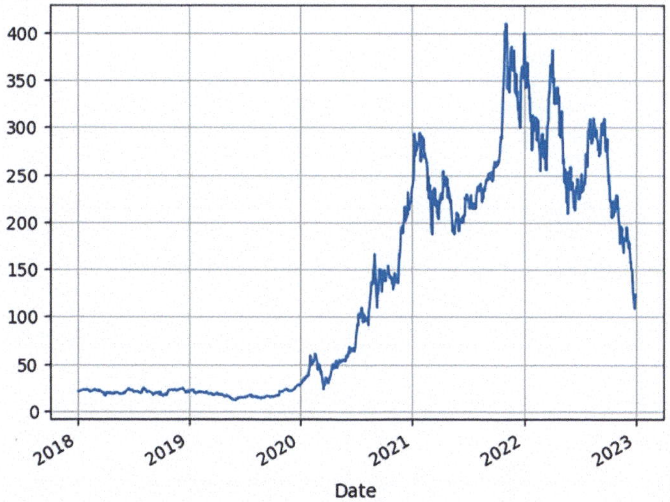


statistical inferences. In financial data, variables like income, market capitalization, or stock prices often span several orders of magnitude. A log transformation compresses large values and expands small ones, making the data easier to visualize, interpret, and model. It also helps reducing the skewness in the data.

Let us examine the advantages of logarithmic transformation and its use. A time series normally shows traces of growth or decline, i.e., non-stationarity. When the characteristics of a time series, such as mean, variance, or covariance, alter with time, it is said to be non-stationary. This shows that prior observations might not be indicative of the future and that the data's behavior is neither steady nor predictable. Non-stationary time series cannot be used in regression models because they may create spurious regression, which is a false relationship.

A non-constant variance series can be stabilized using log transformation. We must remember that log transformation can only be used with positively valued time series. Taking a log reduces the values toward zero. Values close to 1 shrink less, while values higher shrink more, minimizing variance.

Suppose $Y_t$ is an observation of the time series in period $t$, the growth rate ($G_t$) from period $t-1$ is $G_t = \frac{Y_t}{Y_{t-1}}$. If we rearrange this equation and take natural log, we derive at $l_n(1+G_t) = l_n\left(\frac{Y_t}{Y_{t-1}}\right) = l_nY_t - l_nY_{t-1}$.

If we want to understand what is, $l_n(1+G_t)$, we must go back to our fundamental calculus and Taylor's expansion to approximate any functions as $l_n(1+X) = X - \frac{1}{2}X^2 + \frac{1}{3}X^3 - \frac{1}{4}X^4 + \cdots = \sum_{k=1}^{\infty}(-1)^{k+1}\frac{X^k}{k}$.

**Table 13** Compare each years Tesla stock price

```
tesla = pd.DataFrame()
for year in ["2018", "2019", "2020", "2021", "2022"]:
    price_per_year = data.loc[year].reset_index(drop=True)
    price_per_year.name = year + " Close"
    tesla = pd.concat([tesla, price_per_year], axis=1)
print(tesla.head())
```

```
   2018 Close  2019 Close  2020 Close  2021 Close  2022 Close
0   21.368668   20.674667   28.684000  243.256668  399.926666
1   21.150000   20.024000   29.534000  245.036667  383.196655
2   20.974667   21.179333   30.102667  251.993332  362.706665
3   21.105333   22.330667   31.270666  272.013336  354.899994
4   22.427334   22.356667   32.809334  293.339996  342.320007
```

```
tesla.plot(figsize = (14, 8), grid = True)
plt.show()
```

Because the growth rate is generally small, we can use the linear term exclusively in Taylor expansion ($l_n(1 + X) \approx X$) which means log difference approximates the growth rate ($l_n Y_t - l_n Y_{t-1} \approx G_t$).

Table 16 shows how to prepare GDP data for detailed time series analysis, including the creation of lagged variables, calculating growth rates, and applying log transformations. These steps are essential for understanding trends, making forecasts, and performing various statistical analyses on economic data.

The log transformation is an effective approximation technique for small growth rates (<10%). This is due to the property of logarithms where $\log(1 + x) \approx x$ when $x$ is small. However, as growth rates increase, this approximation becomes less correct. For larger growth rates, the log transformation introduces noticeable errors, the approximation $\log(1 + x) \approx x$ becomes less precise. In such situations, alternative methods, such as directly modeling exponential functions or using other transformation techniques needed to capture the growth rate. This understanding is crucial when applying the natural log transformation in financial modeling and

**Table 14** Tesla stock price in monthly frequency

```
data = yf.download('TSLA', start='2018-01-01', end='2023-01-01')['Close']
data.asfreq("M").plot(grid=True)
plt.show()
```

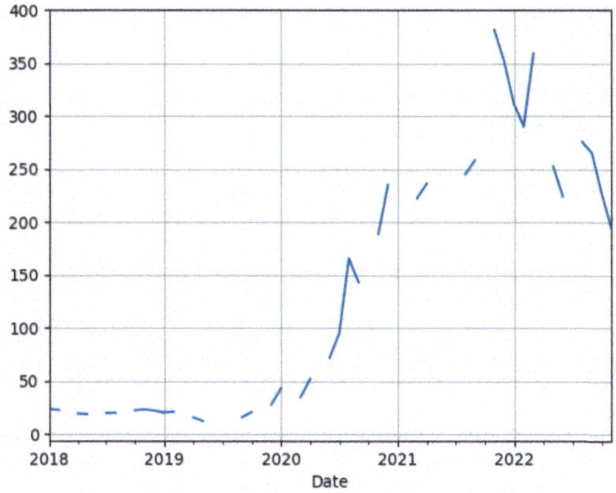


**Table 15** Lagged values and daily changes

```
data = yf.download('TSLA', start = '2018-01-01', end = '2023-01-01')['Close']
tesla = pd.DataFrame(data)
tesla['Lag_1'] = tesla['Close'].shift(1)
tesla['Daily_Change'] = tesla['Close'] / tesla['Lag_1']
tesla.head()
```

| Date | Close | Lag_1 | Daily_Change |
|---|---|---|---|
| **2018-01-02** | 21.368668 | NaN | NaN |
| **2018-01-03** | 21.150000 | 21.368668 | 0.989767 |
| **2018-01-04** | 20.974667 | 21.150000 | 0.991710 |
| **2018-01-05** | 21.105333 | 20.974667 | 1.006230 |
| **2018-01-08** | 22.427334 | 21.105333 | 1.062638 |

time series analysis to ensure the accuracy of the results. Table 17 displays the reliability issue with log transformation.

The first plot on the left-hand side shows the real growth rate versus the approximated growth rate using both the division approach and the natural log approach. For small growth rates (close to 0), the lines overlap, showing that the natural log approach is a good approximation. However, as the growth rate increases, the

**Table 16** Transformation of time series data

```
gdp = pd.read_csv('/content/GDP.csv')


gdp['DATE'] = pd.to_datetime(gdp['DATE'])
gdp.set_index('DATE', inplace = True)
gdp['Lag_1'] = gdp['GDP'].shift(1)
gdp['log_gdp'] = np.log(gdp['GDP'])
gdp["growth_rate"] = gdp["GDP"] / gdp["Lag_1"]
gdp["growth_rate"] = gdp["GDP"] - 1
gdp["log_approx"] = np.log(gdp["GDP"]) - np.log(gdp["Lag_1"])


gdp.dropna(inplace = True)
gdp.head(10)
```

| | GDP | Lag_1 | log_gdp | rate | log_approx |
|---|---|---|---|---|---|
| DATE | | | | | |
| **2010-04-01** | 14980.193 | 14764.610 | 9.614484 | 0.014601 | 0.014496 |
| **2010-07-01** | 15141.607 | 14980.193 | 9.625202 | 0.010775 | 0.010718 |
| **2010-10-01** | 15309.474 | 15141.607 | 9.636227 | 0.011086 | 0.011025 |
| **2011-01-01** | 15351.448 | 15309.474 | 9.638965 | 0.002742 | 0.002738 |
| **2011-04-01** | 15557.539 | 15351.448 | 9.652301 | 0.013425 | 0.013336 |
| **2011-07-01** | 15647.680 | 15557.539 | 9.658078 | 0.005794 | 0.005777 |
| **2011-10-01** | 15842.259 | 15647.680 | 9.670436 | 0.012435 | 0.012358 |
| **2012-01-01** | 16068.805 | 15842.259 | 9.684635 | 0.014300 | 0.014199 |
| **2012-04-01** | 16207.115 | 16068.805 | 9.693206 | 0.008607 | 0.008571 |
| **2012-07-01** | 16319.541 | 16207.115 | 9.700119 | 0.006937 | 0.006913 |

discrepancy between the two approaches becomes more apparent. The second plot on the right-hand side shows the difference between the actual growth rate and the log-transformed growth rate. It shows that for growth rates less than approximately 0.1 (10%), the error introduced by using the log approach is minimal and acceptable. Beyond this point, the error grows, and the log transformation becomes less reliable.

## 4 Key Takeaways

To this end, this chapter introduces fundamental concepts of Econometrics. Econometrics integrates economic theory, mathematical modeling, and statistical inference to analyze real-world economic data. It provides a structured approach

**Table 17** Reliability of natural logarithm

```
g = np.arange(0, 0.8, 0.01)
log(g) = np.log(1 + g)
fig, ax = plt.subplots(nrows = 1, ncols = 2, figsize = (16, 8))
ax[0].plot(g, g, label = "Division Approach")
ax[0].plot(g, log_g, label = "Natural Log Approach")
ax[0].set_xlabel("Real Growth Rate")
ax[0].set_ylabel("Approximated Growth Rate")
ax[0].grid()
ax[0].legend()
ax[1].plot(g, g - log_g, ls = "--", lw = 3, label = "Difference Between Two Approaches")
ax[1].set_xlabel("Real Growth Rate")
ax[1].set_ylabel("Difference (g - log_g)")
ax[1].grid()
ax[1].legend()
plt.show()
```

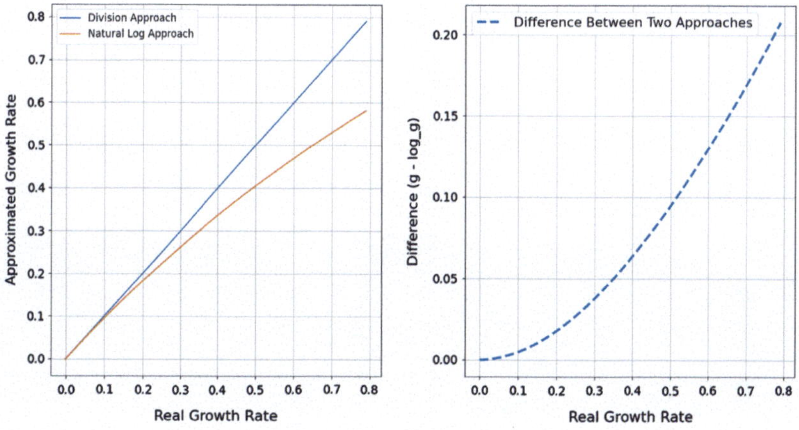


to understanding complex economic phenomena, such as consumer behavior, economic growth, inflation, and market dynamics. Econometrics helps in making predictions and policy decisions by quantifying relationships between variables. The history of Econometrics began with Frisch in 1926, with Tinbergen and Klein and Kuznets all contributing significantly to the field. The first step in Econometrics is to obtain and analyze a dataset and define hypotheses based on existing economic theories. Modeling helps clarify the structure of relationships and test hypotheses.

Models provide a structured method for testing hypotheses, quantifying relations, forecasting future trends, and making evidence-based decisions in economic policy and business strategy. By using a model, we evaluate economic ideas and challenge assumptions, allowing for quantification of relationships between variables. Moreover, models are essential for forecasting, strategic planning, and policy evaluation. This chapter discusses model testing using ordinary least squares regression technique.

## References

Klein, L. R. (1969). The specification of regional Econometric models. *Papers of the Regional Science Association, 23*(1), 105–115. https://doi.org/10.1007/BF01941877

Kuznets, S. (1971). *Modern economic growth: Findings and reflections*. Simon Kuznets Prize Lecture.

# Hypothesis(es) Testing 2

Before delving into hypotheses, let us understand about the significance of data stationary for time series analysis. "Stationary" data means the statistical properties of a time series, i.e., mean, variance, and covariance, do not change over time. Many statistical models require the series to be stationary to make effective predictions. Stationarity.

## 1 Unit Root and Stationarity in Time Series

A time series is considered "stationary" if its statistical properties like mean, variance, and autocorrelation do not change over time. In simpler terms, the series shows a consistent pattern without any predictable trends or seasonality. This property is crucial for many time series analysis techniques.

A unit root is a feature of a time series that indicates non-stationarity. It essentially means that the series has a root of 1 in its characteristic equation. This leads to the series having a stochastic trend, meaning it moves randomly without returning to a long-term mean. Unit root processes are often referred to as "differenced-series" because differencing (subtracting the previous value from the current value) can usually make them stationary.

We will use two statistical tests to check the stationarity of a time series: Augmented Dickey Fuller ("ADF")[1] test and Kwiatkowski-Phillips-Schmidt-Shin ("KPSS")[2] test. To know more about these tests, interested readers may refer to Statsmodel's stationary/detrending[3] documentation.

[1] https://en.wikipedia.org/wiki/Augmented_Dickey%E2%80%93Fuller_test.

[2] https://en.wikipedia.org/wiki/kpss_test.

[3] Stationarity and detrending (ADF/KPSS)—statsmodels 0.15.0 (+571).



S. Maitra, *A Practical Guide to Static and Dynamic Econometric Modelling*, Contributions to Economics, https://doi.org/10.1007/978-3-031-86862-7_2

Now, let us understand the various steps involved in hypotheses testing.

## 2 Steps in Hypotheses Testing

I. Formulate the hypotheses:
   - Null Hypothesis ($H_0$) → there is no effect or no relationship, meaning the coefficient is equal to zero ($\beta = 0$).
   - Alternative Hypothesis ($H_1$) → there is an effect or a relationship, meaning the coefficient is not equal to zero ($\beta \neq 0$).

II. We start with OLS implementation to estimate the regression model and obtain the coefficient estimates ($\widehat{\beta}$)

III. The test statistic for hypothesis testing is usually the $t$-statistic: $t = \frac{\widehat{\beta} - \beta_0}{SE(\widehat{\beta})}$

   where $\widehat{\beta}$ is the estimated coefficient, $\beta_0$ is the hypothesized value of the coefficient (often zero), and $SE(\widehat{\beta})$ is the standard error of the estimated coefficient.

IV. The acceptance or rejection of $H_0$ is determined using a critical value, or the $p$-value which measures the evidence against the null hypothesis.
   - The standard for making a statistical decision is called the level of significance ($\alpha$). The significance level is the probability of rejecting the $H_0$ when it is true (Type I error). Common values are 0.05 (95%), 0.01 (99%), or 0.10 (90%).
   - We reject a hypothesis if the $p$-value < 0.05.

## 3 Assumptions

The Gauss-Markov theorem is a cornerstone in Econometrics and Statistics. It states that under certain conditions, the OLS estimators are the Best Linear Unbiased Estimators (BLUE). The five most important conditions are stated below.

I. Linear regression assumes linearity. Each independent variable is multiplied by a $\beta$ coefficient and summed up to predict the value.

II. The 2nd is endogeneity which occurs when an independent variable is correlated with the error term. This can lead to biased and inconsistent estimates of the coefficients. Endogeneity can arise from several sources:
   - A model may provide the erroneous impression that there is a direct relationship between the independent variables and the dependent variable when it omits a variable that affects both the dependent variable and one or more independent variables.
   - Errors in measuring an independent variable can lead to biased estimates of the relationship between that variable and the dependent variable, as the true relationship is obscured by the inaccuracies in the data.

- Simultaneity occurs when the dependent variable influences the independent variables, leading to a two-way causation that complicates the estimation of the causal effect of the independent variables on the dependent variable.

III. The 3rd assumption is normality and homoscedasticity of the error term. The assumption is that the error term is normally distributed. Homoscedasticity means that the variance of the error term is constant across observations.

IV. The 4th assumption is related to autocorrelation which occurs when the error terms are correlated with each other. This violates the assumption that the covariance of any two error terms is zero.

V. The 5th assumption is that independent variables should not be collinear. Multicolinearity can create issues to determine the individual effect of each independent variable on the dependent variable, leading to inflated standard errors and unreliable coefficient estimates.

## 4 Diagnostic Tests

To ensure a robust model, we must perform a range of diagnostic checks. These tests assess statistical assumptions about the data, the model, and the residuals (errors). Here are the key diagnostic checks:

I. Multicollinearity check: To ensure predictors are not highly correlated. The common checks are quantitative in nature the Variance Inflation Factor (VIF) and Person's correlation test. Variance Inflation Factor (VIF) values over 5 or 10 suggest high multicollinearity and Correlation Matrix examine the correlations among predictors to find highly correlated pairs:

II. Linearity check: To ensure a linear relationship between the predictors and the response variable. The common checks are through visualization:
   - Residuals vs. Fitted Plot: If residuals show random scatter around zero without clear patterns, it suggests linearity. Residuals can only be known after model fitting.
   - Partial Regression Plots: Show the relationship between each predictor and the response variable, accounting for other predictors.

   If linearity is not met, we may need to apply necessary transformations such as polynomial terms or log transformations.

III. Normality of residuals: This is essential for reliable inference in small samples. The common checks here are both visuals and quantitative. The visual tool comprises of a Quantile–Quantile (Q-Q) plot, compares residuals to a normal distribution. If points follow the 45-degree line, normality is likely. Shapiro–Wilk quantitative test checks for normality (though sensitive in large datasets) whereas Jarque–Bera test for normality based on skewness and kurtosis. The D'Agostino–Pearson test combines skewness and kurtosis, provide a comprehensive normality test for residuals.

IV. Homoscedasticity (Constant Variance of Errors): To check that the variance of residuals remains constant across all levels of the predictor variables. The common methods are quantitative checks whereas Breusch–Pagan test checks for heteroscedasticity, White's test checks for non-constant variance and if heteroscedasticity is detected, a transformation like a log transformation can sometimes help.

V. Independence of errors: To confirm that residuals are independent. The common checks are a combination of visual and quantitative where Durbin–Watson test for autocorrelation in residuals and a plot of residuals over time to check if residuals show a pattern over time, which indicates autocorrelation.

VI. Influence and Outlier detection. The common checks are Cook's Distance which measures the influence of each observation on the model's fit. Values above 4/n (where n is the number of observations) or above 1 are typically considered influential and Leverage Points where observations with high leverage (extreme predictor values) can disproportionately affect the regression line.

VII. Assessing model fit: To confirm the model adequately explains the variability in the response variable. The common checks are: (1) $R^2$ and Adjusted $R^2$ which measures of how well the model explains the variance in the data, (2) AIC/BIC (Akaike and Bayesian Information Criteria) which are useful for model comparison, especially when evaluating different sets of predictors, and (3) Cross-Validation where we split data into training and testing sets to evaluate model performance and generalizability.

These diagnostics checks ensure that the model is well specified, interpretable, and provides reliable estimates.

## 4.1 Linearity Test

To assess whether the relationship between the independent and dependent variables is linear, we continue from the model developed (Table 9, Chapter 1). After fitting the OLS model, we plot the residuals (differences between observed and predicted $Y$) against $X$ as displayed in below Table 1. Residuals should randomly scatter around zero without a pattern.

From the plot above, we observe that the residuals are randomly distributed around the zero line, suggesting that the assumption of a linear relationship is reasonable.

### 4.1.1 Normality Test

Understanding normal distribution is important in economics and finance because, (1) stock returns are assumed to follow a normal distribution, and (2) the error terms from a model should follow a normal distribution with a zero mean. However, real-world data often encounter complexities that deviate from this normality

**Table 1** Residual vs fitted plot

```
plt.scatter(model.fittedvalues, model.resid)
plt.axhline(0, color = 'red', linestyle ='--')
plt.title('Residuals vs Fitted Values')
plt.xlabel('Fitted Values')
plt.ylabel('Residuals')
plt.show()
```

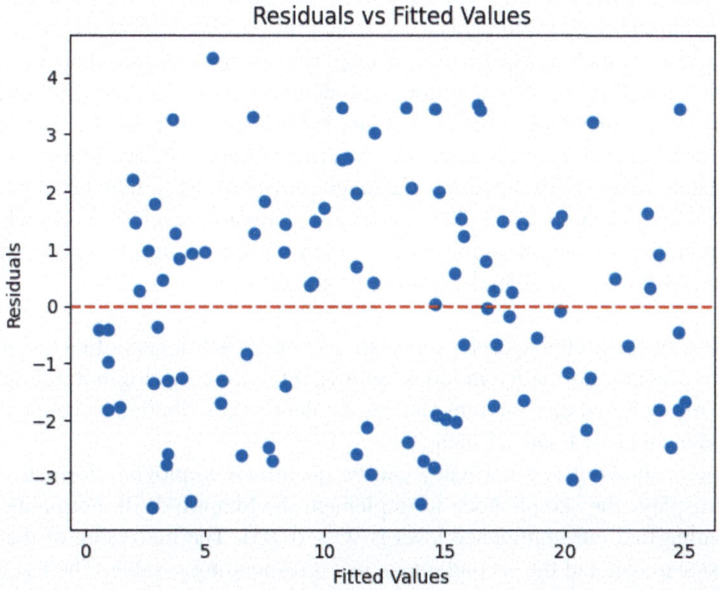


assumption. Let us take some examples to clear our understanding on the statistical assumption of normality vs the real-world characteristics:

I. Income and Wealth distribution often exhibit heavy tails, where extreme values (high incomes or wealth levels) occur more frequently than a normal distribution would predict. Moreover, sudden events like recessions, natural disasters, or geopolitical crises can cause economic variables to exhibit heavy tails.

II. Skewness is observed in various Econometric contexts such as inflation may exhibit right skewness during periods of hyperinflation or left skewness during deflationary phases. During economic downturns, unemployment rates often show a long right tail due to a slow recovery process. Trade balances may display skewness due to structural trade surpluses or deficits in certain economies.

III. Volatility Clustering: GDP growth rates, exchange rates, and inflation often show periods of high variability followed by stability, particularly during economic crises or policy changes. Econometric data can exhibit clusters of volatility due to abrupt changes in monetary or fiscal policy.
IV. Leptokurtosis, or distributions with sharp peaks and fat tails, is prevalent in Econometric data. Employment rates often cluster near certain levels (like full employment) but occasionally experience sharp deviations (e.g., during a recession). Prices of commodities like oil and agricultural products often show leptokurtic distributions due to supply shocks and speculative behaviors.
V. Econometric data is influenced by structural and behavioral factors. Behavioral biases, such as herd behavior or panic buying, can introduce deviations from normality in consumption and demand data. Government interventions (e.g., subsidies, tariffs) and market imperfections (e.g., monopolies, information asymmetry) can distort the distribution of key economic variables.
VI. Variables like GDP, inflation, and unemployment are interdependent, often driven by common shocks or underlying economic cycles. In a globalized economy, national economic data is often correlated due to trade linkages, financial flows, and shared exposure to global risks.

Because of these characteristics, researchers and practitioners often use models that allow for non-normality in stock returns, such as using log-normal distributions, or heavy-tailed distributions like the Student's *t*-distribution to better capture the real dynamics of financial data.

The plots showing non-normalcy can be quantified employing normality tests. Table 2 displays the sample code to implement the Shapiro–Wilk normality test.

Assuming that our confidence level is 95% (0.05). The first value of the result is the test statistic, and the second one is its corresponding *p*-value. The test rejects the hypothesis of normality when the *p*-value $\leq 0.05$. So, we reject the null hypothesis. This suggests that the residuals are not normally distributed. We discussed more about these tests (Jarque–Bera and Shapiro–Wilk) in Chapter 3.

**Table 2** Shapiro–Wilk normality test

```
shapiro_test = stats.shapiro(model.resid)
print('Shapiro-Wilk test statistic:', shapiro_test.statistic)
print('Shapiro-Wilk test p-value:', shapiro_test.pvalue)
```

```
Shapiro-Wilk test statistic: 0.9672574400901794
Shapiro-Wilk test p-value: 0.013686371967196465
```

**Table 3** *T*-test and *F*-test

```
np.random.seed(1235)
x = stats.norm.rvs(size = 10000)
print("T-value P-value (two-tail)")
print(stats.ttest_1samp(x, 0.5))
print(stats.ttest_1samp(x, 0))
```

```
T-value P-value (two-tail)
TtestResult(statistic=-49.76347123142897, pvalue=0.0, df=9999)
TtestResult(statistic=-0.26310321925083024, pvalue=0.7924764437516486, df=9999)
```

## 4.2 *T*-test and *F*-test

The *t*-test can only analyze one regression coefficient at a time, while an *F*-test can examine several coefficients concurrently. If the null hypothesis in the *t*-test is supported, we know that it means the mean for a standard normal distribution is zero. Table 3 displays the implementation of *t*-test and *F*-test.

- For the first test, we test whether the series has a mean of 0.5; we reject the null hypothesis since the *t*-value is 49.76 and the *p*-value is 0.
- For the second test, we accept the null hypothesis since the *t*-value is −0.26 and the *p*-value is $0.79 > 0.05$.

## 4.3 Bartlett Test

The Bartlett test checks if the variances of several groups are equal. It is useful when the assumption of homogeneity of variances (equal variances) is critical for other statistical tests like Analysis of Variance (ANOVA).

- $H_0 \rightarrow$ the variances are equal across all groups,
- $H_1 \rightarrow$ at least one group has a different variance.

Table 4 shows a simple example with using a synthetic dataset with a null hypothesis that all input samples are from populations with equal variances.

With a *t*-value of 7.057 and a *p*-value of $0.007 < 0.05$, we can conclude that these two series having different variances for any significance level.

## 4.4 Heteroscedasticity Test

It is used to check for constant variance of residuals. The common tests are the Breusch-Pagan test and White's test. Table 5 displays the implementation of the Breusch-Pagan heteroscedasticity test.

**Table 4** Bartlett test

```
np.random.seed(0)
group1 = np.random.normal(loc=0, scale=1, size=30)
group2 = np.random.normal(loc=0, scale=2, size=30)

statistic, p_value = stats.bartlett(group1, group2)
print("Bartlett's Test Statistic:", statistic)
print("p-value:", p_value)
alpha = 0.05
if p_value < alpha:
  print("Reject the null hypothesis: The variances are significantly different.")
else:
  print("Fail to reject the null hypothesis: No significant difference in variances.")
```

```
Bartlett's Test Statistic: 7.057436107054651
p-value: 0.007893689035690597
Reject the null hypothesis: The variances are significantly different.
```

**Table 5** Breusch-Pagan heteroscedasticity test

```
bp_test = het_breuschpagan(model.resid, model.model.exog)
labels = ['Lagrange multiplier statistic', 'p-value', 'f-statistic', 'f p-value']
bp_results = dict(zip(labels, bp_test))
print(bp_results)
```

```
{'Lagrange multiplier statistic': 0.03798995844715991, 'p-value': 0.8454633043548758, 'f-statistic': 0.03724430837548936, 'f p-value': 0.847367881175535}
```

- The value is approximately 0.038. This measures the degree of heteroscedasticity in the model, where a value close to 0 suggests little evidence of heteroscedasticity. The $p$-value is $0.845 > 0.05$, so there is no statistically significant evidence of heteroscedasticity. The $F$-statistic is 0.037. This measures the overall significance of the relationship in the context of the heteroscedasticity test. The $p$-value $(0.847) > 0.05$. This reinforces the conclusion that there is no statistical evidence of heteroscedasticity.

### 4.5 Autocorrelation Test

After we run a regression, the error term should have no correlation, with a mean zero. To evaluate whether residuals are correlated across time, normal procedure is to use the Durbin-Watson test or Breusch-Godfrey test. The Durbin-Watson statistic tests the null hypothesis that the residuals are not autocorrelated against

**Table 6** Durbin-Watson test

| Durbin-Watson test | Description |
|---|---|
| ≈2 | Suggests no autocorrelation in the residuals, indicating that the residuals are independent |
| <2 | Values closer to 0 indicate positive autocorrelation |
| >2 | Values closer to 4 indicate negative autocorrelation |

**Table 7** Durbin-Watson autocorrelation test

```
dw_statistic = durbin_watson(model.resid)
print('Durbin-Watson statistic:', dw_statistic)
```

```
Durbin-Watson statistic: 2.0832252321235347
```

the alternative that the residuals follow an AR(1) process. The test statistic ranges from 0 to 4, as shown in Table 6.

Table 7 displays the implementation of Durbin-Watson autocorrelation test. The output displays "Durbin–Watson statistic: 2.083225232125347".

Here, the statistic 2.083 $\approx$ 2, indicating no autocorrelation in the residuals. This supports the assumption of independence of errors. We have discussed other sets of alternative Goodness-of-Fit test during implementation phase in Chapter 5.

## 4.6 Multicollinearity Test

Through this we can assess whether the independent variables are highly correlated with each other using the Variance Inflation Factor (VIF) and Pearson's correlation. This is applicable in the case of multivariate or multiple regression.

## 4.7 Model Specification Test

The Ramsey Regression Equation Specification Error Test (RESET) helps to identify whether the functional form of a regression model is correctly specified or if there are omitted variables, incorrect functional forms, or interaction terms that should be included.

### 4.7.1 How Does RESET Helps in Model Specification?

RESET shows whether the chosen functional form is right. If the test suggests misspecification, it implies that the model might require adjustments such as additional terms (higher-order polynomials or interaction terms) to capture the true relationship between the variables.

**Table 8** Ramsey model specification test

```
reset_test = reset_ramsey(model)
print('RESET test statistic:', reset_test)
```

RESET test statistic: <F-test: F=0.5262291538795965, p=0.716695694985761, df_denom=94, df_num=4>

If important variables are omitted from the model, the RESET helps detect their absence by highlighting specification errors. By diagnosing specification errors, the RESET helps improve the overall fit and validity of the model.

RESET detects nonlinearity in the relationship between the dependent and independent variables. While the RESET is not specifically designed to detect nonlinearity, it shows nonlinearity if the test detects that including higher-order terms significantly improves the model. If the test suggests that the functional form of the model is incorrect, it implies that nonlinearity is present, but it does not directly test for nonlinear relationships.

Table 8 displays the implementation of RESET.

- *F*-statistic (0.5262) is low and suggests that the additional higher-order terms do not explain much of the variation in the dependent variable beyond what is already explained by the original linear model.
- Since the *p*-value > 0.05, we do not reject the null hypothesis. This means there is no statistical evidence that the model is mis-specified.

## 4.8 Outlier Detection

With this test, we identify the influential observations that may disproportionately affect model estimates, using leverage and Cook's distance (Cook, 1977) introduced by American statistician R. Dennis Cook.[4] Cook's distance measures how much an individual data point influences a regression model's results. Specifically, it shows how the model's coefficients would change if that point were removed. It is commonly used to detect outliers in OLS regression. A general rule is that a point is highly influential if its Cook's distance $D(i) > \frac{4}{n}n$, where $n$ is the number of data points. This threshold helps identify potential outliers. The measurement is a combination of each observation's leverage and residual values, the higher the leverage and residuals, the higher the Cook's distance. Table 9 displays the implementation of the OLSInfluence test using Cook's distance.

Points with a large Cook's distance are considered influential because they have a strong effect on the estimated regression coefficients. Here, the influential points are [20, 64, 87]; these points have a significant impact on the regression model's

[4] R. Dennis Cook - Wikipedia.

**Table 9** OLSInfluence test

```
influence = OLSInfluence(model)
cooks_d = influence.cooks_distance[0]
influential_points = np.where(cooks_d > 4 / len(model.model.endog))[0]
plt.stem(np.arange(len(cooks_d)), cooks_d, markerfmt =",", basefmt=" ")
plt.axhline(y = 4/len(model.model.endog))
plt.title('Cook\'s Distance')
plt.xlabel('Observation index')
plt.ylabel('Cook\'s Distance')
plt.show()
print('Influential points:', influential_points)
```

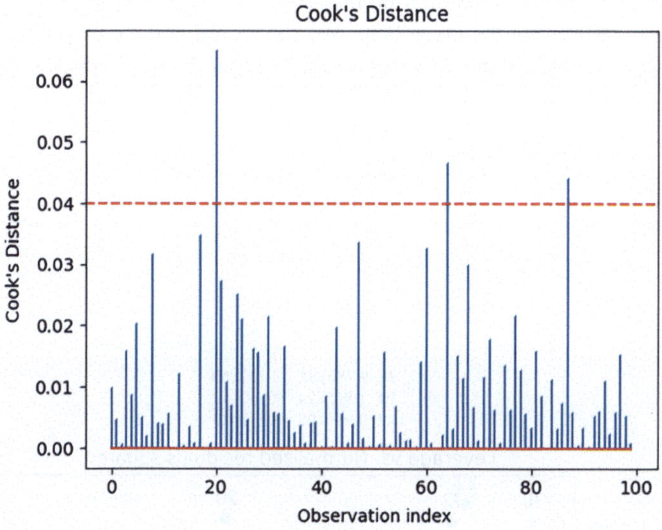


Influential points: [20 64 87]

coefficients. Removing or altering these points would significantly change the fitted model. Influential points might be outliers or leverage points. They could indicate data entry errors, unique conditions, or other anomalies.

### 4.8.1 Mathematical Intuition of Cook's Distance

Cooks distance ($D_i$) for the $i$th data point can be calculated as $D_i = \frac{\sum_{j=1}^{n}(\hat{y}_j - \hat{y}_{j(i)})^2}{p * \text{MSE}}$ where

- $\hat{y}_j$ = the predicted value of the $j$th observation using the full model.
- $\hat{y}_{j(i)}$ = the predicted value of the $j$th observation with the $i$th observation removed.
- $n$ = the number of observations.

- $p =$ the number of parameters (including the intercept) in the model.
- MSE $=$ the mean squared error of the model.

The numerator $\sum_{j=1}^{n}\left(\hat{y}_j - \hat{y}_{j(i)}\right)^2$ measures the aggregate change in predictions for all data points when the $i$th observation is removed. If this value is large, it means that the $i$th point has a significant impact on the regression model's predictions.

The denominator $p * \text{MSE}$ normalizes the difference in predictions. Common thresholds for identifying influential points are $D_i > 1$ or comparing $D_i$ to $\frac{4}{n}$, where $n$ is the number of observations. Points exceeding these thresholds are flagged as potentially influential.

We can further explore these influential points. Table 10 shows the implementation of exploration of influential points.

Several measures can be taken here. We can examine the data points at indices 20, 64, and 87 to understand why they are influential. Need to check for data entry

**Table 10** Exploring influential points

```
print(data.iloc[[20, 64, 87]])
plot_leverage_resid2(model)
plt.show()
```

```
          X          Y
20  9.786183  28.231760
64  1.965824   9.680849
87  0.939405  -0.741029
```

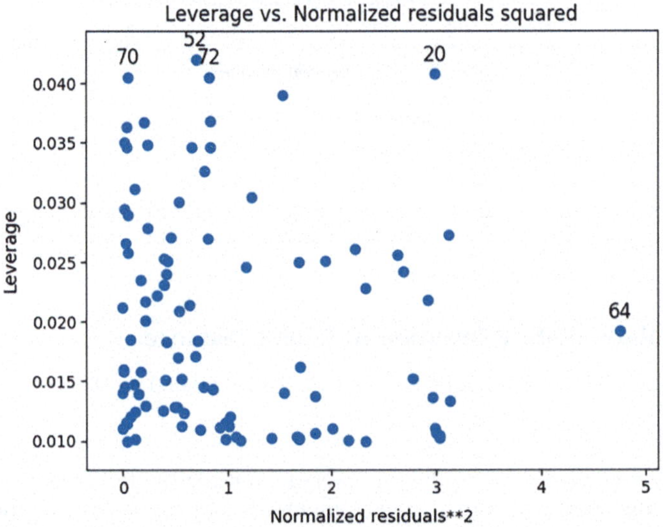

errors or unique conditions that might justify their influence. We may consider refitting the model without these points to see how the model parameters change.

We must note here that Cook's test is theoretically valuable but may not always be applied rigorously in practical Econometric studies. It is particularly relevant in high-stakes modeling, such as economic forecasting or policy evaluation. In large datasets or models with many predictors, Cook's distance may become less effective, as the influence of any single point diminishes. Econometricians often use robust regression techniques or machine learning models that inherently downweigh influential observations, making Cook's test less important.

## 4.9 Parameter Stability Test

Parameter stability test is essential in regression analysis, particularly for time series models. It assesses whether the coefficients of a model remain constant over time or if they change significantly, which indicate structural breaks or shifts in the underlying data-generating process.

### 4.9.1 Importance of Parameter Stability

- Stable parameters ensure that the model can reliably predict outcomes over time. Unstable parameters may lead to unreliable predictions and inferences. Changes in relationships over time can signify structural breaks due to policy changes, economic events, or shifts in market conditions.

Here are some commonly used parameters stability tests:

The Chow Test (Chow, 1960) is used for structural breaks at a known point in time. Here, we divide the data into two (or more) subsets and estimate separate models. Compare the sum of squared residuals to assess whether the parameters differ significantly between the subsets shown in Table 11.

Since the Chow test indicates a significant structural break, it suggests that the relationship between the independent variable ($X$) and the dependent variable ($Y$) changes at the specified breakpoint. This implies that several factors influence the dependent variable before and after this point.

**CUSUM Test** (Page, 1954): Through this test, we can monitor the cumulative sum of residuals to detect gradual changes in parameters. This test (Table 12) compares cumulative sums of residuals to critical bounds. If the cumulative sum exceeds these bounds, it indicates instability.

This $p$-value > 0.05 indicates not enough evidence to reject the null hypothesis of parameter stability. Since the CUSUM test indicates parameter stability, it suggests that the relationship between the independent variable ($X$) and the dependent variable ($Y$) remains consistent throughout the entire dataset. This is a positive outcome for the reliability of your regression model.

**Table 11** Chow test sample script

```
np.random.seed(0)
X = np.random.rand(100, 1) * 10
Y = 2.5 * X + np.random.randn(100, 1) * 2
data = pd.DataFrame({'X': X.flatten(), 'Y': Y.flatten()})
X_with_const = sm.add_constant(X)

model = sm.OLS(Y, X_with_const).fit()
breakpoint = 50
y1 = Y[:breakpoint]
y2 = Y[breakpoint:]
X1 = X_with_const[:breakpoint]
X2 = X_with_const[breakpoint:]

model1 = sm.OLS(y1, X1).fit()
model2 = sm.OLS(y2, X2).fit()
f_stat = ((model1.ssr + model2.ssr) / (model.ssr)) * (len(Y) - 2) / 2
print("Chow Test F-statistic:", f_stat)

df_num = 2
df_denom = len(Y) - 2

p_value = stats.f.sf(f_stat, df_num, df_denom)
print("Chow Test p-value:", p_value)

if p_value < 0.05:
    print("The Chow Test indicates a significant structural break.")
else:
    print("The Chow Test does not indicate a significant structural break.")
```

```
Chow Test F-statistic: 46.0246640706214
Chow Test p-value: 8.046872422550316e-15
The Chow Test indicates a significant structural break.
```

**BDS** (Broock-Dechert-Scheinkman) (Broock et al., 1996) test can be used for detecting serial dependence in time series. The BDS test is linked to chaos theory in the context of detecting nonlinearity and complex dynamics in time series data. However, it primarily checks for nonlinearity and serial dependence in a time series. In finance and economics, nonlinearity can be a sign that the data may exhibit more complex patterns or dependencies that cannot be explained by a simple linear model. However, BDS test cannot directly confirm chaos but can indicate complex dynamics that may point toward chaotic behavior. To detect chaos more

**Table 12** CUMSUM test script

```
np.random.seed(0)
X = np.random.rand(100, 1) * 10
Y = 2.5 * X + np.random.randn(100, 1) * 2

data = pd.DataFrame({'X': X.flatten(), 'Y': Y.flatten()})
X_with_const = sm.add_constant(X)
model = sm.OLS(Y, X_with_const).fit()

cusum_result = breaks_cusumolsresid(model.resid)
print("CUSUM Test statistic:", cusum_result[0])
print("CUSUM Test p-value:", cusum_result[1])

if cusum_result[1] < 0.05:
    print("CUSUM indicates parameter instability.")
else:
    print("CUSUM indicates parameter stability.")
```

```
CUSUM Test statistic: 1.154060357687865
CUSUM Test p-value: 0.13933113046177026
CUSUM indicates parameter stability.
```

definitively, researchers often first use the BDS test to detect nonlinearity, and then examine whether the system behaves in a manner consistent with chaotic systems.

Table 13 displays the implementation of BDS test.

This $p$-value > 0.05 suggests no statistical evidence to reject the null hypothesis of linearity in the residuals. Since the BDS test shows linearity in the residuals, it suggests that the residuals from the model exhibit a linear pattern. This is a desirable outcome as it shows that the model adequately captures the relationship between the independent and dependent variables.

**Engle's ARCH test** (Engle, 1982) for Auto Regressive Conditional Heteroscedasticity (ARCH) detects conditional heteroscedasticity, which occurs when the variance of error terms in a model is not constant but depends on past error terms as shown in the below Table 14. It is relevant in financial and economic time series data, where periods of high volatility (heteroscedasticity) often follow other high-volatility periods (known as volatility clustering).

While the calculation process of the ARCH test involves linear regression, its purpose and implications deal with nonlinear relationships in the data, specifically the time-varying nature of variance. Therefore, Engle's ARCH test is considered a nonlinear diagnostic tool in the broader context of Econometrics and time series analysis.

**Table 13** BDS test script

```
np.random.seed(0)
X = np.random.rand(100, 1) * 10
Y = 2.5 * X + np.random.randn(100, 1) * 2
data = pd.DataFrame({'X': X.flatten(), 'Y': Y.flatten()})
X_with_const = sm.add_constant(X)
model = sm.OLS(Y, X_with_const).fit()

bds_stat, p_value = bds(model.resid)

print("BDS Test statistic:", bds_stat)
print("BDS Test p-value:", p_value)

if p_value < 0.05:
    print("BDS indicates nonlinearity in the residuals.")
else:
    print("BDS indicates linearity in the residuals.")
```

```
BDS Test statistic: -0.6741896383124631
BDS Test p-value: 0.5001907563547601
BDS indicates linearity in the residuals.
```

**Table 14** Arch test

```
np.random.seed(0)
X = np.random.rand(100, 1) * 10
Y = 2.5 * X + np.random.randn(100, 1) * 2
data = pd.DataFrame({'X': X.flatten(), 'Y': Y.flatten()})
X_with_const = sm.add_constant(X)
model = sm.OLS(Y, X_with_const).fit()

arch_test = het_arch(model.resid)
print("ARCH Test statistic:", arch_test[0])
print("ARCH Test p-value:", arch_test[1])

if arch_test[1] < 0.05:
    print("ARCH test indicates the presence of heteroskedasticity.")
else:
    print("ARCH test indicates no significant heteroskedasticity.")
```

```
ARCH test statistic: 11.32575041395169
ARCH test p-value: 0.33270853914692833
ARCH test indicates no significant heteroscedasticity.
```

This $p$-value > 0.05 indicates no statistical evidence to reject the null hypothesis of homoscedasticity. Since the ARCH test indicates no significant heteroscedasticity, it suggests that the variance of the residuals is constant over time, which is a desirable property for the regression model.

## 4.10 Bai-Perron Test (Structural Break Detection)

This test detects structural breaks in the regression model, specifically in the relationship between the dependent and independent variables over time. If we suspect time-dependent changes in the stock's beta (sensitivity to market risk) and if there are significant economic events (e.g., financial crises, policy changes, or industry shifts) that could cause changes in the stock-market relationship, this test is applicable.

## 4.11 Key Takeaways

This chapter provided a theoretical concept about the significance of hypothesis testing in OLS regression. Hypothesis testing involves determining if the estimated coefficients significantly differ from zero or another value, and determining if there is a meaningful relationship between the independent and dependent variables. The process involves formulating hypotheses, which can be null or alternative, and estimating the regression model using the $t$-statistic or $f$-statistics. The acceptance or rejection of a hypothesis is determined using a critical value ($p$-value), and the significance level ($\alpha$) is the standard for statistical decision-making. The Gauss-Markov theorem states that under certain conditions, the OLS estimators are the Best Linear Unbiased Estimators (BLUE). The five most important assumptions include linearity, endogeneity, simultaneousity, normality, and homoscedasticity of the error term autocorrelation and not being collinear. These assumptions help to ensure the accuracy of the estimates and avoid potential biases in the model.

To ensure a robust linear regression model, several diagnostic tests are performed. These tests assess statistical assumptions about data, the model, and residuals. Key checks include multicollinearity checks, which check if predictors are not highly correlated, linearity checks, which ensure a linear relationship between predictors and response variables, normality of residuals, homoscedasticity tests, independence of errors, influence and outlier detection, and assessing model fit.

## References

Brock, W. A., Scheinkman, J. A., Dechert, W. D., & LeBaron, B. (1996). A test for independence based on the correlation dimension. *Econometric Reviews, 15*(3), 197–235. https://doi.org/10.1080/07474939608800353

Chow, G. C. (1960). Tests of equality between sets of coefficients in two linear regressions. *Econometrica, 28*(3), 591. https://doi.org/10.2307/1910133

Cook, R. D. (1977). Detection of influential observation in linear regression. *Technometrics, 19*(1), 15–18. https://doi.org/10.1080/00401706.1977.10489493

Engle, R. F. (1982). Autoregressive conditional heteroscedasticity with estimates of the variance of United Kingdom inflation. *Econometrica, 50*(4), 987. https://doi.org/10.2307/1912773

Page, E. S. (1954). Continuous inspection schemes. *Biometrika, 41*(1/2), 100. https://doi.org/10.2307/2333009

# 3 Dynamic Modeling in Econometrics: Foundational Knowledge

Dynamic modeling plays a crucial role in Econometrics because it allows us to capture and analyze the time-dependent relationships between economic variables. This is critical for understanding how economic systems evolve over time and for making informed forecasts and policy decisions. This chapter discusses about the dynamic modeling and their significance in Econometrics.

We will start with an example. Let us assume, we are analyzing the impact of monetary policy (interest rates) on economic output (GDP). Here, a dynamic model can capture how changes in interest rates affect GDP, not just immediately but over several periods. This is important because in all practical terms, the full effect of a change in interest rates may not be realized immediately and can take several quarters to notice. This is one such reason; however, there are several other reasons pointed out in Table 1 to display why dynamic models can be a viable choice in Econometric analysis:

Common types of dynamic models used in Econometrics are:

I. Auto Regressive (AR) model which uses past values of the dependent variable to predict future values.
II. Distributed Lag (DL) model which includes lagged values of independent variables.
III. Auto Regressive Distributed Lag (ARDL) model which includes both lagged dependent and independent variables.
IV. Moving Average (MA) model where the current value of the dependent variable depends on past errors.
V. Auto Regressive Moving Average (ARMA) model which combines AR and MA components for stationary time series.
VI. Auto Regressive Integrated Moving Average (ARIMA) model which extends ARMA to include differencing for non-stationary series.



S. Maitra, *A Practical Guide to Static and Dynamic Econometric Modelling*, Contributions to Economics, https://doi.org/10.1007/978-3-031-86862-7_3

**Table 1** Benefits of a dynamic model

| Properties | Effect of dynamic modeling |
|---|---|
| Temporal dependencies and autoregressive structure | Economic variables often exhibit lagged effects where past values influence current values. A dynamic model can capture these temporal dependencies in data. Moreover, a dynamic model can capture the autoregressive structure of the data, where past values of the dependent variable are used to predict its current value |
| Adjustment dynamics | A dynamic model can help in understanding how variables adjust over time to changes in other variables. This is crucial in policy analysis to understand the lagged impact of policy changes |
| Speed of adjustment | A dynamic model provides insights into how quickly or slowly economic variables return to equilibrium after a shock |
| Cointegration relationships | In the presence of non-stationary time series data, dynamic models like ARDL (Auto Regressive Distributed Lag) or VAR (Vector Auto Regression) can capture cointegration relationships, allowing for the modeling of both short-term fluctuations and long-term equilibrium relationships |
| Impact assessment | A dynamic model allows economists to assess the impact of economic policies over time, considering the delayed effects of policy interventions |
| Control for endogeneity | By including lagged dependent variables, dynamic models can sometimes help control for endogeneity, which arises when explanatory variables are correlated with the error term |
| Detecting structural breaks | A dynamic model can help identify structural breaks and regime changes in the data, which are periods where the underlying relationships between variables change |

VII. Vector Auto Regression (VAR) model which captures the dynamic relationship between multiple time series.
VIII. Vector Error Correction Model (VECM) where a restricted VAR model for cointegrated series, incorporating long-term equilibrium relationships.

We must remember that in economics and finance, dependent and independent variables rarely respond instantaneously; rather, the dependent variable $Y$ typically responds to changes in the explanatory variable $X$ with a time lag.

While some of these concepts may initially appear mathematically complex, they are built upon fundamental linear algebra principles. Mastering these fundamentals will provide a strong foundation for the practical implementation discussed in Chapters 5, 6, and 7.

## 1 Auto Regressive (AR) Models

Auto Regressive (AR) models are a cornerstone of time series analysis in Econometrics because they capture a fundamental aspect of economic data: persistence. This means that economic variables tend to be influenced by their own past values. Therefore, AR models are estimated via regressing a variable on one or more of its lagged values. An AR model can be univariate (scalar) or multivariate (vector).

An AR model of order $k$, denoted as AR($k$), can be formulated as $Y_t = \alpha + \beta_1 X_{t-1} + \beta_2 X_{t-2} + \ldots \beta_k X_{t-k} + \epsilon_t$ where

- $Y_t$ is the value of the time series at time t.
- $\alpha$ is a constant term.
- $\beta_0, \beta_1, \beta_2, \ldots, \beta_k$ are the autoregressive coefficients.
- $\epsilon_t$ is a white noise error term.

The order k specifies the number of lagged values (past observations) used in the model. For instance, in an AR(1) model, only the previous time period's value is used, while in an AR(2) model, the values from the previous two time periods are used.

For a model to be valid, the time series data must be stationary, meaning that its statistical properties (like mean ($\mu$), variance ($\sigma$)) do not change over time. Application of AR models can be found in various applications, including economic forecasting, signal processing, etc. For AR(1) model, the formula simplifies to $Y_t = \alpha + \beta_1 X_{t-1} + \epsilon_t$.

AR model is a fundamental part of time series analysis and serves as the building block for more complex models such as ARIMA (Auto Regressive Integrated Moving Average) and VAR (Vector Auto Regression) models.

## 2 Distributed Lag (DL) Model

The Distributed Lag (DL) model and the Auto Regressive (AR) model are related but distinct approaches. It is a dynamic model in which the effect of a regressor $X$ on $Y$ occurs over time rather than all at once. A common use case is where the past values of an independent variable influence the dependent variable (e.g., investment affected by past changes in interest rates).

A DL with one explanatory variable $X$ can be formulated as $Y_t = \alpha + \beta_0 X_t + \beta_1 X_{(t-1)} + \beta_2 X_{(t-2)} + \ldots \beta_k X_{(t-k)} + \epsilon_t$. This is called Finite Distributed Lag (FDL) model where coefficient $\beta_0$ attached to $X_t$ is called short run. $\beta_1, \beta_2, \ldots, \beta_k$ are the lag or interim multipliers. $\beta = \sum_{i=0}^{k} \beta_i = \beta_0 + \beta_1 + \cdots + \beta_k$ is the long run. Likewise, we can define Infinite Distributed Lag (IDL) model as $Y_t = \alpha + (\beta_0 X_t + \beta_1 X_{(t-1)} + \beta_2 X_{(t-2)} + \ldots \infty) + \epsilon_t$

The individual coefficient $\beta$ s is called lag weights and collectively comprises the lag distribution. When estimating variables without a clear economic relationship or theoretical basis, an ad hoc estimation method might be used. In each subsequent regression, add lagged values of the explanatory variable (e.g., $X_{(t-i)}$, where$i \geq 1$) to the model. We continue adding these lagged values until we notice that the statistical significance of the lagged terms diminishes, or the coefficients become unstable.

The successive lag values in a time series are often highly correlated with each other. This correlation causes multicollinearity where independent variables are correlated with each other. If we observe high standard errors, we must perform significance tests (e.g., $t$-test). If the $t$-test yields insignificant findings, it is difficult to tell if the lagged factors have a meaningful influence. Therefore, while an ad hoc method can be useful for exploratory purposes, the presence of multicollinearity can lead to inefficiencies and less reliable results.

$$\hat{Y}_t = \alpha + \beta_0 X_t$$

$$\hat{Y}_t = \alpha + \beta_0 X_t + \beta_1 X_{t-1}$$

$$\hat{Y}_t = \alpha + \beta_0 X_t + \beta_1 X_{t-1} + \beta_2 X_{t-2}$$

## 2.1 Koyck Approach to DL Model

Let us consider an Infinite DL (IDL) model as under $Y_t = \alpha + (\beta_0 X_t + \beta_1 X_{t-1} + \beta_2 X_{t-2} + \ldots \infty) + \epsilon_t$. The first-order AR lag model is often called the Koyck (Koyck, 1954) lag. Koyck used the geometric probability distribution to estimate the parameters of above equation. If all the $\beta$ coefficients have the same sign, Koyck assumed that they decline geometrically as in $\beta_k = \beta_0 \lambda^k, k = 0, 1, \ldots; 0 < \lambda < 1$ where $\lambda$ the rate of decline of decay, $(1 - \lambda)$ the speed of adjustment, when $\lambda \approx 1$ means $\beta_k$ declines slowly (i.e., $X$ values in distant past will have some impact on the current value of $Y$), and when $\lambda \approx 0$ means the impact of $X$ in the distant past will have insignificant impact on the current $Y$. In the case of $0 < \lambda < 1$, each successive $\beta$ coefficient is numerically smaller than each preceding $\beta$ and as we go back into the distant past, the effect of that lag on $Y$ becomes progressively smaller.

Therefore, the mathematical intuition of the above can be written as $Y_t = \alpha + (\beta_0 X_t + \beta_0 \lambda X_{t-1} + \beta_0 \lambda^2 X_{t-2} + \beta_0 \lambda^3 X_{t-3} + \ldots \beta_0 \lambda^k X_{t-k} + \ldots \infty) + \epsilon_t$.

Equation $Y_{t-1} = \alpha + (\beta_0 X_{t-1} + \beta_0 X_{t-1} + \beta_0 X_{t-2} + \ldots \beta_0 X_{t-k-1} \ldots \infty) + \epsilon_{t-1}$ can be formed by taking lag of 1 period on both sides and equation $\lambda Y_{t-1} =$

$\lambda\alpha + \beta_0\lambda X_{t-1} + \beta_0\lambda^2 X_{t-2} + \ldots \beta_0\lambda^k X_{t-k-1} \ldots \infty) + \lambda\epsilon_{t-1}$ is formed multiplying by $\lambda$.

Equation $Y_t - \lambda Y_{t-1} = \alpha(1-\lambda) + \beta_0 X_t + (\epsilon_t - \lambda\epsilon_{t-1})$ can be formed by joining with the original equation, wherein equation $Y_t = \alpha(1-\lambda) + \beta_0 X_t + -\lambda Y_{t-1} + (\epsilon_t - \lambda\epsilon_{t-1})$ is a rearranged form.

This is Koyck's transformation of the IDL (Infinite Distributed Lag) model into an AR (Auto Regressive) model of the first order. Since the lagged value of the dependent variable appears as a regressor, it is called AR model. This transformation becomes much simpler than the original model. Instead of estimating an infinite number of parameters, Koyck's transformation estimates only three parameters:

- the short-run impact→ the coefficient of $X$, $\beta_0$
- the long-run impact→ $\beta_0/(1-\lambda)$
- Since $\lambda$ lies between 0 and 1, the long-run impact will be greater than the short-run impact.

However, the Koyck model is not free from limitations; the error term $\epsilon_t$ is autocorrelated, where we may need to test Heteroscedasticity and Autocorrelation Consistent (HAC) standard errors. This has been demonstrated in Chapter 5.

We must be cautious here when adding lags to a regression model. Adding multiple lags to a regression model can have both positive and negative consequences. Including more lags can help capture long-term dependencies and delayed effects that may not be evident with only a few lags. This can lead to a model if the underlying process has a long memory. If the data generation process involves multiple past periods, adding more lags can improve the model fit by reducing residual autocorrelation and better capturing the dynamics of the data. However, adding too many lags can lead to overfitting, where the model becomes overly complex and starts to capture noise rather than the underlying pattern. This reduces the model's ability to generalize to new data.

Moreover, including many lagged variables can increase multicollinearity, which occurs when independent variables are highly correlated with each other. This can make it difficult to estimate the coefficients accurately and interpret their significance. Including many lags also reduces the number of observations available for estimation because lagged values require past data points. For example, if we include 12 monthly lags, we lose the first 12 observations.

## 3 Auto Regressive Distributed Lag (ARDL)

The ARDL model combines the features of Auto Regressive (AR) models and Distributed Lag (DL) models, making it highly versatile for analyzing dynamic relationships in time series data.

We know that the AR(s) influence of the dependent variable's past values ($Y_{t-1}$, $Y_{t-2}$ ...) on itself and the DL(s) influence of the independent variable's current

**Table 2** Comparison of AR, DL, and ARDL models

| Feature | AR model | DL model | ARDL model |
|---|---|---|---|
| Focus | Lagged values of $Y_t$ | Lagged values of $X_t$ | Combines lagged values of $Y_t$ and $X_t$ |
| Stationarity | Requires stationary $Y_t$ | Requires stationary $X_t$ | Allows mix of I(0) and I(1) variables |
| Flexibility | Captures autocorrelation in $Y_t$ | Captures lagged effects of $X_t$ | Captures both autocorrelation and distributed lags |
| Complexity | Simpler | Simpler | More comprehensive and versatile |

and past values ($X_t$, $X_{t-1}$, $X_{t-1}$ ...) on the dependent variable. The general ARDL model can be written as $Y_t = \alpha + \sum_{i=1}^{p} \phi_1 Y_{t-1} + \sum_{j=0}^{q} \beta_j X_{t-j} + \varepsilon_t$ where $Y_t$ is a dependent variable at time $t$, $X_t$ is an independent variable at time $t$, $p$ is the order of the autoregressive part, $q$ is the order of the distributed lag part, $\phi_1$ is the coefficients for the lagged dependent variable ($Y_{t-1}$), $\beta_j$ is the coefficients for the current and lagged independent variable ($X_{t-j}$), and $\varepsilon_t$ is white noise error term.

If we add trend and seasonality, the equation can be rewritten as $Y_t = \alpha + \gamma_t + \sum_{s=1}^{S} \delta_s D_s + \sum_{i=1}^{p} \phi_1 Y_{t-1} + \sum_{j=0}^{q} \beta_j X_{t-j} + \varepsilon_t$ where the added $\gamma_t$ is the trend and $\sum_{s=1}^{S} \delta_s D_s$ is the seasonality. This categorization makes it easier to understand the role of each term in the ARDL model.

Table 2 provides a comparison for easy reckoning the difference among AR, DL, and ARDL models.

While Koyck and ARDL models serve distinct purposes but share similarities in how they deal with lagged relationships in time series data, both approaches are useful in Econometrics for handling dynamic relationships, but ARDL offers more flexibility and robustness, especially in the presence of complex lag structures and potential cointegration. The Koyck transformation, while simpler, imposes a specific form on the decay of past effects, which may not always be appropriate. Table 3 displays a comparison between the two.

## 4 Moving Average (MA)

MA model is crucial for capturing patterns in the residuals (white noise) of a time series. If errors from previous periods influence the current value, an MA model is appropriate. MA model is either complementing Auto Regressive (AR) models in ARMA or ARIMA frameworks, allowing for more accurate modeling of both short-term shocks and long-term dependencies. The MA(q) form can be explained as $Y_t = \mu + \varepsilon_t + \theta_1 \varepsilon_{t-1} + \theta_2 \varepsilon_{t-2} + \cdots + \theta_n \varepsilon_{t-n}$ where $Y_t$ is the value of the time series at time t, $\mu$ is the mean of the series, $\varepsilon_t$ is white noise error term at time t (assumed to be independently and identically distributed), $\theta_1, \theta_2, \ldots, \theta_n$ are the

**Table 3** Comparison between Koyck transformation and ARDL approach

| | Koyck transformation | ARDL |
|---|---|---|
| Model structure | The Koyck model simplifies the infinite lag structure of a distributed lag model into a single equation. It assumes that the effect of past values of the independent variable decays geometrically over time | The ARDL model allows for both autoregressive terms and distributed lags of the explanatory variables. It is more flexible than the Koyck model because it does not impose a geometric decay structure on the lags |
| Formula | $Y_t - \lambda Y_{t-1} = \alpha(1-\lambda) + \beta_0 X_t + (\epsilon_t - \lambda\epsilon_{t-1})$ which can be rewritten as $Y_t = \alpha(1-\lambda) + \beta_0 X_t + \lambda Y_{y-1} + \epsilon_t - \lambda\epsilon_{t-1}$ | $Y_t = \alpha + \sum_{i=1}^{p} \beta_1 Y_{t-1} + \sum_{j=1}^{q} \beta_j X_{t-j} + \epsilon_t$ where $p$ is the number of lags of the dependent variable and $q$ is the number of lags of the independent variable |
| Estimation | Simplifies the model into a single equation that can be estimated using OLS with a transformation. This transformation assumes a specific form for the error terms, which might lead to complications in the presence of autocorrelation | Estimates the model by including multiple lagged terms of both dependent and independent variables. It provides flexible lag structures and capture short-run dynamics and long-run relationships |
| Error terms | Incorporates a lagged error term, which can complicate the estimation if autocorrelation is present | Does not impose such a structure on the error term, making it more robust to different error term behaviors |
| Long-run and short-run dynamics | Focuses more on the immediate and decaying effect of the independent variable | Explicitly models both short-run dynamics and long-run relationships, making it useful for cointegration analysis |

moving average coefficients that measure the influence of past errors, and q is the order of the MA model (number of lagged errors included).

MA models are well suited for systems where shocks (e.g., policy changes, economic crises) have temporary effects that gradually die out over time. In dynamic Econometric models, MA components can address residual autocorrelation, improving model diagnostics and making the results more reliable.

## 5 Auto Regressive Moving Average (ARMA) Model

ARMA models are widely used for forecasting, capturing the temporal evolution of a time series dynamically. It is a combination of two time series processes, the Auto Regressive (AR) process and the Moving Average (MA) process.

The AR component models the current value of a variable ($Y_t$) as a function of its own past values ($Y_{t-1}$, $Y_{t-2}\ldots$). The Moving Average (MA) component models the current value of $Y_t$ as a function of past errors ($\varepsilon_{t-1}$, $\varepsilon_{t-2}\ldots$). Together, these components capture dynamic relationships over time. It has the form $Y_t = \beta_1 Y_{t-1} + \beta_2 Y_{t-2} + \cdots + \theta_1 \varepsilon_{t-1} + \theta_2 \varepsilon_{t-2} + \varepsilon_t$. This dynamic equation highlights how the current value of $Y_t$ depends on both its own lagged values ($Y_{t-1}$, $Y_{t-2}\ldots$) and past error terms ($\varepsilon_{t-1}$, $\varepsilon_{t-2}\ldots$).

So, we see here that ARMA explicitly incorporates lags in its structure, making it suitable for modeling processes where the current outcome depends on past behaviors and noises.

## 6 Auto Regressive Integrated Moving Average (ARIMA)

ARIMA introduces a differencing step (the "Integrated" part) to transform non-stationary data into stationary data, enabling ARMA-like models to work effectively. The ARIMA equation can be presented as $\Delta^d Y_t = \phi_1 Y_{t-1} + \theta_1 \varepsilon_{t-1} + \varepsilon_t$ where $\Delta^d Y_t$ is the differenced series of $Y_t$, applied d times. Difference is used to make a non-stationary time series stationary. $\phi_1 Y_{t-1}$ is the Auto Regressive (AR) component, which relates the current value of $Y_t$ to its past value ($Y_{t-1}$) with a coefficient $\phi_1$.

$\theta_1 \varepsilon_{t-1}$ is the moving average (MA) component, which models the relationship between the current error term ($\varepsilon_t$) and previous error term ($\varepsilon_{t-1}$) with a coefficient $\theta_1$. $\varepsilon_t$ is the white noise, or random shock, in the current period, assumed to be independently and identically distributed.

Difference is critical here when the original series $Y_t$ is non-stationary (e.g., has a trend or seasonality). By applying $\Delta_d$, we remove trends or seasonality and focus on the stationary dynamics of the series. The model can then effectively capture the relationships among stationary components of the time series.

## 7 Vector Auto Regression (VAR)

A primary benefit of employing basic univariate techniques is the ability to predict future values of a single variable based solely on its historical values. But from economic and financial standpoint, most of the variables in real life are dependent on other variables. Therefore, a multivariate time series model is a better way to comprehend the relationships between the various variables throughout time when we have multiple series available. Here, we cover the foundational information needed to understand a Vector Auto Regressive (VAR) model, by using univariate time series framework and extending it to the multivariate case.

We have learned the primary objectives of applied Econometrics:

I. characterize and synthesize macroeconomic data,
II. forecast macroeconomic conditions,

III. quantify the understanding of the underlying macroeconomic structure, and
IV. advise policymakers with data-driven insights.

Stock and Watson (2001), perfectly summarized these four tasks as: *"data description, forecasting, structural inference and policy analysis"*. These tasks were carried out during 1970s utilizing a range of approaches using simple univariate time series models, single-equation models, and massive models with hundreds of equations. However, these approaches proved less reliable, especially in the face of the economic turbulence of the 1970s. During this period, factors such as oil shocks, inflation, and shifting monetary policies led to unexpected changes in economic relationships.

This had motivated Christopher Sims to come up with a new macro Econometric framework. Sims (1980), came up with Vector Auto Regressions (VAR) model with a flexible framework. This has enabled the economists to model the interdependencies among multiple time series without imposing strong theoretical restrictions. VAR allows for better handling of dynamic interactions between variables which makes VAR model more resilient in capturing the evolving economic relationships. While traditional AR models analyze the relationship between a single variable and its lagged values, VAR models consider multiple variables simultaneously.

A VAR model includes lagged values of the variables as predictors. This means that the model accounts for past values of the variables to explain their current and future values. This procedure helps capturing the dynamic nature of the relationships among the variables over time. Let us denote the variables in vector form and then present the VAR equations. Assuming $Y_t$ be a vector of n variables at time t, such that $Y_t = \begin{bmatrix} Y_{1t} \\ Y_{2t} \\ \vdots \\ Y_{nt} \end{bmatrix}$ and $\epsilon_t = \begin{bmatrix} \epsilon_{1t} \\ \epsilon_{2t} \\ \vdots \\ \epsilon_{kt} \end{bmatrix}$ is the vector of error terms (or shocks) at time $t$. The VAR(p) model can be expressed in matrix form $Y_t = \alpha + \beta_1 Y_{t-1} + \beta_2 Y_{t-2} + \cdots + \beta_n Y_{t-n} + \epsilon_t$ where

- $\alpha = n * 1$ vector of constants (intercepts) for each variable.
- $\beta_i = n * n$ matrix of coefficients for the $i$th lag.
- $\epsilon_t = n * 1$ vector of error terms.

In the case of a VAR(2) model with two variables $Y_{1t}$ and $Y_{2t}$, the model equations can be expressed as $\begin{bmatrix} Y_{1t} \\ Y_{2t} \end{bmatrix} = \begin{bmatrix} \alpha_1 \\ \alpha_2 \end{bmatrix} + \begin{bmatrix} \beta_{11,1} & \beta_{12,1} \\ \beta_{21,1} & \beta_{22,1} \end{bmatrix} \begin{bmatrix} Y_{1,t-1} \\ Y_{2,t-1} \end{bmatrix} + \begin{bmatrix} \beta_{11,2} & \beta_{12,2} \\ \beta_{21,2} & \beta_{22,2} \end{bmatrix} \begin{bmatrix} Y_{1,t-2} \\ Y_{2,t-2} \end{bmatrix} + \begin{bmatrix} \epsilon_{1t} \\ \epsilon_{2t} \end{bmatrix}$.

Here

- The first equation is for $Y_{1t}$, and it is influenced by its own past values $Y_{1,t-1}$ and $Y_{1,t-2}$, as well as the past values of $Y_{2t}$.
- The second equation is for $Y_{2t}$, and it is influenced by its own past values $Y_{2,t-1}$ and $Y_{2,t-2}$, as well as the past values of $Y_{1t}$.

The bidirectional nature is evident as each variable $Y_i$ depends on past values of itself as well as past values of other variables in the system. The vectorized form of the VAR model helps to efficiently model and analyze these interactions across multiple time series. Therefore, a VAR model can forecast multiple variables at once, accounting for their interrelationships.

Moreover, VAR models allow for the estimation of Impulse Response Functions (IRF), which show how shocks to one variable affect other variables over time. This helps in understanding the dynamic relationships and feedback mechanisms in the system. VAR models also provide insights into the proportion of the Forecast Error Variance (FEV) of each variable that can be attributed to shocks in other variables. This helps in understanding the relative importance of different variables.

The above example is the reduced form of a VAR model, where each is a function of its own past values and the past values of other variables in the model. While reduced form is the simplest of a VAR model, it comes with disadvantages, such as the fact that contemporaneous variables are not related to one another. Moreover, the error terms will be correlated across equations. This means we cannot consider what impacts individual shocks will have on the system. To have a better understanding, let us consider three endogenous variables: unemploymentRate, inflation, and the interestRate. A reduced form of VAR(2) model would include the following equations:

$$\begin{aligned}\text{unemploymentRate}_t = \beta_{10} &+ \beta_{11}\text{unemploymentRate}_{t-1} + \beta_{12}\text{unemploymentRate}_{t-2} \\ &+ \gamma_{11}\text{inflation}_{t-1} + \gamma_{12}\text{inflation}_{t-2} + \text{Ø}_{11}\text{interateRate}_{t-1} \\ &+ \text{Ø}_{12}\text{interateRate}_{t-2} + \in_{1t}\end{aligned}$$

$$\begin{aligned}\text{inflation}_t = \beta_{20} &+ \beta_{21}\text{unemploymentRate}_{t-1} + \beta_{22}\text{unemploymentRate}_{t-2} \\ &+ \gamma_{21}\text{inflation}_{t-1} + \gamma_{22}\text{inflation}_{t-2} + \text{Ø}_{21}\text{interateRate}_{t-1} \\ &+ \text{Ø}_{22}\text{interateRate}_{t-2} + \in_{2t}\end{aligned}$$

$$\text{interestRate}_t = \beta_{30} + \beta_{31}\text{unemploymentRate}_{t-1} + \beta_{32}\text{unemploymentRate}_{t-2} + \gamma_{31}\text{inflation}_{t-1} + \gamma_{32}\text{inflation}_{t-2} + \emptyset_{31}\text{interateRate}_{t-1} + \emptyset_{32}\text{interateRate}_{t-2} + \in_{3t}$$

- In the reduced form of VAR, each equation for an endogenous variable only includes lagged values of the other variables, not their current values. For instance, in the first equation for the unemployment rate, the model includes lagged values of unemployment, inflation, and interest rates but does not include the current values of inflation or interest rates at time $t$. This simplification means that, by design, it does not capture any instantaneous (or contemporaneous) effects that these variables might have on one another.
- Since each equation in the reduced form of VAR treats the error terms as if they only affect the individual variable's equation (i.e., each $\epsilon_{1t}$, $\epsilon_{2t}$, and $\epsilon_{3t}$), it assumes that the equations are independent in terms of how errors or shocks influence them. However, shocks affecting one variable (like a sudden increase in inflation) often influence others (such as interest rates and unemployment). This interdependence can lead to correlated error terms across equations, as each shock could potentially affect multiple variables, making it difficult to treat these shocks as independent for each variable.

In a structural VAR model, contemporaneous relationships are specified, often based on theoretical economic reasoning, to isolate how each variable uniquely responds to shocks in the other variables. The reduced-form VAR lacks these assumptions, which limits the ability to analyze the effect of an individual shock in one variable (e.g., a monetary policy shock affecting interest rates) on the system. Therefore, reduced-form models do not allow the clear identification of structural shocks and their propagation through the system, which is a key objective in many macroeconomic applications.

In Structural VAR (SVAR), the contemporaneous relationships between $Y_{1t}$ and $Y_{2t}$ are explicitly modeled by imposing restrictions. The structural model becomes $B\begin{bmatrix} Y_{1t} \\ Y_{2t} \end{bmatrix} = \begin{bmatrix} \alpha_1 \\ \alpha_2 \end{bmatrix} + \begin{bmatrix} \beta_{11,1} & \beta_{12,1} \\ \beta_{21,1} & \beta_{22,1} \end{bmatrix}\begin{bmatrix} Y_{1,t-1} \\ Y_{2,t-1} \end{bmatrix} + \begin{bmatrix} \beta_{11,2} & \beta_{12,2} \\ \beta_{21,2} & \beta_{22,2} \end{bmatrix}\begin{bmatrix} Y_{1,t-2} \\ Y_{2,t-2} \end{bmatrix} + \begin{bmatrix} \epsilon_{1t} \\ \epsilon_{2t} \end{bmatrix}$. Here, $B$ is a matrix capturing contemporaneous relationships between $Y_{1t}$ and $Y_{2t}$, such as $B = \begin{pmatrix} 1 & -b_{12} \\ -b_{21} & 1 \end{pmatrix}$. The structural errors ($\epsilon_t$ ) are uncorrelated, and their interpretation as structural shocks requires identification via restrictions (e.g., Cholesky decomposition or theoretical assumptions). Restrictions are necessary to estimate $B$ and disentangle the structural shocks. The structural and reduced forms are linked by $u_t = B^{-1}\epsilon_t$ where $u_t$ represents the structural shocks in SVAR. Table 4 presents a comparative study in a tabular format.

The choice between reduced form and structural techniques is often influenced by the study's objective, available data, and desired level of comprehension. Reduced form models are simpler and more data-driven, whereas structural models

**Table 4** Comparison: reduced form VAR and structural VAR

| Aspect | Reduced form VAR | Structural VAR (SVAR) |
|---|---|---|
| Error terms | Reduced-form residuals ($u_t$), correlated | Structural shocks ($\epsilon_t$ ), uncorrelated |
| Contemporaneous relationships | Not modeled explicitly | Explicitly modeled through $B$ |
| Causal interpretation | Lacks causal interpretation | Provides causal relationships based on restrictions |
| Identification | Does not require restrictions | Requires theoretical restrictions for identification |
| Ease of estimation | Simpler to estimate using OLS | More complex due to identification assumptions |

strive for deeper insights but may need more robust assumptions and sophisticated analysis. If we have a dataset that is ideal for a reduced-form approach to answering certain questions, adding extra structure may undermine the answers.

Reduced form of VAR is used for forecasting and understanding dynamic relationships without focusing on causality, such as forecasting GDP and inflation based on past values. Structural VAR is used for policy analysis and understanding the impact of structural shocks, such as analyzing the effect of monetary policy shocks on inflation and unemployment.

## 7.1 Vector Error Correction Model (VECM)

In a VAR model, all variables are assumed to be stationary (either in levels or after differencing). If variables are non-stationary but cointegrated, fitting a regular VAR model to the data can lead to spurious results because it ignores the cointegration relationship. A VECM addresses this issue by incorporating the cointegration relationship explicitly, allowing the model to handle both short-term dynamics (via differenced terms) and long-term equilibrium relationships (via the error correction term).

Thus, Vector Error Correction Model (VECM) is applied when we want to model a long-term relationship between non-stationary variables that are cointegrated. Even though the individual series may drift over time, they tend to move together in the long run, and this is captured by the cointegration relationship. VECM helps to separate the long-term equilibrium relationship (captured by the cointegration term) from short-term dynamics (captured by differencing). This error correction term measures the "error" or deviation from the long-run equilibrium. When there is a shock, it adjusts the variables over time to bring them back to equilibrium.

If we remember the simple regression equation from Chapter 1, where both the variables $X_t$ and $Y_t$ are non-stationary, the error $\epsilon_t$ is also non-stationary as a linear combination of two non-stationary variables. The error term can be presented as:

$$\varepsilon_t = Y_t - \beta_0 - \beta_1 X_t$$

This violates some assumptions about errors in the model, as well as the assumption that $\{\epsilon_t \sim N(1,0)\}$ errors have a normal distribution with mean 0 and std 1. However, if we find that $\epsilon_t$ is stationary, then the variables $Y_t$ and $X_t$ are cointegrated and the regression in that case, is not spurious. Also, it means that these signals have a long-run relationship between them. However, even if two series are cointegrated, it is still likely that $\epsilon_t$ will be serially correlated. To capture the serial correlation, we can think of fitting $Y_t = \beta_0+\beta_1 X_t+\alpha_2 Y_{t-1}+\beta_2 X_{t-1}+\epsilon_t$.

We can rearrange this model to ensure that we have only stationary variables by adding $-Y_{t-1}$ on both sides and $\beta_1 X_t - \beta_1 X_{t-1}$ on the right side. After rearranging, the formula will look like:

$$Y_t - Y_{t-1} = \beta_0 + \beta_1(X_t - X_{t-1}) + (\alpha_2 - 1)Y_{t-1} + X_{t-1}(\beta_1 + \beta_2) + \varepsilon_t$$

$$\Delta Y_t = \beta_1 \Delta X_t + \varphi(Y_{t-1} - \emptyset_1 - \emptyset_2 X_{t-1}) + \varepsilon_t$$

where $\varphi = (\alpha_2 - 1)$, $\varnothing_1 = \frac{\beta_0}{1-\alpha_2}$, and $\varnothing_2 = \frac{\beta_1+\beta_2}{1-\alpha_2}$.

This model is known as the error correction model.

- The term $\Delta X_t$ represents the model's short-run dynamics.
- The term $\varphi(Y_{t-1} - \varnothing_1 - \varnothing_2 X_{t-1})$ is known as the error correction mechanism and $\varphi$ is the error correction parameter that measures how $Y_t$ and $X_t$ react to deviations from long-run equilibrium.

Error Correction Model (ECM) from the simple VAR(1) will look like:

$$\Delta Y_t = \alpha_1 + \beta_{11}\Delta Y_{t-1} + \beta_{12}\Delta X_{t-1} + \varphi_Y(Y_{t-1} - \emptyset_1 - \emptyset_2 X_{t-1}) + \varepsilon_{Y,t}$$

$$\Delta X_t = \alpha_2 + \beta_{21}\Delta Y_{t-1} + \beta_{22}\Delta X_{t-1} + \varphi_X(Y_{t-1} - \emptyset_1 - \emptyset_2 X_{t-1}) + \varepsilon_{X,t}$$

Here, $\alpha_1$ and $\alpha_2$ are constraints, $\beta_{11}$ and $\beta_{21}$ represent short-run dynamics for $Y$ and $X$, $\varphi_Y$ and $\varphi_X$ are the error correction coefficients for $Y$ and $X$, and $\epsilon_{Y,t}$ and $\epsilon_{X,t}$ are the error terms for $Y$ and $X$, respectively.

In a macroeconomic context, we can use cointegration and ECM to explore the relationship between consumption ($C_t$) and disposable income ($I_t$). If these series are cointegrated, it implies they share a long-term relationship even though they may both be non-stationary individually.

Assume that the long-run average propensity to consume is 90%, which we can express as $C_t = 0.9I_t$. This equation suggests that consumption tends to adjust around 90% of disposable income in the long run. We can frame this long-term relationship as a linear regression model $C_t = \beta I_t + \varepsilon_t$, where $\beta = 0.9$ represents the average propensity to consume, and $\varepsilon_t$ is the error term capturing deviations from this equilibrium.

In this context, cointegration implies that although both $C_t$ and $I_t$ are non-stationary over time, the errors in the regression model ($\varepsilon_t$) should be stationary. This stationarity of $\varepsilon_t$ confirms that the two series move together in the long run, maintaining a stable relationship despite short-term fluctuations.

Let us illustrate how the ECM responds to both transitory and permanent shocks.

**Case 1: Transitory Shock to Disposable Income:** Suppose disposable income ($I_t$) experiences a temporary increase of 10 units in period t, then returns to its previous level ($I_{t-1}$) in subsequent periods.

- **Immediate Impact (Period t):** The change in disposable income in period $t$ is $\Delta I_t = 10$. Given a short-run effect of 0.5 on disposable income, the immediate impact on consumption is $0.5 * \Delta I_t = 0.5 * 10 = 5$. Thus, consumption ($C_t$) increases by 5 in the current period.
- **Error Correction Adjustment:** Since the model was initially in equilibrium, $\varepsilon_t = 0$. The error correction mechanism activates with:$-0.2 * (C_{t-1} - 0.9 * I_{t-1})$. Given $C_{t-1} = 0.9 * I_{t-1}$' the error correction term works to adjust $C_t$ back toward the long-run equilibrium as $I_t$ returns to its previous level in the next period.
- **Subsequent Adjustment (Period $t + 1$ and beyond):** When $I_t$ reverts to $I_{t-1}$, the change in income ($\Delta I_t$) becomes zero for future periods. The consumption adjusts downward due to the error correction term: $\Delta C_{t+1} = -0.2 * 5 = -1$. Over time, $C_t$ gradually decreases, returning to its original level and converges to $C_{t-1}$, restoring the equilibrium.

**Case 2: Permanent Shock to Disposable Income:** Now, let us consider a permanent increase in disposable income ($I_t$) by 10 units. This permanent change leads to the following adjustments:

- **Immediate Impact:** The immediate change in disposable income is still $\Delta I_t = 10$, with an immediate increase in consumption of: $0.5 * \Delta I_t = 0.5 * 10 = 5$.
- **Long-Run Adjustment to New Equilibrium:** With the permanent increase in $I_t$, the long-run equilibrium for consumption adjusts. The new target for consumption is: $C_t = 0.9 * (I_{t-1} + 10) = C_{t-1} + 0.9 * 10$. Thus, consumption will eventually converge to a level that is 9 units higher than $C_{t-1}$, reflecting the long-term impact of the income change: $C_t = C_{t-1} + 9$.
- **Gradual Adjustment to New Equilibrium:** Over time, $C_t$ will incrementally adjust toward this new equilibrium, reflecting a permanent increase in consumption by 9 units, consistent with the sustained rise in disposable income.

To incorporate short-run adjustments and align the two series with their long-run equilibrium, we use the ECM, which adjusts for any short-term deviations by partially correcting the dependent variable based on this error. This correction factor

shows how quickly the series returns to the long-term equilibrium following disruptions in the relationship between $C_t$ and $I_t$. The ECM model can be represented as $\Delta C_t = \alpha * \varepsilon_{t-1} + \gamma * \Delta I_t + \varepsilon_t$
where

- $\Delta C_t$ is the change in consumption,
- $\Delta I_t$ is the change in disposable income,
- $\varepsilon_{t-1}$ is the lagged error term from the cointegration equation, representing the deviation from equilibrium in the prior period,
- $\alpha$ captures the speed of adjustment back to equilibrium,
- $\gamma$ captures the short-run impact of changes in disposable income on consumption,
- $\varepsilon_t$ is the error term.

This framework effectively captures both short-term dynamics and long-term stability, illustrating how consumption $C_t$ adjusts in response to changes in income $I_t$ while respecting the underlying long-term relationship between the two series.

To summarize, the VECMs are widely used in economics and finance to model the relationship between macroeconomic variables (e.g., GDP, inflation, and interest rates), analyze the dynamics of financial markets, including long-term equilibrium relationships between stock prices and fundamentals, study causality and impulse response functions in systems where long-term and short-term dynamics coexist, etc.

## 7.2 VAR Model Specification

To fit a VAR model, a single parameter which is the model order or lag length ($p$) must be chosen. Most VAR models are estimated with symmetric lags, which means that the same lag length is used for all variables in the model's equations. This lag period is typically determined by an explicit statistical criterion, such as the Akaike Information Criterion (AIC), Schwarz's Bayesian Information Criterion (BIC), Hannan-Quinn Criterion (HQ), and Akaike's Final Prediction Error Criterion (FPE).

## 7.3 Developing VAR Model

We shall discuss more on the VAR model during the implementation phase in Chapter 6. A broader overview of the steps is provided below.

**Table 5** Autoregressive models

| VAR (Vector Auto Regression) | VECM (Vector Error Correction Model) | ARDL (Auto Regressive Distributed Lag) |
|---|---|---|
| VAR models are used to model the dynamic interrelationships among multiple time series. Here, each variable is regressed on its own lagged values as well as lagged values of other variables in the system. VAR models do not consider long-term equilibrium relationships among variables | VECM model accounts for long-terms equilibrium relationships among variables. It includes an error correction term that captures the adjustment process of the variables back to their long-term equilibrium after a shock of deviation | ARDL models are used for analyzing the relationship between two or more variables in a single equation framework. ARDL models are useful when variables are integrated of different orders |
| Use VAR if the focus is on short-term dynamics and all variables are stationary or have been differenced to achieve stationarity | Use VECM if the variables are cointegrated, meaning there is a long-term equilibrium relationship among them. It captures both the short-term adjustments and the long-term equilibrium | Use ARDL if we need a flexible approach that can handle variables integrated of different orders and if we are interested in both short-term and long-term relationships within a single equation framework |

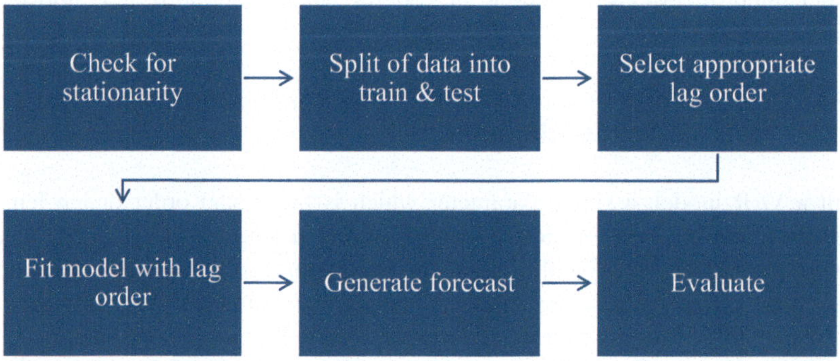


Now, let us summarize our understanding of different Auto Regressive models. The Auto Regressive dynamic category has three distinct models and has different applications, as shown in Table 5.

## 8 Key Takeaways

This chapter provided a foundational knowledge on dynamic linear models. Dynamic models allow researchers and analysts to capture the temporal interdependence and evolution of economic variables. These models account for how current decisions, actions, and outcomes are influenced by past behaviors or shocks, making them essential for understanding real-world economic phenomena.

Economic processes often exhibit time dependencies where past values influence current outcomes (e.g., inflation, GDP growth, or stock prices). Dynamic models, such as ARIMA or Vector Auto Regression (VAR), explicitly incorporate lagged relationships to analyze such dependencies.

We will discuss the implementation of dynamic models in Chapters 6 and 7.

## References

Koyck, L. M. (1954). Distributed lags and investment analysis (Vol. 4, p. 145). North-Holland Publishing Company.

Sims, C. A. (1980). Macroeconomics and reality. *Econometrica, 48*(1), 1. https://doi.org/10.2307/1912017

Stock, J. H., & Watson, M. W. (2001). Vector autoregressions. *Journal of Economic Perspectives, 15*(4), 101–115. https://doi.org/10.1257/jep.15.4.101

# Theoretical Overview: Capital Asset Pricing and Arbitrage Pricing Theory

# 4

So far, we have gone through the foundational concepts about Econometric models and the quantification process through various statistical analyses. In this chapter we explore the theoretical overview of two popular models in the field of asset pricing, portfolio management, and risk-return analysis: (1) Capital Asset Pricing (CAP) model or CAPM and (2) Arbitrage Pricing Theory (APT) model. They are widely used for valuing financial assets, estimating the cost of capital, and making investment decisions. This chapter primarily focuses on the history and background of CAP and APT.

## 1 Capital Asset Pricing (CAP) Model

CAPM is the most popular asset pricing model. It helps to quantify the trade-off between risk (beta) and expected return. It is the first model that allowed economists to theorize their ideas about the risk / return trade-off in a systematic manner. This asset price model with just one element generally used as a prototype for later, like Fama–French 3-factor, 4-factor, and 5-factor models.

The theory of CAPM was initially designed to be descriptive; it also has normative implications, suggesting that individual investors should, at a minimum must maintain well-diversified portfolios. It was introduced by Sharpe (1964) and Lintner (1975) to investigate the relationship between the expected Rate of Return (RoR) and systematic risk. The practical implementation of the CAP began in the late 1960s and early 1970s, shortly after its formal introduction by William Sharpe and John Lintner. An early example of the use of CAP concepts in financial products was the Vanguard 500 Index Fund, which was introduced in 1976. Empirical studies in the 1970s and 1980s tested CAP's predictions in real-world data, providing mixed evidence but cementing its role as a starting point for asset

 
S. Maitra, *A Practical Guide to Static and Dynamic Econometric Modelling*,
Contributions to Economics, https://doi.org/10.1007/978-3-031-86862-7_4

pricing models. By the 1980s, CAP was widely taught in business schools and adopted as a tool for investment analysis, portfolio management, and corporate finance.

CAP provided the foundation for widely used financial metrics like alpha (excess returns) and beta (systematic risk). It is based on the relationship between an asset's market risk ($\beta$), the risk-free rate ($R_f$), and the equity risk premium, or the expected return on the market minus the risk-free rate can be presented as ($\mathrm{ER}_m - R_f$). Beta quantifies how much a stock's returns move relative to the overall market. According to the CAP model, the expected returns of a stock are linearly correlated with expected market returns.

The CAP is commonly used for pricing risky securities and estimating projected returns for assets based on their risk and the cost of capital. The expected return is the profit or loss from an investment based on past RoR, which is calculated by multiplying potential outcomes by their likelihood of occurring and adding the results. To simplify, assuming an investment has a 50% chance of gaining 20% and a 50% chance of losing 10%, the expected return would be $(0.5 * 20\%) + (0.5 * -10\%) = 10\% - 5\% = 5\%$.

## 1.1 Key Components of CAP Model

The formula for calculating the expected return of an asset given its risk is $\mathrm{ER}_i = R_f + \beta_i(\mathrm{ER}_m - R_f)$ where,

- $E(R_i)$ is the expected return on an asset over a period.
- $R_f$ is the risk-free rate, typically represented by government bonds, such as U.S. Treasury bills. This rate serves as a benchmark for other investments and accounts for the time value of money.
- $E(R_m)$ is expected market return which represents the overall market performance. This is usually measured by a broad market index such as S&P 500.
- $\beta_i$ is asset's systematic risk relative to the market. If a stock is riskier than the market, it will have a $\beta > 1$ which means it is more volatile than the overall market. If $\beta < 1$, the formula assumes it will reduce the risk of a portfolio which means the stock either has lower volatility than the market, or it is a volatile asset whose price movements are not highly correlated with the overall market. $\beta = 1$ indicates asset's price moves with the market.
- ($\mathrm{ER}_m - R_f$) is market risk premium which is the additional return expected from the market above the risk-free rate. This premium compensates investors for taking on the higher risk of investing in the market.

We can simplify the above equation where the expectation could be dropped as $R_i = R_f + \beta_i(R_m - R_f)$. We could think about the connection between excess returns on stocks and excess returns on the market. It has a better and more understandable interpretation $R_i - R_f = \alpha + \beta_i(R_m - R_f)$.

CAPM assumes that investors hold diversified portfolios, so idiosyncratic risk (firm-specific or unsystematic risk) is eliminated through diversification. Only systematic risk remains, and investors are compensated for bearing this risk through the equity risk premium. The risk premium of individual stock depends on two components: (1) its market risk and (2) the market risk premium. Mathematically, the slope of $R_i - R_f = \alpha + \beta_i(R_m - R_f)$ can be written as $\beta_i = \frac{\sigma_{i,m}}{\sigma_m^2}$ where, $\sigma_{i,m}$ is the covariance between stock returns and the market index returns and $\sigma_m^2$ is the variance of the market returns. Since $\sigma_{i,m} = \rho_{i,m}\sigma_i\sigma_m$ where $\rho_{i,m}$ is the correlation between stock return and the index returns, $\beta_i = \frac{\sigma_{i,m}}{\sigma_m^2}$ can be written as $\beta_i = \frac{\rho_{i,m} * \sigma_i}{\sigma_m}$.

The meaning of $\beta$ is that when the expected risk-premium increases by 1%, the stock's expected return would increase by $\beta$% and vice versa. Hence, $\beta$ (market risk) could be viewed as an amplifier. The average beta of all stocks is one. Thus, if a stock's $\beta > 1$, it means that its market risk is higher than that of an average stock. Let us revisit a simple OLS model fitting procedure (Table 1).

Let us focus on the values of the coefficients and their corresponding t-statistics and *p*-values. The $\beta$ is 0.3571, with *t*-value of 2.152 > 2, which is significantly

**Table 1** OLS regression model fitting

```
Y = [1, 2, 3, 4, 5, 6, 7]; X = range(1, 8)
X = sm.add_constant(X)
model = sm.OLS(Y, X).fit()
print(model.summary())
print('*****************')
print(model.params)
```

```
                            OLS Regression Results
==============================================================================
Dep. Variable:                      y   R-squared:                       0.481
Model:                            OLS   Adj. R-squared:                  0.377
Method:                 Least Squares   F-statistic:                     4.630
Date:                Wed, 31 Jul 2024   Prob (F-statistic):             0.0841
Time:                        03:38:36   Log-Likelihood:                -7.8466
No. Observations:                   7   AIC:                             19.69
Df Residuals:                       5   BIC:                             19.59
Df Model:                           1
Covariance Type:            nonrobust
==============================================================================
                 coef    std err          t      P>|t|      [0.025      0.975]
------------------------------------------------------------------------------
const          1.2857      0.742      1.732      0.144      -0.622       3.194
x1             0.3571      0.166      2.152      0.084      -0.070       0.784
==============================================================================
Omnibus:                          nan   Durbin-Watson:                   1.976
Prob(Omnibus):                    nan   Jarque-Bera (JB):                0.342
Skew:                           0.289   Prob(JB):                        0.843
Kurtosis:                       2.083   Cond. No.                         10.4
==============================================================================

Notes:
[1] Standard Errors assume that the covariance matrix of the errors is correctly specified.
*****************
[1.28571429 0.35714286]
```

different from zero. Alternatively, based on the $P$-value of 0.084 < 0.05, we will have the same conclusion if we choose a 10% as our cut-off point. We will discuss more on this during the implementation phase at Chapter 5.

### 1.2 Significance of CAP Model

The CAP model is important for several reasons:

- It provides a theoretical framework to understand the relationship between the expected return of an asset and its systematic risk (beta). This helps investors make informed decisions based on their risk tolerance.
- It helps in assessing whether an asset is valued. By comparing the expected return from an asset with the required return given its risk, we can identify underpriced or overpriced securities.
- Business uses the CAP model to estimate the cost of equity; this is crucial for capital budgeting and investment decisions. Understanding the required rate of return can influence decisions on new investments.
- The model supports the concept of market equilibrium, where the expected returns are aligned with risk, helping to explain market dynamics and pricing behavior of assets.

### 1.3 Assumptions of CAP Model

The CAP model relies on several assumptions, such as:

- Investors are rational and risk-averse.
- Markets are efficient, with all investors having access to the same information.
- There are no taxes or transaction costs, and investors can lend and borrow at the risk-free rate.

While these assumptions simplify the model, they may not always hold true in the real world, which can limit CAPM's applicability in certain situations.

## 2 Fama–French Model

Let us familiarize ourselves with multi-factor model. A multi-factor model attempts to explain complex phenomena using a small number of underlying factors. The CAP model uses only one variable to compare the returns of a portfolio or stock with the returns of the market. In contrast, Fama–French (Fama & French, 1992) introduced an extension of the CAP model that aims to explain stock returns better by incorporating additional factors.

## 2.1 3-Factor Model

In this model (Fama & French, 1993; 1996), the $\beta$ is the same as in the CAPM. Besides, this model considers additional factors such as size (SMB, i.e., small minus big), which is the historic excess returns of small-cap companies over large-cap companies, and value (HML, i.e., High Minus Low), which is the historic excess returns of value stocks (high book-to-price ratio) over-growth stocks (low book-to-price ratio). The 3-factor model can be formulated as $R_i - R_f(\text{ExcessReturn}_i) = \alpha_i + \beta_{im}(R_m - R_f) + \beta_{i(\text{SMB})}\text{SMB} + \beta_{i(\text{HML})}\text{HML} + \epsilon_i$. Chapter 5 covers the implementation of Fama–French model.

## 2.2 4-Factor Model

The Fama–French 4-factor model extends the 3-factor model by adding a momentum factor. An additional Momentum (MOM) factor is included here. This return difference between past winners (stocks with high past returns) and past losers (stocks with low past returns) $[R_i - R_f = \alpha_i + \beta_{im}(R_m - R_f) + \beta_{i(\text{SMB})}\text{SMB} + \beta_{i(\text{HML})}\text{HML} + \beta_{i(\text{MOM})}\text{MOM} + \epsilon_i]$.

## 2.3 5-Factor Model

In 2015, (Fama & French, 2015) expanded their model to include two additional factors: (1) Profitability (RMW, i.e., Robust Minus Weak), which captures the premium associated with companies with high profitability versus those with low profitability; and (2) Investment (CMA, i.e., Conservative Minus Aggressive), which reflects the performance difference between firms that invest conservatively and those that invest aggressively. $[R_i - R_f = \alpha_i + \beta_{im}(R_m - R_f) + \beta_{i(\text{SMB})}\text{SMB} + \beta_{i(\text{HML})}\text{HML} + \beta_{i(\text{RMW})}\text{RMW} + \beta_{i(\text{CMA})}CMA + \epsilon_i]$.

where the additional factors:

- $\beta_{i(RMW)}$ is the sensitivity of the stock's excess return to the profitability factor.
- RMW = Robust Minus Weak, the return spread between firms with high and low profitability.
- $\beta_{i(CMA)}$ is the sensitivity of the stock's excess return to the investment factor.
- CMA = Conservative Minus Aggressive, the return spread between firms with conservative and aggressive investment policies.

While the 5-Factor model offers a more comprehensive framework for understanding stock returns than the original 3-Factor model, it is not without limitations. The added factors help explain a broader range of stock returns, but challenges remain in fully capturing the returns of certain portfolios, especially those with specific characteristics such as high investment but low profitability.

## 3 Arbitrage Pricing Theory (APT)

APT is a multi-factor model that extends CAP Model by considering multiple sources of risk that can affect an asset's returns. Developed by economist Stephen Ross in the 1970s, APT offers a more flexible approach compared to the CAP model to asset pricing by considering multiple factors that influence returns. The CAPM and the APT are both models for estimating the expected return of an asset, but they differ fundamentally in their assumptions, complexity, and the types of risk factors they incorporate.

### 3.1 Key Concepts of APT

The key concept involves that the expected return of an asset can be modeled as a linear function of various macroeconomic factors or theoretical market indices. The APT formula can be expressed as $E(R_i) = R_f + \beta_{i1}F_1 + \beta_{i2}F_2 + \cdots + \beta_{ij}F_j$ where,

- $E(R_i)$ = expected return of asset $I$,
- $R_f$ = risk-free rate,
- $\beta_{ij}$ = sensitivity of asset $i$ to factor $j$, and
- $F_j$ = risk premium associated with factor $j$.

APT starts with the risk-free rate which is the return on a risk-free asset. Each $\beta_{ij}$ measures how sensitive the asset is to changes in the $j$th factor. Higher sensitivities indicate that the asset's returns are affected by that factor. Each $F_j$ represents the additional return expected for taking on the risk associated with that factor. These include various macroeconomic variables like inflation rates, interest rates, GDP growth, or industry-specific factors.

### 3.2 Key Features of APT

- APT recognizes that asset returns are influenced by multiple sources of risk, not just market risk.
- APT is based on the principle that arbitrage opportunities will be exploited by investors, leading to prices that align with the model's predictions. If an asset is mispriced, arbitrageurs will buy or sell it until its price reflects the expected return as per APT.
- APT does not specify which factors should be used, allowing for flexibility. Investors can choose factors based on empirical evidence or theoretical considerations.

**Table 2** Summary table CAPM vs APT

| Feature | CAPM | APT |
|---|---|---|
| Risk factors | Single (market risk) | Multiple (macroeconomic factors) |
| Sensitivity (beta) | One beta (market beta) | Multiple betas (one for each factor) |
| Formula | $\mathrm{ER}_i = R_f + \beta_i(\mathrm{ER}_m - R_f)$ | $E(R_i) = R_f + \beta_{i1}F_1 + \beta_{i2}F_2 + \cdots + \beta_{ij}F_j$ |
| Ease of use | Simpler, easier to apply | More complex; it requires identification of relevant factors |
| Real-world use | Widely used in portfolio and asset pricing | Useful for advanced asset pricing with multi-factor exposures |

### 3.3 Assumptions of APT

APT assumes that markets are efficient, meaning prices fully reflect all available information. There are no arbitrage opportunities in equilibrium, as they would be quickly exploited by investors. The returns of assets can be described by a linear function of multiple factors.

### 3.4 Disadvantages

Determining the relevant factors and their risk premiums can be challenging and may require extensive data analysis. The model's flexibility comes at the cost of increased complexity compared to simpler models like CAP. Table 2 summarizes the difference between CAPM and APT models.

## 4 Key Takeaways

This chapter explored the conceptual ideas of two popular asset pricing model: Capital Asset Pricing (CAP) model and Arbitrage Pricing Theory (APT) model. Both models are cornerstones of financial theory, forming the basis for more advanced pricing models. CAPM provides simplicity and insight into the market risk-return relationship, while APT extends this framework to accommodate multiple risk dimensions, making them indispensable tools for both theoretical research and practical applications in economics and finance.

CAP is the first model to organize economists' ideas about the risk/return tradeoff in a systematic manner, focusing on the relationship between an asset's market risk ($\beta$), the risk-free rate ($R_f$), and the equity risk premium. It is commonly used for pricing risky securities and estimating projected returns based on their risk and cost of capital. CAP is important for several reasons, such as providing a theoretical framework to understand the relationship between an asset's expected return and its systematic risk, assessing asset valuation, and supporting market equilibrium. APT, developed by economist Stephen Ross in the 1970s, is a multi-factor model for asset pricing that considers multiple factors influencing returns. It recognizes that asset returns are influenced by multiple sources of risk, not just market risk, and assumes that markets are efficient. However, determining the relevant factors and their risk premiums can be challenging and may require extensive data analysis.

We have discussed the theoretical underpinnings, context, benefits, and drawbacks of the APT and CAP models. In Chapter 5, we will explore how these concepts are put into practice.

## References


Fama, E. F., & French, K. R. (1992). The cross-section of expected stock returns. *The Journal of Finance, 47*(2), 427–465. https://doi.org/10.1111/j.1540-6261.1992.tb04398.x

Fama, E. F., & French, K. R. (1993). Common risk factors in the returns on stocks and bonds. *Journal of Financial Economics, 33*, 3–56.

Fama, E. F., & French, K. R. (1996). Multifactor explanations of asset pricing anomalies. *The Journal of Finance, 51*(1), 55–84.

Fama, E. F., & French, K. R. (2015). A five-factor asset pricing model. *Journal of Financial Economics, 116*(1), 1–22.

Lintner, J. (1975). The valuation of risk assets and the selection of risky investments in stock portfolios and capital budgets. In *Stochastic optimization models in finance* (pp. 131–155). Elsevier. https://doi.org/10.1016/B978-0-12-780850-5.50018-6

Sharpe, W. F. (1964). Capital asset prices: A theory of market equilibrium under conditions of risk*. *The Journal of Finance, 19*(3), 425–442. https://doi.org/10.1111/j.1540-6261.1964.tb02865.x

# Model Implementation and Testing 5

This chapter shows how to implement bivariate and multivariate regression models and test hypotheses for CAPM and APT models. Link of all the necessary **source code**[1] repository can be found in the footnote section.

## 1 CAP Model Implementation

Investors cannot eliminate systematic risk, since it is the inherent risk tied to market movements that affect all assets. However, they can manage their exposure to this risk through strategies like hedging. An optimal hedge ratio determines the percentage of a hedging instrument, i.e., a hedging asset that an investor should hedge.

$$\text{Optimal Hedge Ratio} = \rho * \frac{\sigma_s}{\sigma_f}$$

where

- $\rho$ = The correlation coefficient of the changes in the spot and futures prices,
- $\sigma_s$ = Standard deviation of changes in the spot price '$s$', and
- $\sigma_f$ = Standard deviation of changes in the futures price '$f$'.

Let us try to simplify this. CAPM's expected return on an asset depends on its beta, or its sensitivity to market movements. Higher beta implies greater sensitivity to market fluctuations. The optimal hedge ratio effectively reduces the impact of

[1] PracticalGuideEconometrics/Chapter_5.ipynb at main · saritmaitra/PracticalGuideEconometrics.



S. Maitra, *A Practical Guide to Static and Dynamic Econometric Modelling*,
Contributions to Economics, https://doi.org/10.1007/978-3-031-86862-7_5

these fluctuations by using hedging instruments that offset potential losses. This creates a smoother return profile, which aligns with CAPM's goal of achieving predictable returns based on systematic risk alone, without unpredictable asset-specific fluctuations.

Moreover, CAPM assumes that investors hold diversified portfolios to eliminate unsystematic risk. The optimal hedge ratio complements this by helping investors manage the systematic risk that remains even after diversification. This allows investors to maintain their target portfolio beta and risk level more effectively, as hedging helps mitigate unexpected losses while preserving returns. In CAP terms, this helps investors to achieve an "efficient" portfolio, where returns are maximized for a given level of market risk.

CAP also supports the creation of a market equilibrium where each asset is priced according to its risk relative to the market. The optimal hedge ratio fits into this framework by helping investors ensure that short-term volatility does not disrupt their long-term risk-return expectations. This stability supports the CAP model's assumption of a stable risk-return relationship, as hedging reduces the impact of short-term market shocks.

$$\text{Optimal Hedge Ratio (OHR)} = \rho * \frac{\sigma_s}{\sigma_f}$$

where,

- $\rho$ = correlation coefficient of the changes in the spot and futures prices,
- $\sigma_s$ = standard deviation of changes in the spot price, and
- $\sigma_f$ = standard deviation of changes in the futures price.

The optimal hedge ratio is typically estimated by running a bivariate regression between the returns of the stock and the returns of the corresponding futures contracts.

The regression model is of the form $R_{\text{stock}} = \alpha + \beta R_{\text{futures}} + \epsilon$ where, $R_{\text{stock}}$ is the return on the stock, $R_{\text{futures}}$ is the return on the futures contract, β is the hedge ratio, α is the intercept, and ϵ is the error term. β is the number of futures contracts needed to hedge one unit of the stock. It is calculated to minimize the variance of the portfolio, thereby reducing the overall risk.

To calculate the CAPM for Apple stock (or any stock), we need to convert the price series into continuously compounded returns and then transform these returns into excess returns over the risk-free rate. To generate constantly compounded returns, we apply the log difference of the series and subtract the risk-free rate from the log returns to get the excess returns.

We will perform a simple linear regression analysis to investigate the relationship between the log returns of Apple's stock (AAPL_Returns) and the log returns of the S&P 500 index (SP_returns). Table 1 displays the code snippet.

**Table 1** Linear regression and beta estimate

```
data['AAPL_Returns'] = np.log(data['AAPL']).diff()
data['SP_returns'] = np.log(data['^GSPC']).diff()
data.dropna(inplace = True)


(beta,alpha,r_value,p_value,std_err) = stats.linregress(data['SP_returns'], data['AAPL_Returns'])


print(alpha,beta)
print("R-squared =", r_value**2)
print("p-value =", p_value)
```

```
0.010860724794190294 1.1308604524157015
R-squared= 0.39233181054402816
p-value = 1.3939912030356463e-19
```

- Alpha (Intercept) 0.0108 is the expected return of AAPL when the return of the S&P 500 is zero. In other words, it is the base return of AAPL that is not explained by the movements of the S&P 500.
- Beta (Slope) 1.130 shows that for every 1% increase in the S&P 500 returns, the returns of AAPL are expected to increase by approximately 1.13%. This suggests that AAPL is more volatile than the S&P 500 index.
- R-squared 0.392 shows that around 39% of the variance in AAPL returns can be explained by the variance in S&P 500 returns. The remaining 61% is due to other factors not included in this model.
- *p*-value 1.393e−19 is extremely low (close to zero) and suggests that the relationship between S&P 500 returns and AAPL returns is statistically significant. There is a low probability that the observed relationship occurred by random chance.

Let us understand the Beta ($\beta$) dynamics prior to diving into the CAP Model implementation. We already know by now the importance of $\beta$ in the model. To simplify, it estimates the expected return of an asset based on its risk compared to the market. Understanding beta and its changes over time allows investors to make informed decisions regarding their investment strategies and risk management. A rising $\beta$ indicates increasing volatility or risk, while a declining $\beta$ suggests a stable or defensive position.

## 1.1 Rolling Beta

Sometimes, we need to generate a $\beta$-series based on moving window, for example, a three-year moving window. The advantage here is that a moving $\beta$ provides a dynamic view of the relationship between a stock and the market over time. Table 2

**Table 2** Rolling window regression analysis

```
stock = 'AAPL'
market_index = '^GSPC'
data = yf.download([stock, market_index], start = '2010-01-01', end = '2024-01-01', interval='1mo')['Adj
Close']
data.index = pd.to_datetime(data.index)
log_returns = np.log(data).diff().dropna()
def calculate_beta(X, Y):
    (beta, alpha, r_value, p_value, std_err) = stats.linregress(X, Y)
    return beta
window_size = 36

rolling_betas = pd.DataFrame(index = log_returns.index[window_size-1:], columns=[stock])

for i in range(len(log_returns) - window_size + 1):
    window_data = log_returns.iloc[i:i + window_size]
    beta = calculate_beta(window_data[market_index], window_data[stock])
    rolling_betas.iloc[i] = beta

print(rolling_betas.head())
```

```
                AAPL
Date
2013-01-01  0.715988
2013-02-01   0.70674
2013-03-01  0.631915
2013-04-01    0.6203
2013-05-01  0.664915
```

displays how to calculate the rolling beta of AAPL with respect to the S&P 500 index over a 3-year moving window.

## 1.2 Adjusted Beta

Adjusted $\beta$ accounts for mean reversion and provides a realistic expectation of the future $\beta$. Mean reversion is a foundational concept in finance, helps investors to understand the price dynamics and make informed decisions based on the expectation that extreme prices or returns will eventually revert to the mean. It is a modified version of the traditional $\beta$ coefficient, which provides better estimate of a stock's future $\beta$. The adjustment of $\beta$ to account for mean reversion involves a process known as "regression to the mean". In finance, this adjustment is used to modify a stock's $\beta$ based on historical $\beta$ values and the general tendency of all $\beta$s to gravitate toward the market average $\beta$ of 1 over time. The most common formula for calculating adjusted $\beta$ is $\beta_{\text{adjusted}} = \frac{1}{3} * \beta_{\text{raw}} + \frac{2}{3} * 1 = 0.67 * \beta_{\text{raw}} + 0.33 * 1$.

**Table 3** Difference between adjusted beta and SW adjusted beta

| Simple adjusted beta | Scholes and Williams adjusted beta |
|---|---|
| Adjusts for mean reversion of the beta over time | Corrects for nonsynchronous trading bias |
| Uses a weighted average formula | Uses contemporaneous, lagged, and lead market returns to correct for timing discrepancies |
| Easier to calculate and understand, requiring only the raw beta | More complex, requiring additional data points (lagged and lead returns) and calculations |
| Commonly used in general financial analysis to adjust for mean reversion | Specifically used to address nonsynchronous trading issues, making it more relevant for markets or stocks with significant trading discrepancies |

The formula gives two-thirds weight to the market $\beta$ (1) and one-third weight to the stock's historical $\beta$. The adjustment assumes that over time, the $\beta$ of a stock will move closer to the market $\beta$ of 1 reflecting the mean-reverting nature.

### 1.2.1 Scholes and Williams Adjusted Beta

Developed by economists Myron Scholes[2] and Joseph Williams, this approach allows for a better estimation of $\beta$ by considering the characteristics of stock returns and their relationship to the market. When estimating the $\beta$ of a stock, the OLS regression can be biased if the stock and the market index do not trade at the same time. This is known as nonsynchronous trading. The Scholes and Williams method (Scholes & Williams, 1977) corrects this bias by using not just the contemporaneous market returns but also the lagged and lead market returns.

The Scholes and Williams $\beta$ can be calculated using the following steps:

I. Calculate contemporaneous beta $\left\{\beta_0 = \operatorname{cov}\left(R_i, R_{m,-1}\right)/\sigma(R_m)\right\}$

II. Calculate lagged beta $\left\{\beta_{-1} = \operatorname{cov}(R_i, R_m)/\sigma(R_m)\right\}$

III. Calculate lead beta $\left\{\beta_{+1} = \operatorname{cov}\left(R_i, R_{m,+1}\right)/\sigma(R_m)\right\}$

IV. Combine beta $\left\{\beta_{sw} = (\beta_0 + \beta_{-1} + \beta_{+1})/3\right\}$.

Table 3 tabulates the difference between Adjusted beta and Scholes and Williams (SW) Adjusted Beta.

Table 4 displays the implementation of Scholes and Williams Adjusted Beta.

A contemporaneous beta of 1.13 suggests that on an average return moves slightly more than the market, which means if the market rises by 1%, return

[2] Myron Scholes - Wikipedia.

**Table 4** Scholes and Williams adjusted beta

```
stock = 'AAPL'
market_index = '^GSPC'


data = yf.download([stock, market_index], start = '2010-01-01', end = '2024-01-01', interval = '1mo')['Adj
Close']
data['AAPL_Returns'] = np.log(data[stock]).diff()
data['SP_returns'] = np.log(data[market_index]).diff()
data.dropna(inplace = True)


(beta_0, alpha_0, r_value_0, p_value_0, std_err_0) = stats.linregress(data['SP_returns'],
data['AAPL_Returns'])
(beta_lag, alpha_lag, r_value_lag, p_value_lag, std_err_lag) =
stats.linregress(data['SP_returns'].shift(1).dropna(), data['AAPL_Returns'][1:])
(beta_lead, alpha_lead, r_value_lead, p_value_lead, std_err_lead) = stats.linregress(data['SP_returns'][:-1],
data['AAPL_Returns'][1:])
beta_SW = (beta_0 + beta_lag + beta_lead) / 3


print(f"Contemporaneous Beta: {beta_0}")
print(f"Lagged Beta: {beta_lag}")
print(f"Lead Beta: {beta_lead}")
print(f"Scholes and Williams Adjusted Beta: {beta_SW}")
```

```
[*********************100%%**********************]  2 of 2 completedContemporaneous Beta: 1.1308604524157015
Lagged Beta: -0.04612734097466388
Lead Beta: -0.04612734097466388
Scholes and Williams Adjusted Beta: 0.34620192348879125
```

is expected to increase by about 1.13%, reflecting a moderate sensitivity to market fluctuations. The negative lagged beta (−0.046) here implies that return is inversely affected by the market returns from the prior period. However, the small magnitude indicates a weak relationship, suggesting returns do not significantly respond to past market movements.

Lead Beta (−0.046127) is the correlation between returns and the following period's S&P 500 returns. The small, negative lead beta also suggests a minor inverse relationship between Apple's current returns and the next period's market returns, showing that Apple's stock might not strongly predict future market movements.

SW Adjusted Beta (0.346202 $\approx$ 35%) indicates that, on average, AAPL's returns are positively correlated with the market returns, but the sensitivity is lower compared to the contemporaneous beta alone. For every 1% change in the market index, AAPL's returns change by approximately 0.35%.

**Table 5** Data ingestion—TSLA close market price from Jan-2022 till Jan-2024

```
stock_data = yf.download('TSLA', start = '2022-01-01', end = '2024-01-01')
stock_data = stock_data['Close']
futures_data = stock_data * 0.95 + np.random.normal(0, 2, len(stock_data))
data = pd.DataFrame({'Stock': stock_data, 'Futures': futures_data})

data.head()
```

| | Stock | Futures |
|---|---|---|
| **Date** | | |
| **2022-01-03** | 399.926666 | 377.096521 |
| **2022-01-04** | 383.196655 | 365.774749 |
| **2022-01-05** | 362.706665 | 345.125076 |
| **2022-01-06** | 354.899994 | 335.212785 |
| **2022-01-07** | 342.320007 | 325.833641 |

## 2 Hypotheses Testing: CAP Model

Let us revisit our data ingestion procedure. Table 5 displays the ingestion process from Yahoo Finance. The output table shows the data having three different columns, i.e., Date, Price, and Futures, respectively. We will run a regression of 'Stock' on a 'constant' and 'Futures' and examine the parameter estimates. The constant term is the value at which the regression line crosses the *Y* axis and is also known as the *Y* intercept. Here, we will use Tesla stock and generate hypothetical futures data to demonstrate the implementation.

The relationship between stock prices and futures prices can be analyzed both in terms of price levels and returns. The price-level regressions are suitable for understanding long-term relationships; the returns are for short-term hedging strategies. Here, at first, we regressed the futures prices on the stock prices at price level to find the hedge ratio as displayed in Table 6. We have added a constant to the independent variable for the intercept term. Interested readers may look through **statsmodel documentations.**[3]

- The regression results show a strong model fit, with an $R^2$ of 0.999, suggesting that the independent variable ('Futures') explains all the variance in the dependent variable (Stock).
- The 'intercept' is the expected value of the stock when the 'Futures' variable is zero. The coefficient is 0.7754 with a standard error of 0.413.
- The *p*-value of 0.061 is marginally significant, suggesting the intercept might not be significantly different from zero at the 5% level. The 'Futures' coefficient

[3] https://www.statsmodels.org/dev/example_formulas.html.

**Table 6** OLS regression

```
formula = 'Stock ~ Futures'
model = sm.ols(formula, data).fit()
print(model.summary())
```

```
                            OLS Regression Results
==============================================================================
Dep. Variable:                  Stock   R-squared:                       0.999
Model:                            OLS   Adj. R-squared:                  0.999
Method:                 Least Squares   F-statistic:                 3.548e+05
Date:                Sat, 03 Aug 2024   Prob (F-statistic):               0.00
Time:                        16:13:26   Log-Likelihood:                -1076.2
No. Observations:                 501   AIC:                             2156.
Df Residuals:                     499   BIC:                             2165.
Df Model:                           1
Covariance Type:            nonrobust
==============================================================================
                 coef    std err          t      P>|t|      [0.025      0.975]
------------------------------------------------------------------------------
Intercept      0.7754      0.413      1.879      0.061      -0.035       1.586
Futures        1.0506      0.002    595.682      0.000       1.047       1.054
==============================================================================
Omnibus:                        1.538   Durbin-Watson:                   2.060
Prob(Omnibus):                  0.463   Jarque-Bera (JB):                1.620
Skew:                          -0.109   Prob(JB):                        0.445
Kurtosis:                       2.827   Cond. No.                     1.04e+03
==============================================================================

Notes:
[1] Standard Errors assume that the covariance matrix of the errors is correctly specified.
[2] The condition number is large, 1.04e+03. This might indicate that there are
strong multicollinearity or other numerical problems.
```

(1.0546) is significant ($p < 0.01$), showing for every unit increase in Futures, the Stock price increases by approximately 1.05 units.

- The *F*-statistics (3.548e+05) and Prob (*F*-statistics) (0.00) showing the model is statistically significant.
- The Omnibus and Jarque–Bera tests show *p*-values > 0.05, suggesting no statistical evidence against normality in the residuals.
- The Condition Number is high (1.04e+03), which suggests potential multicollinearity or numerical issues. This might indicate that there could be redundancy in our predictors, although we currently only have one predictor (Futures).
- The Durbin-Watson statistic (2.06) is close to 2, suggesting there is no significant autocorrelation in the residuals.
- Jarque–Bera (JB) test (1.620) with *p*-value (0.445) suggests the residuals do not significantly deviate from normality.
- The Akaike Information Criterion (AIC) measures the relative quality of a model for a given set of data and has the formula $AIC = 2k - 2L$ where, $k$ is the number of coefficients to be estimated in the model and $L$ is the value of the log-likelihood. Here in this case $k = 1$ and $L = -544.16$, so, $AIC = 2 * 1 - 2 * (-544.16) = 1092$. AIC would test whether this is a good model in an absolute term. If we have several models, the preferred model is the one with the minimum AIC value. AIC rewards goodness-of-fit (as assessed

**Table 7** Hedge ratio extraction

```
hedge_ratio = model.params.iloc[1]
print(f'Optimal Hedge Ratio: {hedge_ratio}')
```

```
Optimal Hedge Ratio: 1.0505767074107426
```

by the likelihood function), but it also includes a penalty that is an increasing function of the number of estimated parameters ($k$).

- Bayesian Information Criterion $\text{BIC} = \log(n) * k - \log(L)$ where, $n$ is the number of observations and $k$ is the number of parameters to be estimated including the intercept.

Table 7 shows how to extract the hedge ratio from the slope.

The optimal hedge ratio of 1.0506 shows that for each unit of the underlying stock, this means that we should hold approximately 1.0506 futures contracts to hedge against price movements effectively. If we are holding 100 shares of a stock and need to hedge our position using futures contracts, with an optimal hedge ratio of 1.0506, we would calculate:

$$\begin{aligned} \text{Number of Futures Contracts} &= \text{Number of Shares} * \text{Optimal Hedge Ratio} \\ &= 100 * 1.0506 = 105.06 \end{aligned}$$

Next, we conduct $F$-test to test linear restrictions on the parameters of the model. Null Hypothesis ($H_0$) is the parameter associated with Futures is equal to 1 ($\beta_{\text{Futures}} = 1$). Alternative Hypothesis ($H_1$) is that the parameter associated with Futures is not equal to 1 ($\beta_{\text{Futures}} \neq 1$). Table 8 shows the hypothesis test.

The $F$-statistic for this test is extremely high (822.38). This shows a substantial deviation from $H_0$. The $p$-value ($1.36\text{e}{-107} < 0.05$) implies we can confidently reject $H_0$. This means that the data provides statistical evidence that the true coefficient of the 'Futures' variable is different from 1.

In the next step, we transform the 'Stock' and 'Futures' prices into percentage returns. Here we apply logarithmic returns instead of simple returns as displayed in Table 9.

**Table 8** Hypothesis test

```
hypotheses = 'Futures = 1'
f_test = model.f_test(hypotheses)
print(f_test)
```

```
<F test: F=822.3848648761457, p=1.3626793694355158e-107, df_denom=499, df_num=1>
```

**Table 9** Log differences (returns)

```
data['Stock_Returns'] = np.log(data['Stock']).diff()
data['Futures_Returns'] = np.log(data['Futures']).diff()
data = data.dropna()
```

```
data.describe()
```

| | Stock | Futures | Stock_Returns | Futures_Returns |
|---|---|---|---|---|
| **count** | 500.000000 | 500.000000 | 500.000000 | 500.000000 |
| **mean** | 240.010493 | 227.713288 | -0.000952 | -0.000984 |
| **std** | 54.977550 | 52.280051 | 0.038102 | 0.040110 |
| **min** | 108.099998 | 101.067007 | -0.130590 | -0.139799 |
| **25%** | 197.367496 | 188.227335 | -0.021259 | -0.023070 |
| **50%** | 241.661667 | 230.037576 | 0.000997 | 0.000432 |
| **75%** | 276.017509 | 261.757880 | 0.020431 | 0.023578 |
| **max** | 383.196655 | 363.190319 | 0.104362 | 0.116313 |

**Fig. 1** Statistical summary

Let us investigate the results obtained from the statistical run. We see that based on their mean values, both the return series (Stock_Returns and Futures_Returns) are quite similar, as are the standard deviations and their minimum and maximum values as displayed in Fig. 1.

We run the regression again using the return series. Tables 10 and 11 displays the implementation which is followed by the model output and hedge ratio.

The optimal hedge ratio value (0.88) suggests there is a strong relationship between the stock and futures prices. This means that for every dollar invested in the stock, we should invest about $0.88 in futures.

The null hypothesis ($H_0$) is that the $\beta_{\text{Future\_returns}} = 1$ and alternate hypothesis ($H_1$) is $\beta_{\text{Future\_returns}} \neq 1$. $F$-statistic 54.69 obtained from Table 12 suggests the model significantly improves when $\beta_{\text{Future\_returns}} \neq 1$. This shows statistical evidence that the relationship captured by the model is meaningful. The $p$-value $<0.05$ provides strong statistical evidence favoring $H_1$.

Utilizing our learning from above testing, let us estimate and test some hypotheses about the CAP model for several US stocks. Table 13 displays the data ingestion from Yahoo Finance having average monthly prices for Apple (AAPL), Microsoft (MSFT), Google (GOOGL), Amazon (AMZN), and S&P 500 (^GSPC). We download only the adjusted close (Adj Close) column. The adjusted close price is the closing price after dividend payouts, stock splits, or the issue of additional

**Table 10** OLS regression using log difference data

```
formula = 'Stock_Returns ~ Futures_Returns'
model = sm.ols(formula, data).fit()
print(model.summary())
```

```
                            OLS Regression Results
==============================================================================
Dep. Variable:          Stock_Returns   R-squared:                       0.877
Model:                            OLS   Adj. R-squared:                  0.877
Method:                 Least Squares   F-statistic:                     3547.
Date:                Sat, 03 Aug 2024   Prob (F-statistic):          1.18e-228
Time:                        16:36:58   Log-Likelihood:                 1448.4
No. Observations:                 500   AIC:                            -2893.
Df Residuals:                     498   BIC:                            -2884.
Df Model:                           1
Covariance Type:            nonrobust
===================================================================================
                      coef    std err          t      P>|t|      [0.025      0.975]
-----------------------------------------------------------------------------------
Intercept       -7.661e-05      0.001     -0.128      0.898      -0.001       0.001
Futures_Returns     0.8895      0.015     59.556      0.000       0.860       0.919
==============================================================================
Omnibus:                       36.297   Durbin-Watson:                   2.942
Prob(Omnibus):                  0.000   Jarque-Bera (JB):              108.243
Skew:                           0.284   Prob(JB):                     3.13e-24
Kurtosis:                       5.207   Cond. No.                         25.0
==============================================================================

Notes:
[1] Standard Errors assume that the covariance matrix of the errors is correctly specified.
```

**Table 11** Hedge ratio estimation

```
hedge_ratio = model.params.iloc[1]
print(f'Optimal Hedge Ratio: {hedge_ratio}')
```

```
Optimal Hedge Ratio: 0.8895416810232564
```

**Table 12** Hypothesis ($f$-test)

```
hypotheses = 'Futures_Returns = 1'
f_test = model.f_test(hypotheses)
f_test
```

```
<class 'statsmodels.stats.contrast.ContrastResults'>
<F test: F=54.69014833175215, p=6.025202851037571e-13, df_denom=498, df_num=1>
```

shares have been considered. This price provides better sign of the stock's value than the closing price.

Let us revisit our previous analysis wherein we created AAPL and ^GSPC series with their returns. We add risk-free data with these as shown in Table 14.

**Table 13** Multiple series ingestion

```
stocks = ['AAPL', 'MSFT', 'GOOGL', 'AMZN']
market_index = '^GSPC'
data = yf.download(stocks + [market_index], start='2010-01-01', end='2024-01-01', interval='1mo')['Adj Close']
data.index = pd.to_datetime(data.index)
print(data)
```

```
Ticker            AAPL        AMZN       GOOGL        MSFT        ^GSPC
Date
2010-01-01    5.799201    6.270500   13.246559   21.296070  1073.869995
2010-02-01    6.178446    5.920000   13.168070   21.666374  1104.489990
2010-03-01    7.095763    6.788500   14.175922   22.238413  1169.430054
2010-04-01    7.883547    6.855000   13.140574   23.187479  1186.689941
2010-05-01    7.756424    6.273000   12.138970   19.588638  1089.410034
...                ...         ...         ...         ...          ...
2023-08-01  186.877548  138.009995  136.013901  325.215973  4507.660156
2023-09-01  170.535538  127.120003  130.709991  313.962494  4288.049805
2023-10-01  170.097275  133.089996  123.937759  336.195923  4193.799805
2023-11-01  189.201691  146.089996  132.378067  376.764923  4567.799805
2023-12-01  192.024185  151.940002  139.529861  374.670074  4769.830078

[168 rows x 5 columns]
```

Table 15 displays line plots and a scatter plot for the returns of Apple and the S&P 500 to check if both the plots are moving together.

From the above plot, we can see a positive relationship between the two series, which is consistent with the idea that Apple's stock tends to move in the same direction as the broader market. Apple's returns show higher volatility compared to the S&P 500 index, reflecting higher risk. The scatter plot suggests that while Apple's returns are influenced by the market, there is still a substantial amount of idiosyncratic risk that investors need to consider.

Let us revisit the CAP formula $\mathrm{ER}_i = R_f + \beta_i(\mathrm{ER}_m - R_f)$ where, $\mathrm{ER}_i$ = expected return on investment, $R_f$ = risk-free rate, $\beta_i$ = beta of the investment, $\mathrm{ER}_m - R_f$ = market risk premium. To simplify, $\text{excessreturn} = \text{regularreturn} - \text{riskfreereturn}$. We apply this logic to transform the data shown in Table 16.

Table 17 shows the calculation of excess returns (AAPL_Returns and SP_Returns). We ran OLS regression on the excess return series, where the dependent variable is the excess return of Apple (Apple_ExcessReturns), regressed on a constant and the excess market return (SP_ExcessReturns).

This summary provides insights into the relationship between AAPL_ExcessReturns and the SP_ExcessReturns. Both the parameters' coefficients are highly statistically significant with *p*-values close to 0.

- $R^2 = 99.8\%$, which shows 99.8% of the variation in AAPL_ExcessReturns can be explained by the variation in SP_ExcessReturns.

**Table 14** Return series

```
stock = 'AAPL'
market_index = '^GSPC'

data = yf.download([stock, market_index], start = '2010-01-01', end = '2024-01-01', interval='1mo')['Adj
Close']
data['AAPL_Returns'] = np.log(data[stock]).diff()
data['SP_returns'] = np.log(data[market_index]).diff()

start = dt.datetime(2010, 1, 1)
end = dt.datetime(2024,1,1)

data['risk_free_rate'] = pdr.get_data_fred('DGS3MO', start=start, end=end)
data['risk_free_rate'].index = pd.to_datetime(data['risk_free_rate'].index)
data
```

| Ticker | AAPL | ^GSPC | AAPL_Returns | SP_returns | risk_free_rate |
|---|---|---|---|---|---|
| Date | | | | | |
| **2010-01-01** | 5.799201 | 1073.869995 | NaN | NaN | NaN |
| **2010-02-01** | 6.178447 | 1104.489990 | 0.063347 | 0.028115 | 0.10 |
| **2010-03-01** | 7.095765 | 1169.430054 | 0.138431 | 0.057133 | 0.13 |
| **2010-04-01** | 7.883547 | 1186.689941 | 0.105280 | 0.014651 | 0.16 |
| **2010-05-01** | 7.756425 | 1089.410034 | -0.016256 | -0.085532 | NaN |
| **...** | ... | ... | ... | ... | ... |
| **2023-08-01** | 186.877533 | 4507.660156 | -0.044658 | -0.017875 | 5.54 |
| **2023-09-01** | 170.535538 | 4288.049805 | -0.091510 | -0.049946 | 5.53 |
| **2023-10-01** | 170.097260 | 4193.799805 | -0.002573 | -0.022225 | NaN |
| **2023-11-01** | 189.201691 | 4567.799805 | 0.106443 | 0.085424 | 5.57 |
| **2023-12-01** | 192.024185 | 4769.830078 | 0.014808 | 0.043279 | 5.43 |

168 rows × 5 columns

- A high *F*-statistic (97,140) shows the overall model is highly significant.
- Intercept ($\beta_0 = 0.02$) is the expected AAPL_ExcessReturns when the SP_ExcessReturns are zero. It suggests that, on average, AAPL generates an excess return of 2% even when the market excess return is zero. This also indicates a slight positive bias or alpha in AAPL's returns, which is a measure of performance on a risk-adjusted basis.

**Table 15** Visualization returns series (line and scatter plots)

```
fig, (ax1, ax2) = plt.subplots(1, 2, figsize = (14, 6))
ax1.plot(data['AAPL_Returns'], label = 'Apple returns')
ax1.plot(data['SP_Returns'], label = 'S&P returns')
ax1.set_xlabel('Date')
ax1.set_ylabel('Returns')
ax1.set_title('Returns Over Time')
ax1.grid(True)
ax1.legend()

ax2.scatter(data['SP_Returns'], data['AAPL_Returns'], alpha = 0.5)
ax2.set_xlabel('S&P Returns')
ax2.set_ylabel('Apple Returns')
ax2.set_title('Apple Returns vs S&P Returns')
ax2.grid(True)
plt.tight_layout()
plt.show()
```

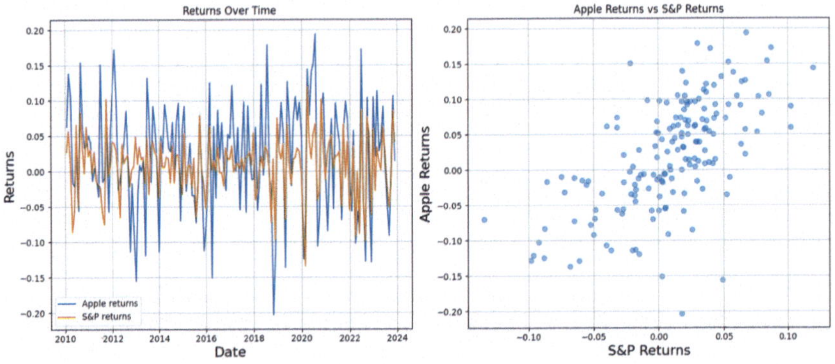


- Slope ($\beta_1 = 1.004$) is the change in AAPL_ExcessReturns for a one-unit change in SP_ExcessReturns. It suggests for every 1% increase in SP_ExcessReturns, AAPL_ExcessReturns increase by approximately 1.004%. This value being close to 1 indicates a nearly one-to-one relationship, implying that AAPL's performance closely follows the market movements represented by the S&P 500.
- Omnibus (8.268) and Prob (Omnibus) (0.01) suggest the residuals are not normally distributed.
- Jarque–Bera (8.89), Prob (JB) (0.01) further confirms the non-normality of residuals.
- Skew (−0.48) shows slight left skewness in the residuals. Kurtosis (3.99) suggests heavier tails compared to a normal distribution.

**Table 16** Implementation of excess returns

```
data = data.dropna()
data.loc[:,'AAPL_ExcessReturns'] = data.loc[:,'AAPL_Returns'] - data.loc[:,'risk_free_rate']
data.loc[:, 'SP_ExcessReturns'] = data.loc[:,'SP_returns'] - data.loc[:,'risk_free_rate']
data.head()
```

| Ticker | AAPL | ^GSPC | AAPL_Returns | SP_returns | risk_free_rate | AAPL_ExcessReturns | SP_ExcessReturns |
|---|---|---|---|---|---|---|---|
| Date | | | | | | | |
| **2010-02-01** | 6.178447 | 1104.489990 | 0.063347 | 0.028115 | 0.10 | -0.036653 | -0.071885 |
| **2010-03-01** | 7.095765 | 1169.430054 | 0.138431 | 0.057133 | 0.13 | 0.008431 | -0.072867 |
| **2010-04-01** | 7.883547 | 1186.689941 | 0.105280 | 0.014651 | 0.16 | -0.054720 | -0.145349 |
| **2010-06-01** | 7.594883 | 1030.709961 | -0.021047 | -0.055388 | 0.16 | -0.181047 | -0.215388 |
| **2010-07-01** | 7.767601 | 1101.599976 | 0.022487 | 0.066516 | 0.17 | -0.147513 | -0.103484 |

**Table 17** OLS regression on excess returns

```
formula = 'AAPL_ExcessReturns ~ SP_ExcessReturns'
model = sm.ols(formula, data).fit()
print(model.summary())
```

```
                            OLS Regression Results
==============================================================================
Dep. Variable:     AAPL_ExcessReturns   R-squared:                       0.998
Model:                            OLS   Adj. R-squared:                  0.998
Method:                 Least Squares   F-statistic:                 6.498e+04
Date:                Fri, 02 Aug 2024   Prob (F-statistic):          3.85e-153
Time:                        09:46:42   Log-Likelihood:                 150.43
No. Observations:                 111   AIC:                            -296.9
Df Residuals:                     109   BIC:                            -291.4
Df Model:                           1
Covariance Type:            nonrobust
====================================================================================
                       coef    std err          t      P>|t|      [0.025      0.975]
------------------------------------------------------------------------------------
Intercept            0.0200      0.007      2.837      0.005       0.006       0.034
SP_ExcessReturns     1.0041      0.004    254.914      0.000       0.996       1.012
==============================================================================
Omnibus:                        8.268   Durbin-Watson:                   1.942
Prob(Omnibus):                  0.016   Jarque-Bera (JB):                8.893
Skew:                          -0.484   Prob(JB):                       0.0117
Kurtosis:                       3.993   Cond. No.                         2.34
==============================================================================

Notes:
[1] Standard Errors assume that the covariance matrix of the errors is correctly specified.
```

- Durbin-Watson (1.94) shows there is no significant autocorrelation in the residuals (close to 2).
- Condition Number (2.34) shows no serious multicollinearity issues.

$$H_0 \rightarrow \text{“SP\_ExcessReturns} = 1\text{"}$$

$H_0 : \beta = 1$ suggests the S&P 500's excess returns fully explain Apple's excess returns at a one-to-one ratio. $H_1 : \beta \neq 1$ would imply Apple's excess returns do not have a direct one-to-one relationship with the S&P 500's excess returns, showing either greater or lesser sensitivity to market changes.

$$H_0 \rightarrow \text{“SP\_ExcessReturns} = \text{Intercept} = 1\text{"}$$

$H_0$ : Intercept $= 1$ Implies even when S&P 500's excess returns are zero, Apple's excess returns are expected to be 1, being a baseline return or consistent $\alpha$ of 1. $H1$ : Intercept $\neq 1$ suggests the intercept is different from 1, meaning Apple's returns do not have a baseline level of 1% (or 1 unit) independently of market returns.

This is useful in finance when assessing whether an investment consistently outperforms (or underperforms) compared to the market. A statistically significant intercept implies a persistent performance level above or below the market, independent of market movements. Table 18 displays the hypotheses test.

- In the first test, the $F$-statistic is low (1.06), and the $p$-value (0.304) is > 0.05, showing we do not reject the $H_0$. This implies we do not have enough evidence to state that the coefficient for SP_ExcessReturns significantly differs from 1.
- In the second test $F$-statistic is extremely high (13,547.46), and the $p$-value is extremely small (close to 0), showing against the null hypothesis. Therefore, we reject the null hypothesis. There is statistical evidence that at least one of the coefficients (either SP_ExcessReturns or the Intercept) is significantly different from 1.

**Table 18** Hypotheses testing

```
hypotheses = 'SP_ExcessReturns = 1'
f_test = model.f_test(hypotheses)
print(f_test)

hypotheses = 'SP_ExcessReturns = Intercept = 1'
f_test = model.f_test(hypotheses)
print(f_test)
```

```
<F test: F=1.0635155130370995, p=0.30469758498565036, df_denom=109, df_num=1>
<F test: F=13547.465262624151, p=2.2507063093832185e-131, df_denom=109, df_num=2>
```

# 3 Quantile Regression (QR)

OLS regression and related methods assume that associations between independent and dependent variables are the same at all levels. Here, Quantile Regression (QR) provides an alternative approach. QR was first presented by Koenker and Bassett (1978). It builds upon the traditional least squares estimation of a conditional mean model to estimate an ensemble model for multiple conditional quantile functions. QR offers a comprehensive understanding of how the independent factors affect the dependent variable at different quantiles. Quantiles and percentiles are synonymous; the 0.99 quantile is the 99th percentile. The best-known quantile is the median.

In OLS regression, the goal is to minimize the distances between the values predicted by the regression line and the original values. However, QR differentially weighs the distances between the values predicted by the regression line and the observed values, then tries to minimize the weighted distances. The main advantage of QR is that it allows to understand the relationships between variables outside of the mean (average) of the data. This is useful for understanding outcomes that are not normally distributed.

To demonstrate how to run QR, let us employ a simple CAP model beta estimation. Table 19 shows the code snippet, which provides results from multiple quantile regressions followed by the output. quantiles = np.arange(0.10, 1.00, 0.10) sets the quantiles from 0.10 to 0.90 with a step of 0.10.

The output reveals a strong and consistent linear relationship between AAPL_ExcessReturns and SP_ExcessReturns across different quantiles. The intercept varies slightly across quantiles but stays close to zero. This suggests when the S&P 500's excess returns are zero, Apple's excess returns are also close to zero on average, implying minimal alpha or baseline return independent of the market across different market conditions. The coefficient for SP_ExcessReturns is consistently close to 1 across all quantiles, showing a steady relationship between Apple's excess returns and the S&P 500's excess returns. This means for each 1% change in the S&P 500's excess returns, Apple's excess returns tend to move approximately 1%, signifying strong linearity in their relationship.

The intercept varies significantly in higher quantiles (e.g., it is more positive in the 0.7 to 0.9 quantiles), which reflects Apple's slightly higher baseline returns during periods of stronger market performance. The consistency of the slope across quantiles shows that the relationship between the returns remains stable, regardless of the returns' magnitude (whether low or high). This insight is useful for risk management and investment strategy development. Table 20 displays the code snippet to get the QR plots from the above model, which is followed by the plots.

I. Coefficients plot: The coefficients of the SP_ExcessReturns across different quantiles are relatively stable and around 1. This shows the relationship between AAPL_ExcessReturns and SP_ExcessReturns is consistent across different quantiles. However, there are slight variations suggesting the effect of SP_ExcessReturns on AAPL_ExcessReturns may vary slightly depending

**Table 19** Quantile regression implementation

```
stocks = ['AAPL']
market_index = '^GSPC'
data = yf.download(stocks + [market_index], start = '2010-01-01', end = '2024-01-01', interval = '1mo')['Adj
Close']
data.index = pd.to_datetime(data.index)

data['risk_free_rate'] = pdr.get_data_fred('DGS3MO', start=start, end=end)
data['risk_free_rate'].index = pd.to_datetime(data['risk_free_rate'].index)

data['AAPL_ExcessReturns'] = np.log(data['AAPL']).diff() - data['risk_free_rate']
data['SP_ExcessReturns'] = np.log(data['^GSPC']).diff() - data['risk_free_rate']
data = data.dropna()
quantiles = np.arange(0.10, 1.00, 0.10)
results_list = []
```

(continued)

**Table 19** (continued)

```
for q in quantiles:
    model = sm.quantreg('AAPL_ExcessReturns ~ SP_ExcessReturns', data).fit(q=q)
    summary_df = model.summary2().tables[1]
    summary_df['Quantile'] = q
    results_list.append(summary_df)

combined_results = pd.concat(results_list)

combined_results.reset_index(inplace = True)
combined_results
```

(continued)

**Table 19** (continued)

| | index | Coef. | Std.Err. | t | P>\|t\| | [0.025 | 0.975] | Quantile |
|---|---|---|---|---|---|---|---|---|
| 0 | Intercept | -0.053940 | 0.010494 | -5.140257 | 1.215760e-06 | -0.074738 | -0.033142 | 0.1 |
| 1 | SP_ExcessReturns | 1.005802 | 0.005284 | 190.360153 | 2.386367e-139 | 0.995330 | 1.016274 | 0.1 |
| 2 | Intercept | -0.026990 | 0.009826 | -2.746804 | 7.042651e-03 | -0.046464 | -0.007515 | 0.2 |
| 3 | SP_ExcessReturns | 1.002612 | 0.005717 | 175.374657 | 1.764451e-135 | 0.991281 | 1.013942 | 0.2 |
| 4 | Intercept | -0.017008 | 0.010358 | -1.642066 | 1.034585e-01 | -0.037537 | 0.003521 | 0.3 |
| 5 | SP_ExcessReturns | 1.002128 | 0.006029 | 166.225853 | 5.935854e-133 | 0.990179 | 1.014077 | 0.3 |
| 6 | Intercept | 0.000012 | 0.010091 | 0.001166 | 9.990719e-01 | -0.019988 | 0.020012 | 0.4 |
| 7 | SP_ExcessReturns | 1.004821 | 0.005752 | 174.689112 | 2.700019e-135 | 0.993421 | 1.016221 | 0.4 |
| 8 | Intercept | 0.024839 | 0.009629 | 2.579519 | 1.122518e-02 | 0.005754 | 0.043924 | 0.5 |
| 9 | SP_ExcessReturns | 1.005595 | 0.005383 | 186.799213 | 1.857545e-138 | 0.994925 | 1.016264 | 0.5 |
| 10 | Intercept | 0.035692 | 0.009631 | 3.706101 | 3.325329e-04 | 0.016604 | 0.054780 | 0.6 |
| 11 | SP_ExcessReturns | 1.001270 | 0.005356 | 186.938945 | 1.712582e-138 | 0.990655 | 1.011886 | 0.6 |
| 12 | Intercept | 0.051600 | 0.009199 | 5.609561 | 1.553670e-07 | 0.033368 | 0.069831 | 0.7 |
| 13 | SP_ExcessReturns | 1.001981 | 0.005053 | 198.286141 | 2.832505e-141 | 0.991965 | 1.011996 | 0.7 |
| 14 | Intercept | 0.071777 | 0.008534 | 8.410905 | 1.737989e-13 | 0.054864 | 0.088691 | 0.8 |
| 15 | SP_ExcessReturns | 1.005105 | 0.004222 | 238.076908 | 6.527225e-150 | 0.996738 | 1.013473 | 0.8 |
| 16 | Intercept | 0.090980 | 0.009221 | 9.867101 | 8.585536e-17 | 0.072705 | 0.109255 | 0.9 |
| 17 | SP_ExcessReturns | 1.002422 | 0.004901 | 204.533088 | 9.720964e-143 | 0.992708 | 1.012136 | 0.9 |

**Table 20** Quantile regression plots

```
quantiles = np.arange(0.1, 1.0, 0.1)
models = [sm.quantreg('AAPL_ExcessReturns ~ SP_ExcessReturns', data).fit(q = q) for q in quantiles]

coefs = pd.DataFrame([model.params for model in models], index = quantiles)
conf_ints = pd.DataFrame([model.conf_int().loc['SP_ExcessReturns'] for model in models], index=quantiles,
columns = ['2.5%', '97.5%'])

fig, axes = plt.subplots(3, 2, figsize = (15, 10))
axes[0, 0].plot(coefs.index, coefs['SP_ExcessReturns'], label = 'Slope', marker = 'o')
axes[0, 0].set_xlabel('Quantiles')
axes[0, 0].set_ylabel('Coefficient')
axes[0, 0].set_title('Quantile Regression Coefficients')
axes[0, 0].legend()

residuals = pd.DataFrame({'Residuals': models[4].resid, 'Quantile': 0.5})
for model in models:
   residuals = pd.concat([residuals, pd.DataFrame({'Residuals': model.resid, 'Quantile': model.q})])
sns.scatterplot(x = residuals.index, y = 'Residuals', hue='Quantile', data = residuals, palette = 'viridis', ax =
axes[0, 1])
axes[0, 1].axhline(0, color = 'k', linestyle = '--')
axes[0, 1].set_xlabel('Index')
axes[0, 1].set_ylabel('Residuals')
axes[0, 1].set_title('Quantile Regression Residuals')
axes[0, 1].legend(loc='upper right')
quantile = 0.5
model_median = smf.quantreg('AAPL_ExcessReturns ~ SP_ExcessReturns', data).fit(q = quantile)
data['Predicted'] = model_median.predict(data['SP_ExcessReturns'])
sns.scatterplot(x = 'SP_ExcessReturns', y = 'AAPL_ExcessReturns', data = data, ax = axes[1, 0], label =
'Actual')
sns.lineplot(x = 'SP_ExcessReturns', y = 'Predicted', data = data, color = 'r', ax = axes[1, 0], label =
'Predicted')
axes[1, 0].set_xlabel('SP_ExcessReturns')
axes[1, 0].set_ylabel('AAPL_ExcessReturns')
axes[1, 0].set_title('Predicted vs. Actual Returns')
axes[1, 0].legend()
axes[1, 1].plot(coefs.index, coefs['SP_ExcessReturns'], label = 'Slope', marker = 'o')
axes[1, 1].fill_between(conf_ints.index, conf_ints['2.5%'], conf_ints['97.5%'], color = 'b', alpha = 0.2)
axes[1, 1].set_xlabel('Quantiles')
axes[1, 1].set_ylabel('Coefficient')
axes[1, 1].set_title('Quantile Regression Slopes with Confidence Bands')
axes[1, 1].legend()
```

(continued)

**Table 20** (continued)

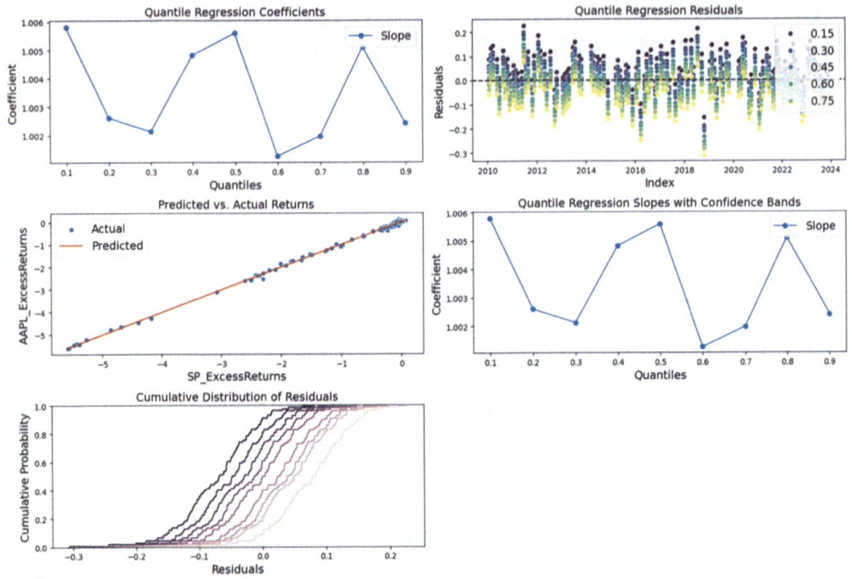


```
sns.ecdfplot(data = residuals, x = 'Residuals', hue = 'Quantile', ax = axes[2, 0])
axes[2, 0].set_xlabel('Residuals')
axes[2, 0].set_ylabel('Cumulative Probability')
axes[2, 0].set_title('Cumulative Distribution of Residuals')
axes[2, 0].legend(loc='lower right')
axes[2, 1].axis('off')
plt.tight_layout()
plt.show()
```

on the quantile. Such as, at the 0.8 quantile, the coefficient is slightly higher, suggesting a stronger relationship in the upper quantiles.

II. Residuals plot: The residuals are randomly scattered around zero, which is desirable in a well-fitted model. The spread of residuals is consistent across time, with no obvious patterns, which shows that the model fits the data well. Different quantiles show different residual distributions, with some quantiles having more spread than others.

III. Predicted vs. Actual Returns plot: The predicted values from the median (0.5 quantile) quantile regression closely follow the actual values, indicating a good fit for the median model. The points are closely clustered around the line, suggesting that the model's predictions are accurate for the median quantile.

IV. Slopes with confidence bands: This plot shows the slope of SP_ExcessReturns across different quantiles with confidence intervals. The confidence intervals are narrow, indicating that the estimates are precise. The slight variations in slopes across quantiles suggest that the relationship between AAPL_ExcessReturns and SP_ExcessReturns is consistent but have slight differences depending on the quantile.

V. Cumulative Distribution of Residuals: The cumulative distribution functions (CDFs) of the residuals for different quantiles are plotted to compare the distribution of residuals across quantiles. The distribution of residuals varies slightly across quantiles, with some quantiles showing more spread or skewness than others.

## 4 Three-Factor Model Implementation

Let us revisit the equation $R_i - R_f = \alpha_i + \beta_{im}(R_m - R_f) + \beta_{i(\mathrm{SMB})}\mathrm{SMB} + \beta_{i(\mathrm{HML})}\mathrm{HML} + \epsilon_i$.

Tables 21 and 22 display the data ingestion which we had done earlier. Let us implement a 3-factor model on this data.

We need to merge the above ingested datasets in a single frame for further analysis. Table 23 displays the merging procedure of the two datasets.

Developing the Fama–French 3 factors directly from the stock data alone is not straightforward. The Fama–French factors, such as Market Excess Return (MKT), Small Minus Big (SMB), and High Minus Low (HML) derived from broad market

**Table 21** Data ingestion for 3-factor model

```
start = dt.datetime(2010, 1, 1)
end = dt.datetime.now()

stock = 'AAPL'
market_index = '^GSPC'
data = yf.download([stock, market_index], start = start, end = end, interval = '1mo')['Adj Close']
data['AAPL_Returns'] = np.log(data[stock] / data[stock].shift(1))
data['Market_Returns'] = np.log(data[market_index] / data[market_index].shift(1))
data = data.dropna()
data.reset_index(inplace = True)
data.head()
```

| Ticker | Date | AAPL | ^GSPC | AAPL_Returns | Market_Returns |
|---|---|---|---|---|---|
| 0 | 2010-02-01 | 6.178447 | 1104.489990 | 0.063346 | 0.028115 |
| 1 | 2010-03-01 | 7.095764 | 1169.430054 | 0.138431 | 0.057133 |
| 2 | 2010-04-01 | 7.883543 | 1186.689941 | 0.105280 | 0.014651 |
| 3 | 2010-05-01 | 7.756427 | 1089.410034 | -0.016256 | -0.085532 |
| 4 | 2010-06-01 | 7.594882 | 1030.709961 | -0.021047 | -0.055388 |

**Table 22** 3-month treasury bill

```
start = dt.datetime(2010, 1, 1)
end = dt.datetime.now()

rf_data = pdr.get_data_fred('DGS3MO', start = start, end = end)
rf_data = rf_data.resample('M').last() / 100
rf_data.reset_index(inplace = True)
rf_data.columns = ['Date', 'RF']
rf_data
```

| | Date | RF |
|---|---|---|
| **0** | 2010-01-31 | 0.0006 |
| **1** | 2010-02-28 | 0.0011 |
| **2** | 2010-03-31 | 0.0015 |
| **3** | 2010-04-30 | 0.0016 |
| **4** | 2010-05-31 | 0.0016 |
| **...** | ... | ... |
| **169** | 2024-02-29 | 0.0524 |
| **170** | 2024-03-31 | 0.0524 |
| **171** | 2024-04-30 | 0.0524 |
| **172** | 2024-05-31 | 0.0525 |
| **173** | 2024-06-30 | 0.0524 |

174 rows × 2 columns

**Table 23** Merge the risk-free rate with the main dataset

```
data = pd.concat([data, rf_data['RF']], axis = 1)
data.set_index('Date', inplace = True)
data['AAPL_ExcessReturns'] = data['AAPL_Returns'] - data['RF']
data.head()
```

| | AAPL | ^GSPC | AAPL_Returns | Market_Returns | RF | AAPL_ExcessReturns |
|---|---|---|---|---|---|---|
| **Date** | | | | | | |
| **2010-02-01** | 6.178448 | 1104.489990 | 0.063347 | 0.028115 | 0.0008 | 0.062547 |
| **2010-03-01** | 7.095762 | 1169.430054 | 0.138431 | 0.057133 | 0.0013 | 0.137131 |
| **2010-04-01** | 7.883545 | 1186.689941 | 0.105280 | 0.014651 | 0.0016 | 0.103680 |
| **2010-05-01** | 7.756422 | 1089.410034 | -0.016257 | -0.085532 | 0.0016 | -0.017857 |
| **2010-06-01** | 7.594885 | 1030.709961 | -0.021046 | -0.055388 | 0.0016 | -0.022646 |

data and not from a single stock. SMB and HML factors are based on the returns of portfolios that are constructed from a broad universe of stocks, not just a single stock. To construct SMB and HML, we need a detailed dataset that includes information on stock characteristics (like size and book-to-market ratio).

Ken French's data library provides historical returns for the Fama–French factors and other risk factors used in asset pricing research. This data is widely used by researchers and practitioners for empirical studies and investment analysis. Many financial data providers and academic platforms offer access to Fama–French factor data as part of their services. This dataset can be accessed here **getFamaFrenchFactors**.[4]

The Fama–French 3-factor model is well-suited to explaining returns across a broad cross-section of stocks, especially portfolios or groups of stocks. However, it may not fully capture the return dynamics of individual, large-cap stocks like Apple (Table 24).

Once we have the factors, we merge them with the original data on the date index as shown in Table 25.

Table 26 generates a visual comparison between the excess returns of the stock (AAPL) and the three Fama–French factors.

- The first plot on the left-hand side compares the AAPL_ExcessReturns (blue line) with the market risk premium (Mkt-RF, orange line). We can see periods where AAPL's returns align closely with the market risk premium, suggesting that AAPL's returns are significantly influenced by overall market movements. Both the market risk premium and AAPL's returns exhibit high volatility, with spikes and drops, which suggests a significant level of risk associated with the stock, influenced by market conditions.
- The second plot in the middle compares the excess returns of AAPL with the size premium (SMB, orange line). This is the difference in returns between small-cap stocks and large-cap stocks. The plot shows some alignment, but not as strongly as with the market risk premium, showing a moderate influence. The SMB factor also shows volatility, though it is less evident compared to the market factor.
- The third plot on the left-hand side compares the excess returns of AAPL with the value premium (HML, orange line). The value premium is the difference in returns between high book-to-market (value) stocks and low book-to-market (growth) stocks. Co-movement with the HML factor would suggest that AAPL's returns are influenced by the value premium, the difference in returns between high book-to-market and low book-to-market stocks. The plot shows occasional alignment, indicating some influence but less than the market factor.

[4] https://pypi.org/project/getFamaFrenchFactors/.

**Table 24** Fama–French factors

```
ff3 = pd.DataFrame(gff.famaFrench3Factor(frequency='m'))
ff3['date_ff_factors'] = pd.to_datetime(ff3['date_ff_factors'], format = '%Y%m')
ff3 = ff3.set_index('date_ff_factors')
ff3.index = ff3.index + pd.offsets.MonthBegin(1)
ff3 = ff3.tail(174)
print(ff3)
```

| | Mkt-RF | SMB | HML | RF |
|---|---|---|---|---|
| date_ff_factors | | | | |
| **2010-02-01** | -0.0336 | 0.0040 | 0.0043 | 0.0000 |
| **2010-03-01** | 0.0340 | 0.0119 | 0.0323 | 0.0000 |
| **2010-04-01** | 0.0631 | 0.0148 | 0.0221 | 0.0001 |
| **2010-05-01** | 0.0200 | 0.0487 | 0.0289 | 0.0001 |
| **2010-06-01** | -0.0789 | 0.0009 | -0.0244 | 0.0001 |
| **...** | ... | ... | ... | ... |
| **2024-03-01** | 0.0506 | -0.0016 | -0.0354 | 0.0042 |
| **2024-04-01** | 0.0283 | -0.0246 | 0.0416 | 0.0043 |
| **2024-05-01** | -0.0467 | -0.0234 | -0.0054 | 0.0047 |
| **2024-06-01** | 0.0434 | 0.0061 | -0.0137 | 0.0044 |
| **2024-07-01** | 0.0278 | -0.0302 | -0.0331 | 0.0041 |

174 rows × 4 columns

**Table 25** Merging Fama–French factors with the original data

```
merged_data = pd.merge(data, ff3, left_index = True, right_index = True, how = 'inner')
print('Missing values in the data: ', merged_data.isna().sum())
```

```
Missing values in the data:  AAPL
^GSPC                 0
AAPL_Returns          0
Market_Returns        0
RF_x                  0
AAPL_ExcessReturns    0
Mkt-RF                0
SMB                   0
HML                   0
RF_y                  0
dtype: int64
```

**Table 26** Visual comparison plots

```
stock = 'AAPL_ExcessReturns'
factors = ['Mkt-RF', 'SMB', 'HML']
plt.figure()
fig3, axs = plt.subplots(1, 3,figsize=(15, 4))
axs[0].plot(merged_data['Mkt-RF'].rolling(3).mean(),linewidth=2.5)
axs[0].plot(merged_data[stock])
axs[0].set_title('Stock compared to market returns')
axs[0].grid()
axs[1].plot(merged_data['SMB'].rolling(3).mean(),linewidth=2.5)
axs[1].plot(merged_data[stock])
axs[1].grid()
axs[1].set_title('Stock compared to small comp returns')
axs[2].plot(merged_data['HML'].rolling(3).mean(),linewidth=2.5)
axs[2].plot(merged_data[stock])
axs[2].grid()
axs[2].set_title('Stock compared to value stocks index')
plt.show()
```

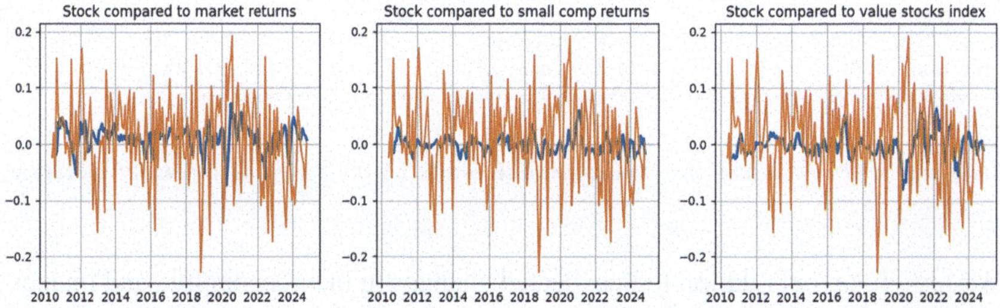


In all the cases, a rolling average of 3 months is used to smooth out the short-term fluctuations. Table 27 displays the three-factor model fitting using OLS regression.

A low adjusted $R^2$(0.003) suggests these factors do not explain much of the variation in AAPL's returns. The $F$-statistic tests the overall significance of the model. With a $p$-value of 0.317, it suggests that the model is not statistically significant in explaining AAPL_ExcessReturns. In this case, the Fama–French 3-factor model, does not provide a strong explanation of AAPL_ExcessReturns. This could be due to the unique characteristics of AAPL, or other factors not included in the model.

## 5 Arbitrage Pricing Theory (Multi-Factor Model)

Here we extend our knowledge from simple Linear Regression to employ multiple regression using Arbitrage Pricing Theory (APT) multi-factor model. In our hypothesis, we shall investigate the monthly returns on Crude-Oil stocks

**Table 27** Fama–French 3-factor model

```
X = sm.add_constant(merged_data[['Mkt-RF', 'SMB', 'HML']])
Y = merged_data['AAPL_ExcessReturns']
model = sm.OLS(Y, X).fit()
print(model.summary())
```

```
                            OLS Regression Results
==============================================================================
Dep. Variable:     AAPL_ExcessReturns   R-squared:                       0.020
Model:                            OLS   Adj. R-squared:                  0.003
Method:                 Least Squares   F-statistic:                     1.185
Date:                Fri, 02 Aug 2024   Prob (F-statistic):              0.317
Time:                        10:50:52   Log-Likelihood:                 196.91
No. Observations:                 174   AIC:                            -385.8
Df Residuals:                     170   BIC:                            -373.2
Df Model:                           3
Covariance Type:            nonrobust
==============================================================================
                 coef    std err          t      P>|t|      [0.025      0.975]
------------------------------------------------------------------------------
const          0.0107      0.006      1.729      0.086      -0.002       0.023
Mkt-RF        -0.1132      0.145     -0.782      0.435      -0.399       0.173
SMB            0.3252      0.252      1.291      0.199      -0.172       0.822
HML           -0.2500      0.183     -1.364      0.174      -0.612       0.112
==============================================================================
Omnibus:                        2.435   Durbin-Watson:                   1.719
Prob(Omnibus):                  0.296   Jarque-Bera (JB):                2.414
Skew:                          -0.235   Prob(JB):                        0.299
Kurtosis:                       2.664   Cond. No.                         43.2
==============================================================================

Notes:
[1] Standard Errors assume that the covariance matrix of the errors is correctly specified.
```

(Western-Texas) in relation to unexpected changes in macroeconomic and financial variables.

- $H_0$: The monthly returns on Crude-Oil stocks (Western-Texas) are not significantly explained by unexpected changes in the set of macroeconomic and financial variables.
- $H_1$ : The monthly returns on Crude-Oil stocks (Western-Texas) are significantly explained by unexpected changes in the set of macroeconomic and financial variables.

We will use macroeconomic variables such as Consumer Price Index (CPIAUCSL), Industrial Production Index (INDPRO), Treasury Bill Yields (3 months and 10 years (DGS3MO and DGS10), Unemployment Rate (UNRATE), and Total Consumer Credit Owned and Securitized (TOTALSL). All these variables are taken on a monthly frequency and the date range spanning from Jan 2010 till Dec 2023. Table 28 shows the code snippet to obtain CL $= F$ and SP 500 monthly data.

**Table 28** Crude oil and SP 500 series

```
stocks = ['CL=F']
market_index = '^GSPC'
data = yf.download(stocks + [market_index], start = '2010-01-01', end = '2024-01-01', interval = '1mo')['Adj
Close']
data.index = pd.to_datetime(data.index)
data.reset_index(inplace = True)
print(data)
```

| Ticker | Date | CL=F | ^GSPC |
|---|---|---|---|
| **0** | 2010-01-01 | 72.889999 | 1073.869995 |
| **1** | 2010-02-01 | 79.660004 | 1104.489990 |
| **2** | 2010-03-01 | 83.760002 | 1169.430054 |
| **3** | 2010-04-01 | 86.150002 | 1186.689941 |
| **4** | 2010-05-01 | 73.970001 | 1089.410034 |
| ... | ... | ... | ... |
| **163** | 2023-08-01 | 83.629997 | 4507.660156 |
| **164** | 2023-09-01 | 90.790001 | 4288.049805 |
| **165** | 2023-10-01 | NaN | 4193.799805 |
| **166** | 2023-11-01 | 75.959999 | 4567.799805 |
| **167** | 2023-12-01 | 71.650002 | 4769.830078 |

168 rows × 3 columns

If you notice, we are using WTI Futures series (CL $= F$). While spot prices provide a snapshot of the current market value, WTI futures prices are better suited for Arbitrage Pricing Theory (APT) analysis due to their direct link to arbitrage opportunities, sensitivity to macroeconomic factors, data availability, and liquidity.

Rest of the dataset obtained from **Federal Reserve Economic Data (FRED)**.[5] Table 29 displays the code snippet.

Now that we have ingested the dataset, we can start with the analysis followed by investigation. The first stage is to apply differencing process for each of the variables, since APT theorizes that the stock returns can be explained by reference to the unexpected changes in the macroeconomic variables rather than their levels.

The question then arises "How do we measure investors' expectations"?

[5] https://fred.stlouisfed.org/.

**Table 29** FRED macroeconomic data ingestion

```
start = dt.datetime(2010, 1, 1); end = dt.datetime(2024,1,1)
cpiaucsl = pdr.get_data_fred('CPIAUCSL', start = start, end = end)
cpiaucsl.reset_index(inplace=True)
dgs3mo = pdr.get_data_fred('DGS3MO', start = start, end = end)
dgs3mo = dgs3mo.resample('M').last() / 100
dgs3mo.reset_index(inplace = True)
DGS10 = pdr.get_data_fred('DGS10', start = start, end = end)
DGS10 = DGS10.resample('M').last() / 100
DGS10.reset_index(inplace = True)
gdp = pdr.get_data_fred('GDP', start = start, end = end)
gdp = gdp.resample('M').bfill().ffill()
gdp.reset_index(inplace = True)

unrate = pdr.get_data_fred('UNRATE', start = start, end = end)
unrate.reset_index(inplace=True)

indpro = pdr.get_data_fred('INDPRO', start = start, end = end)
indpro.reset_index(inplace=True)

totalsl = pdr.get_data_fred('TOTALSL', start = start, end = end)
totalsl.reset_index(inplace=True)

m2sl = pdr.get_data_fred('M2SL', start = start, end = end)
m2sl.reset_index(inplace=True)

unrate = pdr.get_data_fred('UNRATE', start = start, end = end)
unrate.reset_index(inplace = True)

vix = yf.download ('^VIX',   start='2010-01-01', end='2024-01-01', interval = '1mo')['Adj Close']
vix = vix.reset_index()
vix.rename(columns={'Adj Close': 'VIX'}, inplace = True)

data = pd.concat([data, cpiaucsl['CPIAUCSL'], dgs3mo['DGS3MO'], DGS10['DGS10'],\ gdp['GDP'],
unrate['UNRATE'], indpro['INDPRO'], totalsl['TOTALSL'], m2sl['M2SL'], \ vix['VIX']], axis = 1)
data = data.set_index('Date')
print(data.head())

data.to_csv('data.csv')
```

(continued)

**Table 29** (continued)

| Date | CL=F | ^GSPC | CPIAUCSL | DGS3MO | DGS10 | GDP \ |
|---|---|---|---|---|---|---|
| 2010-01-01 | 72.889999 | 1073.869995 | 217.488 | 0.0008 | 0.0363 | 14980.193 |
| 2010-02-01 | 79.660004 | 1104.489990 | 217.281 | 0.0013 | 0.0361 | 14980.193 |
| 2010-03-01 | 83.760002 | 1169.430054 | 217.353 | 0.0016 | 0.0384 | 14980.193 |
| 2010-04-01 | 86.150002 | 1186.689941 | 217.403 | 0.0016 | 0.0369 | 15141.607 |
| 2010-05-01 | 73.970001 | 1089.410034 | 217.290 | 0.0016 | 0.0331 | 15141.607 |

| Date | UNRATE | INDPRO | TOTALSL | M2SL | VIX |
|---|---|---|---|---|---|
| 2010-01-01 | 9.8 | 89.1897 | 2543.50802 | 8458.1 | 24.620001 |
| 2010-02-01 | 9.8 | 89.5046 | 2530.02428 | 8507.4 | 19.500000 |
| 2010-03-01 | 9.9 | 90.1356 | 2536.55195 | 8504.5 | 17.590000 |
| 2010-04-01 | 9.9 | 90.4607 | 2532.76479 | 8535.2 | 22.049999 |
| 2010-05-01 | 9.6 | 91.7014 | 2521.68794 | 8589.9 | 32.070000 |

While there are many ways to construct measures of expectations, the easiest is to assume that investors expect the next period's value to be equal to the current value, which is a naïve forecasting approach. This means they believe that no significant changes will occur, leading to the conclusion that any actual change in value from one period to the next is unexpected.

Table 30 displays some simple, yet powerful data transformations as explained below.

I. DGS3MO and DGS10 represent the 3-month and 10-year Treasury Bill rate; these are annualized rates. We converted these to monthly rate dividing by 12.
II. The difference between the yields is the spread of yields. This spread is a commonly used indicator in finance and economics for various purposes. Such as, a negative term spread (when the yield on the 3-month bill exceeds the yield on the 10-year note) is often considered a signal of an upcoming recession. This is known as an inverted yield curve. A positive and widening term spread is associated with economic expansion and growth expectations.
III. The period-to-period change in the yield spread considered here, which provides insights into the changes in market expectations such as how the market's expectations of future interest rates and economic conditions are evolving over time. Periods of high volatility in interest rates may result in larger changes in the yield spread. Sudden changes in the spread of yield can be indicative of shifts in economic sentiment or responses to new information.
IV. Excess returns help to evaluate whether taking on the risk of the asset is worthwhile compared to a no-risk alternative. $\text{CL}_{\text{ExcessReturns}} = \text{LogReturns of CL} = F - \text{Monthly Risk} - \text{Free Rate}$ represents the return of $\text{CL} = F$ above what could be earned from a risk-free investment (Treasury bills).
V. Likewise, the excess returns for the S&P 500 index are computed: $\text{SP}_{\text{ExcessReturns}} = \text{Log Returns of GSPC} - \text{Monthly Risk} - \text{Free Rate}$

**Table 30** Data transformation

```
data = data.dropna()
df = pd.DataFrame()
df['CL_ExcessReturns'] = np.log(data['CL = F']).diff() - data['DGS3MO']/12
df['SP_ExcessReturns'] = np.log(data['^GSPC']).diff() - data['DGS3MO']/12
df['indpro'] = data['INDPRO'] - data['INDPRO'].shift(1)
df['inflation'] = (data['CPIAUCSL'].diff() / data['CPIAUCSL'].shift(1)) * 100
df['ConsumerCredit'] = np.log(data['TOTALSL']) - np.log(data['TOTALSL'].shift(1))
df['termSpread'] = (data['DGS10'] - data['DGS3MO']) - (data['DGS10'] - data['DGS3MO']).shift(1)
df['yieldSpread'] = data['DGS10'] - data['DGS3MO']
df['m2sl'] = np.log(data['M2SL']) - np.log(data['M2SL']).shift(1)
df['vix'] = data['VIX']- data['VIX'].shift(1)
df['unrate'] = data['UNRATE'] - data['UNRATE'].shift(1)

df.dropna(inplace = True)
print(df.head())
```

```
            CL_ExcessReturns  SP_ExcessReturns  indpro  inflation  \
Date
2010-02-01          0.088708          0.028006  0.3149  -0.095178
2010-03-01          0.050055          0.056999  0.6310   0.033137
2010-04-01          0.028001          0.014518  0.3251   0.023004
2010-05-01         -0.152564         -0.085665  1.2407  -0.051977
2010-06-01          0.022043         -0.055538  0.2019  -0.041880

            ConsumerCredit  termSpread  yieldSpread  m2sl        vix
Date
2010-02-01       -13.48374     -0.0007       0.0348  49.3  -5.120001
2010-03-01         6.52767      0.0020       0.0368  -2.9  -1.910000
2010-04-01        -3.78716     -0.0015       0.0353  30.7   4.459999
2010-05-01       -11.07685     -0.0038       0.0315  54.7  10.020000
2010-06-01        -3.27153     -0.0036       0.0279  19.1   2.470001
```

VI. Inflation Rate $= \frac{(\mathrm{CPI})_t - (\mathrm{CPI})_{t-1}}{(\mathrm{CPI})_{t-1}} * 100.$

## 5.1 Multicollinearity

Multicollinearity exists when two or more of the predictors are correlated with one another. When multicollinearity exists, any of the following outcomes can be worsened:

- The estimated regression coefficient ($\beta$) of any one variable depends on which other predictors are included in the model.

**Table 31** Pearson correlation

```
df[['SP_ExcessReturns', 'inflation', 'termSpread', 'yieldSpread', 'indpro', 'ConsumerCredit']].corr(method =
'pearson')
```

| | SP_ExcessReturns | inflation | termSpread | yieldSpread | indpro | ConsumerCredit |
|---|---|---|---|---|---|---|
| **SP_ExcessReturns** | 1.000000 | 0.075480 | 0.163152 | 0.027303 | 0.084118 | 0.124863 |
| **inflation** | 0.075480 | 1.000000 | -0.049246 | -0.045384 | 0.365653 | 0.399467 |
| **termSpread** | 0.163152 | -0.049246 | 1.000000 | 0.215993 | -0.261985 | 0.000015 |
| **yieldSpread** | 0.027303 | -0.045384 | 0.215993 | 1.000000 | 0.070258 | 0.062563 |
| **indpro** | 0.084118 | 0.365653 | -0.261985 | 0.070258 | 1.000000 | 0.276254 |
| **ConsumerCredit** | 0.124863 | 0.399467 | 0.000015 | 0.062563 | 0.276254 | 1.000000 |

- The precision of the estimated regression coefficients decreases as more predictors are added to the model.
- The marginal contribution of any one predictor variable in reducing the error sum of squares depends on which other predictors are already in the model.
- Hypothesis tests for $\beta_k = 0$ may yield different conclusions depending on which predictors are in the model.

Table 31 employs Pearson's correlation to quantify and investigate the multicollinearity issue in the dataset.

The largest observed correlation is 0.39 (inflation and ConsumerCredit). However, it does not exceed the common statistical threshold (0.5), so we ignore the multicollinearity issues in this case and conclude that predictors are truly independent.

We perform the OLS regression, taking some of the variables from Table 30.

$$\text{formula} = \text{'CL\_ExcessReturns} \sim \text{SP\_ExcessReturns} + \text{inflation} + \text{indpro} \\ + \text{termSpread} + \text{yieldSpread} + \text{ConsumerCredit'}$$

Since we are familiar with OLS equations, here, we add multiple variables. The formula string will automatically add a constant term shown in Table 32.

- In the case of multivariate analysis, we are interested in Adjusted $R^2$ (approximate 0.42) which accounts for the number of predictors in the model. Adjusted $R^2$ adjusts for the number of predictors in the model, but more accurately, it penalizes the $R^2$ value based on the number of predictors. This adjustment helps prevent the misleading inflation of $R^2$ that can occur when adding more predictors, regardless of their relevance.
- $F$-statistics (17.16) and Prob ($F$-statistics) (1.52e−14) show the overall model is statistically significant.

**Table 32** OLS multi-factor model

```
formula = 'CL_ExcessReturns ~ SP_ExcessReturns + inflation + indpro + termSpread + yieldSpread'
model1 = sm.ols(formula, df).fit()
print(model1.summary())
```

```
                            OLS Regression Results
==============================================================================
Dep. Variable:       CL_ExcessReturns   R-squared:                       0.442
Model:                            OLS   Adj. R-squared:                  0.416
Method:                 Least Squares   F-statistic:                     17.16
Date:                Sat, 03 Aug 2024   Prob (F-statistic):           1.52e-14
Time:                        17:14:15   Log-Likelihood:                 122.65
No. Observations:                 137   AIC:                            -231.3
Df Residuals:                     130   BIC:                            -210.9
Df Model:                           6
Covariance Type:            nonrobust
======================================================================================
                       coef    std err          t      P>|t|      [0.025      0.975]
--------------------------------------------------------------------------------------
Intercept           -0.0309      0.018     -1.738      0.085      -0.066       0.004
SP_ExcessReturns     0.8795      0.205      4.283      0.000       0.473       1.286
inflation            0.0756      0.029      2.583      0.011       0.018       0.134
indpro               0.0354      0.006      6.036      0.000       0.024       0.047
termSpread           9.4639      3.632      2.606      0.010       2.278      16.649
yieldSpread          0.0143      0.840      0.017      0.986      -1.648       1.677
ConsumerCredit       0.6491      1.487      0.437      0.663      -2.293       3.591
==============================================================================
Omnibus:                       57.111   Durbin-Watson:                   2.288
Prob(Omnibus):                  0.000   Jarque-Bera (JB):              452.522
Skew:                           1.185   Prob(JB):                     5.45e-99
Kurtosis:                      11.583   Cond. No.                         717.
==============================================================================

Notes:
[1] Standard Errors assume that the covariance matrix of the errors is correctly specified.
```

- Some of the parameter estimates are not significantly different from zero, e.g., yieldSpread and ConsumerCredit.
- Omnibus test statistics (57.111) and *p*-value = 0.000. The significant *p*-value indicates non-normal residuals.
- Jarque–Bera test statistics 452.522 (*p*-value = 5.45e−99). The low *p*-value suggests significant deviations from normality.
- Skew 1.185 (positive skew) and Kurtosis 11.583 (leptokurtic, showing heavy tails).

This model offers moderate explanatory power for CL_ExcessReturns, and significant predictors include SP_ExcessReturns, inflation, indpro, and termSpread. However, the non-significance of yieldSpread and ConsumerCredit suggests these may be less relevant in this setup, potentially worth re-evaluation for model refinement.

We further employ the Variance Inflation Factor (VIF) to ensure that multicollinearity is not affecting the regression model (Table 33). This is another statistical quantification process which measures how much the variance of a

**Table 33** Variable inflation factor implementation

```
X = df[['SP_ExcessReturns', 'inflation', 'termSpread', 'yieldSpread', 'indpro', 'ConsumerCredit']]
vif = pd.DataFrame()
vif["Variable"] = X.columns
vif["VIF"] = [variance_inflation_factor(X.values, i) for i in range(X.shape[1])]
print(vif)
```

```
           Variable       VIF
0  SP_ExcessReturns  1.092803
1         inflation  1.771247
2        termSpread  1.112797
3       yieldSpread  1.446858
4            indpro  1.213607
5    ConsumerCredit  1.845463
```

regression coefficient is inflated due to multicollinearity among the predictors. A general guideline for interpreting VIF values is shown below.

- VIF = 1: No correlation between the predictor and other variables.
- 1 < VIF < 5: Moderate correlation, but not severe enough to warrant corrective measures.
- VIF > 5: High correlation that might be problematic.
- VIF > 10: High correlation, indicating serious multicollinearity problems.

Despite the non-significant VIF values, the high condition number (717 > 100) from Table 32 suggests there may be some underlying numerical issues that should be explored further.

- We test the null hypothesis that the parameters on these two variables are jointly zero using $F$-test. Below hypothesis meaning both coefficients are not significantly different from zero, implying they have no substantial effect on CL_ExcessReturns.

$$H_0 \rightarrow \beta_{\text{yieldSpread}} = \beta_{\text{ConsumerCredit}} = 0$$

- At least one of these coefficients is significantly different from zero, suggesting it may contribute meaningfully to the model.

$$H_1 \rightarrow \beta_{\text{yieldSpread}} \neq 0 \text{ and } \beta_{\text{ConsumerCredit}} \neq 0$$

By conducting an $F$-test on these variables, we assess if removing them would lead to a statistically unfit model. If the test shows they do not significantly affect the model, this could justify removing them, potentially simplifying the model without sacrificing explanatory power. Table 34 employs the hypothesis test.

**Table 34** Null hypothesis test

```
hypotheses = 'ConsumerCredit = yieldSpread = 0'
fTest = model1.f_test(hypotheses)
print(fTest)
```

```
<F test: F=0.09627854326549806, p=0.9082757025434491, df_denom=130, df_num=2>
```

The obtained $F$-test statistic (0.096), $p$-value 0.908, suggest we do not have sufficient evidence to reject $H_0$. This suggests that these variables do not significantly contribute to the explanation of CL_ExcessReturns in this model. Simplifying the model by removing non-significant predictors can improve interpretability without affecting the model's predictive power.

## 5.2 Diagnostic Tests

Let us start performing a detailed diagnostic test. First is the visual inspection, wherein we look at the residuals to understand the non-normality and explore. If the residuals of the regression have systematically changing variability, it is a sign of heteroscedasticity.

Table 35 shows the code snippet to get the residuals pattern from the model. The plot obtained from this code showing the patterns in the residuals over time.

Since there is not much of a pattern here, we must use a rigorous statistical test to measure our comprehension. We also plot a histogram of the residuals. This histogram provides a visual assessment of the distribution of residuals. Table 36 provides the code snippet to plot a histogram from the residuals.

Visual inspection reveals the residuals are normally distributed. Normally distributed residuals allow us to make valid statistical inferences about the coefficients. It also ensures that the t-tests and F-tests for significance are valid. However, we see a large positive outlier, which might lead to a considerable positive skewness.

Table 37 displays the plots with different bin sizes to obtain a more differentiated histogram for better visualization.

### 5.2.1 Normality Test

Let us now move on to statistical tests to quantify and validate our above assumption. The commonly applied test for normality is the Shapiro–Wilk and Jarque–Bera test. Here we test whether the normality assumption is satisfied for the residuals of Apple stock on the unexpected changes in the financial and economic factors (Table 38).

- Shapiro–Wilk test: The null hypothesis is, the residuals are normally distributed. The $p$-value $\approx 0$ indicates we reject the null hypothesis and accept alternate hypothesis that the residuals are not normally distributed.

**Table 35** Residuals pattern

```
plt.plot(model1.resid)
plt.xlabel('Months')
plt.ylabel('Residuals')
plt.grid(True)
plt.show()
```

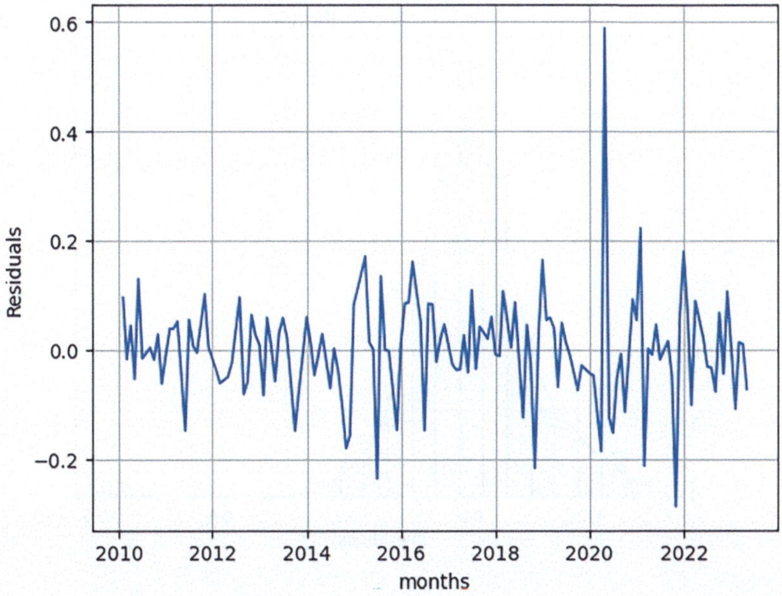


- Jarque–Bera test: This evaluates whether the residuals have skewness and kurtosis matching a normal distribution. Here too, the *p*-value is extremely small, which also suggests we reject the null hypothesis. This reinforces the finding that the residuals are not normally distributed, as the test detects significant deviations from normality in terms of skewness and kurtosis.

In this case, the workable solutions are to use robust standard errors to account for non-normal residuals or use non-parametric methods or Generalized Least Squares (GLS) if normality is a critical concern for the analysis.

### 5.2.2 Homoscedasticity

To assess if the residuals have constant variance, we further perform Breusch-Pagan (Breusch & Pagan, 1979) and White tests (White, 1980). Table 39 displays the code snippet followed by residuals vs. fitted scatter plot. Both the tests use the Lagrange multiplier framework to assess the presence of heteroscedasticity.

**Table 36** Distribution of residuals

```
sns.histplot(model1.resid, kde = True)
plt.xlabel('Residuals')
plt.ylabel('Density')
plt.title('Residuals Distribution')
plt.show()
```

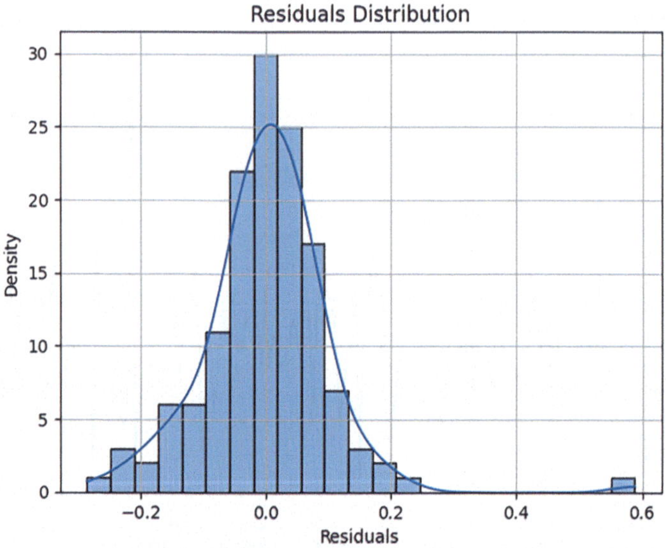


- The Breusch-Pagan test checks for heteroscedasticity by testing whether the variance of residuals is related to the independent variables. A $p$-value of $0.422 > 0.05$ shows we do not reject the null hypothesis of homoscedasticity. This suggests that there is no considerable evidence of heteroscedasticity in the residuals.
- The White test also tests for heteroscedasticity but is more general as it does not assume any specific form of heteroscedasticity. Given the small $p$-values for both the Lagrange multiplier and the $F$-test, there is statistical evidence to reject the null hypothesis of homoscedasticity. This suggests that the model residuals show heteroscedasticity.

The discrepancy between the tests suggests that while the Breusch-Pagan test does not find significant heteroscedasticity, the White test does. The Breusch-Pagan test is designed to detect linear forms of heteroscedasticity while the White test can detect more complex forms of heteroscedasticity, including those that are not linearly related to the explanatory variables. Moreover, the White test can be less effective in smaller sample sizes as the limited number of observations is spread across a larger number of estimated parameters, reducing the power of the test.

**Table 37** Histogram with different bins

```
fig, axes = plt.subplots(nrows = 1, ncols = 2, figsize = (14, 6))
sns.histplot(model1.resid, kde = True, bins = 50, ax = axes[0])
axes[0].set_xlabel('Residuals')
axes[0].set_ylabel('Density')
axes[0].set_title('Residuals Distribution (Increased Bins)')
axes[0].grid()

sns.histplot(model1.resid, kde=True, binwidth=0.1, ax=axes[1])
axes[1].set_xlabel('Residuals')
axes[1].set_ylabel('Density')
axes[1].set_title('Residuals Distribution (Smaller Bin Width)')
axes[1].grid()

plt.tight_layout()
plt.show()
```

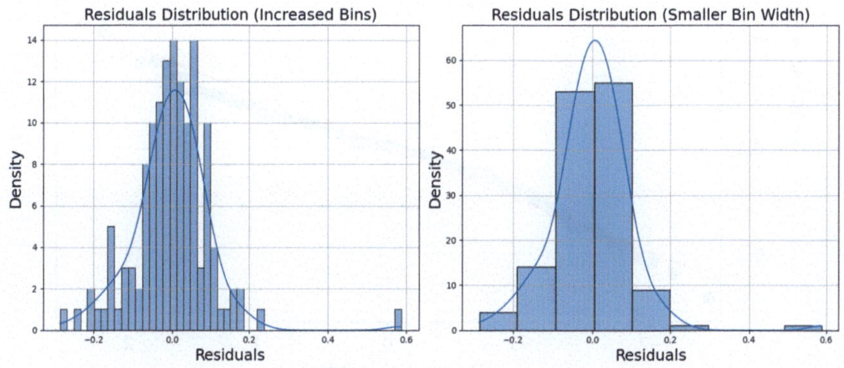


To address heteroscedasticity, we can consider heteroscedasticity-robust standard errors to correct for the bias in the standard errors. The different types of Heteroscedasticity-Consistent (HC) standard errors available to adjust for heteroscedasticity in regression models. Each type has its own method for estimating robust standard errors, and the choice among them often depends on the specifics of the data and the model. Table 40 provides a breakdown of when to use each type.

Table 41 shows the implementation of HC3. This was proposed by MacKinnon and White (1985). It helps to account for potential heteroscedasticity, which adjusts the standard errors of the coefficients and so affects the $t$-statistics and $p$-values.

While the coefficient estimates remain unchanged, the significance levels ($p$-values) of some variables shift when heteroscedasticity-robust standard errors are used. This reflects the importance of accounting for heteroscedasticity to avoid overstated significance and obtain more reliable statistical inferences.

**Table 38** Shapiro–Wilk and Jarque–Bera tests

```
shapiro_test = shapiro(model1.resid)
print("Shapiro-Wilk Test:", shapiro_test)
jarque_bera_test = jarque_bera(model1.resid)
print("Jarque-Bera Test:", jarque_bera_test)

sm.qqplot(model1.resid, line='s')
plt.grid()
```

```
Shapiro-Wilk Test: ShapiroResult(statistic=0.8999113415017607, pvalue=4.0649488980125665e-08)
Jarque-Bera Test: SignificanceResult(statistic=452.52201748092216, pvalue=5.446185557627817e-99)
```

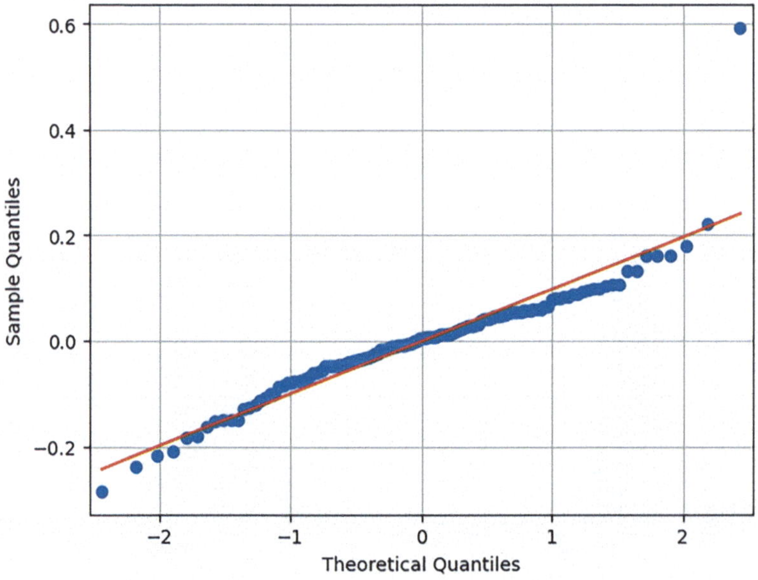


### 5.2.3 Autocorrelation

Whereas the Durbin-Watson Test (Durbin & Watson, 1971) is restricted to detecting first-order autoregression, the Breusch-Godfrey (BG) Test can detect autocorrelation up to any predesignated order *p*. The null hypothesis of BG test is that there is no serial correlation of any order up to *p*. Table 42 displays the DW and BG test procedures. Here we go back to our model1.

The DW test suggests that while first-order autocorrelation might not be an issue, there are indications of autocorrelation at higher orders. The presence of higher-order autocorrelation detected by the BG test ($p < 0.05$) implies the model may benefit from including lagged values of the dependent variable or using other techniques to address autocorrelation. The results of the BG test suggest that there

**Table 39** Homoscedasticity tests

```
name = ['Lagrange multiplier statistic', 'p-value', 'f-value', 'f p-value']

bp_test = het_breuschpagan(model1.resid, model.model.exog)
print("Breusch-Pagan Test:", lzip(name, bp_test))

white_test = het_white(model1.resid, model.model.exog)
print("White Test:", lzip(name, white_test))

plt.scatter(model1.fittedvalues, model.resid)
plt.xlabel('Fitted values')
plt.ylabel('Residuals')
plt.title('Residuals vs Fitted')
plt.grid()
plt.show()
```

- Breusch-Pagan Test: [('Lagrange multiplier statistic', 6.006635896741766), ('p-value', 0.4224471331985067), ('f-value', 0.9935142795489218), ('f p-value', 0.4325138508289139)]
- White Test: [('Lagrange multiplier statistic', 52.288921758187826), ('p-value', 0.0024498750784851782), ('f-value', 2.4919091829047675), ('f p-value', 0.0004724816581086481 6)]

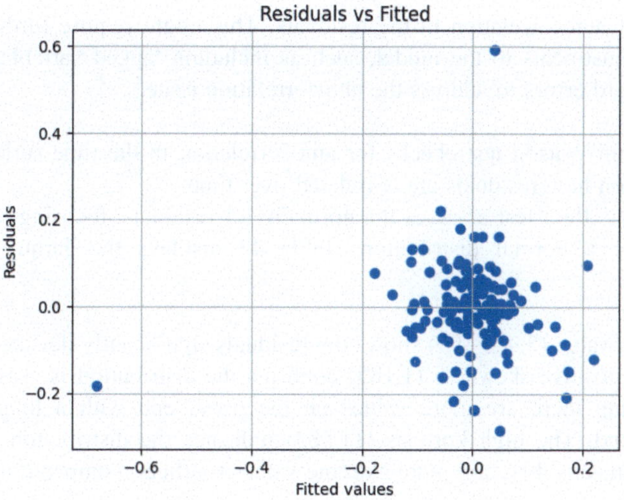

**Table 40** Heteroscedasticity-Consistent (HC) variations and applications

| HC variations | Application |
|---|---|
| HC0 | It is the simplest form of heteroscedasticity-consistent standard error estimation. It provides a consistent estimate of the covariance matrix of the regression coefficients under heteroscedasticity but does not include any adjustments for sample size or leverage. It can be used when we want a basic correction for heteroscedasticity without any additional adjustments |
| HC1 | It adjusts HC0 standard errors by a factor related to the sample size. It is a straightforward correction, accounting for the fact that the variance of the residuals is estimated with a finite sample size. This adjustment is like using the finite-sample correction in OLS. It can be used when we want a version of robust standard errors that adjusts for sample size |
| HC2 | It modifies HC0 by scaling the residuals to account for leverage points. This version provides more robust standard errors by reducing the impact of high-leverage points on the estimation of the variance–covariance matrix. It is useful when we have influential data points that might unduly affect the regression results |
| HC3 | It provides a stronger adjustment for heteroscedasticity by applying a more substantial down-weighting of observations with high leverage. It is particularly effective when dealing with influential observations or small sample sizes. HC3 is recommended for its robustness in various scenarios, especially when you suspect that heteroscedasticity and leverage points might be an issue |

is significant autocorrelation in the residuals. This might require further investigation or adjustments to the model, such as including lagged variables or using robust standard errors to address the autocorrelation issue.

- The Durbin-Watson test checks for autocorrelation in the time series models, focusing on how residuals are correlated over time.
- The Jarque–Bera test assesses the normality of residuals, focusing on whether they have a normal distribution. Table 43 displays the Jarque–Bera test procedure.

A small *p*-value (5.45e−99) shows the residuals significantly deviate from normality. The positive skewness (1.185) confirms the distribution is skewed to the right, meaning there are more values on the lower end with a longer tail on the higher end. The high kurtosis (11.583) indicates the distribution has heavy tails, which means there are more extreme values (outliers) compared to a normal distribution.

At this stage, we can conclude that model1 explains a moderate portion of the variance in Crude-Oil returns and is statistically significant overall. SP_ExcessReturns, Inflation, Indpro, and TermSpread are significant predictors. YieldSpread and ConsumerCredit are not significant. There is evidence of non-normality, which may affect the validity of the regression results. The presence of autocorrelation and heteroscedasticity are reported in the above diagnostic tests.

**Table 41** Heteroscedasticity Consistent (HC3) model

```
formula = 'CL_ExcessReturns ~ SP_ExcessReturns + inflation + indpro + termSpread + yieldSpread +
ConsumerCredit'
model2 = sm.ols(formula, df).fit(cov_type = 'HC3')
print(model2.summary())
```

(continued)

**Table 41** (continued)

```
                           OLS Regression Results
==============================================================================
Dep. Variable:        CL_ExcessReturns   R-squared:                       0.442
Model:                             OLS   Adj. R-squared:                  0.416
Method:                  Least Squares   F-statistic:                     10.63
Date:                 Sat, 03 Aug 2024   Prob (F-statistic):           1.36e-09
Time:                         13:44:57   Log-Likelihood:                 122.65
No. Observations:                  137   AIC:                            -231.3
Df Residuals:                      130   BIC:                            -210.9
Df Model:                            6
Covariance Type:                   HC3
====================================================================================
                       coef    std err          z      P>|z|      [0.025      0.975]
------------------------------------------------------------------------------------
Intercept           -0.0309      0.029     -1.077      0.282      -0.087       0.025
SP_ExcessReturns     0.8795      0.195      4.519      0.000       0.498       1.261
inflation            0.0756      0.033      2.302      0.021       0.011       0.140
indpro               0.0354      0.032      1.110      0.267      -0.027       0.098
termSpread           9.4639      3.074      3.079      0.002       3.440      15.488
yieldSpread          0.0143      0.802      0.018      0.986      -1.557       1.585
ConsumerCredit       0.6491      2.185      0.297      0.766      -3.633       4.931
==============================================================================
Omnibus:                       57.111   Durbin-Watson:                   2.288
Prob(Omnibus):                  0.000   Jarque-Bera (JB):              452.522
Skew:                           1.185   Prob(JB):                     5.45e-99
Kurtosis:                      11.583   Cond. No.                         717.
==============================================================================

Notes:
[1] Standard Errors are heteroscedasticity robust (HC3)
```

**Table 42** Autocorrelation test

```
durbin_watson_test = durbin_watson(model1.resid)
print("Durbin-Watson Test:", durbin_watson_test)


bg_test = diag.acorr_breusch_godfrey(model1, nlags=10)
print('Breusch-Godfrey Test:')
print('Lagrange Multiplier statistic:', bg_test[0])
print('p-value:', bg_test[1])
print('F-statistic:', bg_test[2])
print('F-test p-value:', bg_test[3])
```

```
Durbin-Watson Test: 2.288056955421003
Breusch-Godfrey Test:
Lagrange Multiplier statistic: 18.032212410659604
p-value: 0.006152196931040702
F-statistic: 3.1324926747399964
F-test p-value: 0.00681341464818838
```

**Table 43** Jarque–Bera normality test

```
name = ['Jarque-Bera', 'Chi^2 two-tail prob.', 'Skew', 'Kurtosis']
test = sm.jarque_bera(model1.resid)
lzip(name, test)
```

```
[('Jarque-Bera', 452.52201748092216),
 ('Chi^2 two-tail prob.', 5.446185557627817e-99),
 ('Skew', 1.1846364921044215),
 ('Kurtosis', 11.582568123583332)]
```

### 5.2.4 Heteroscedasticity and Autocorrelation Consistent (HAC) Standard Errors

If diagnostic tests or plots suggest residuals are autocorrelated (e.g., the Durbin-Watson test shows significant autocorrelation), HAC standard errors provide robust estimates of standard errors that are valid even in the presence of changing variance. When standard errors are adjusted for both heteroscedasticity and autocorrelation, the inference drawn from the model (e.g., confidence intervals, *p*-values) is more reliable.

There might be different economic motivations for choosing the maximum lag length. Table 44 shows the implementation with a maximum lag length of six, which means the potential autocorrelation in the data does not go beyond six months.

We must note that, the HAC adjustment addresses the presence of heteroscedasticity and autocorrelation issues by providing robust standard errors but does not directly correct the underlying problems in the residuals.

**Table 44** Newly west procedure

```
model3 = sm.ols(formula, data = df).fit(cov_type = 'HAC', cov_kwds = {'maxlags': 6})

print(model3.summary())
```

```
                            OLS Regression Results
==============================================================================
Dep. Variable:         CL_ExcessReturns   R-squared:                       0.442
Model:                              OLS   Adj. R-squared:                  0.416
Method:                   Least Squares   F-statistic:                     37.31
Date:                  Sat, 03 Aug 2024   Prob (F-statistic):           4.86e-26
Time:                          13:51:22   Log-Likelihood:                 122.65
No. Observations:                   137   AIC:                            -231.3
Df Residuals:                       130   BIC:                            -210.9
Df Model:                             6
Covariance Type:                    HAC
=====================================================================================
                        coef    std err          z      P>|z|      [0.025      0.975]
-------------------------------------------------------------------------------------
Intercept            -0.0309      0.012     -2.610      0.009      -0.054      -0.008
SP_ExcessReturns      0.8795      0.171      5.154      0.000       0.545       1.214
inflation             0.0756      0.027      2.827      0.005       0.023       0.128
indpro                0.0354      0.010      3.486      0.000       0.015       0.055
termSpread            9.4639      2.043      4.633      0.000       5.461      13.467
yieldSpread           0.0143      0.484      0.030      0.976      -0.933       0.962
ConsumerCredit        0.6491      1.556      0.417      0.677      -2.401       3.699
==============================================================================
Omnibus:                       57.111   Durbin-Watson:                   2.288
Prob(Omnibus):                  0.000   Jarque-Bera (JB):              452.522
Skew:                           1.185   Prob(JB):                     5.45e-99
Kurtosis:                      11.583   Cond. No.                         717.
==============================================================================

Notes:
[1] Standard Errors are heteroscedasticity and autocorrelation robust (HAC) using 6 lags and without small sample correction
```

### 5.2.5 Cook's Distance

Cook's Distance (Cook, 1979) measures the influence of each data point on the regression model. The large influential datasets may be outliers, and datasets with a sizeable number of highly influential points may not be right for Linear Regression without further processing, such as imputation or outlier elimination. Table 45 displays the implementation of Cook's distance.

The plots above display Cook's Distance plot and Influence plot. A general rule of thumb is that observations with Cook's Distance greater than $4/n$ ($n$ is the number of observations) or greater than 1 might be considered influential. Influential points are not necessarily bad data points but could indicate further investigation to see if they reflect meaningful variation or if they are errors, outliers, or other issues.

In the influence plot, there is one large bubble (high Cook's distance) that shows a highly influential observation with both high leverage and high studentized residuals. The data point around 2020–04-01 is an influential observation with high leverage and high studentized residuals. By addressing the influential observations, we can improve the reliability and robustness of our analysis. Table 46 displays how to identify the influential points.

### 5.2.6 We Already Know from Residual Plot

The non-normality in the residuals can be attributed to a few outliers in the sample, as shown in the normality test. Like that, such non-normality can be found by charting the residuals and actual values of the regression as displayed in Table 47.

**Table 45** Cook's distance and leverage plot

```
influence = model1.get_influence()
cooks_d, _ = influence.cooks_distance
plt.figure(figsize = (15, 5))

plt.subplot(1, 2, 1)
plt.stem(np.arange(len(cooks_d)), cooks_d, markerfmt = ",")
plt.xlabel('Observation Index')
plt.ylabel("Cook's Distance")
plt.grid()
plt.title("Cook's Distance Plot")
plt.subplot(1, 2, 2)
sm.graphics.influence_plot(model1, ax = plt.gca())
plt.grid()
plt.tight_layout()

plt.show()
```

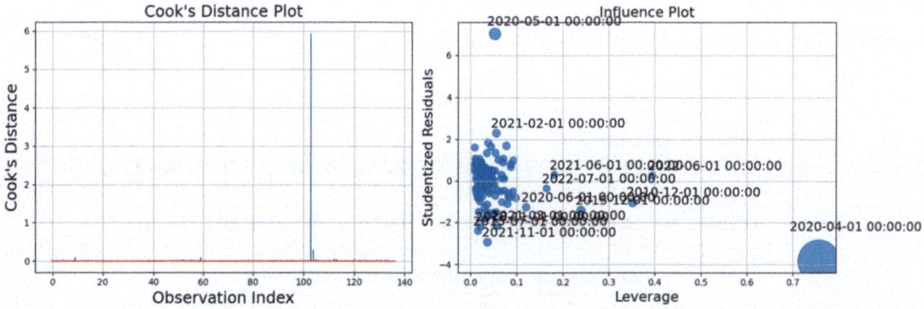


The above plot shows the residuals and the linear prediction over time. The residuals are the difference between the observed values and the values predicted by the model. We already know from Chapter 1 that ideally residuals should be randomly scattered around the horizontal axis (zero line) without any discernible pattern.

From the graph, several positive and negative outliers can be seen, but the largest occurred in 2020 (during the pandemic period). These correspond to months where the actual return was much smaller than the model's prediction. The residuals become more volatile from 2000 to 2022, suggesting the model's predictions are less accurate during this period. This change could be due to several factors, such as structural breaks, changes in the underlying data generation process, or external shocks (e.g., pandemic period). We could experiment by adding nonlinearity in the model by including polynomial terms to capture potential nonlinear relationships. Table 48 displays the polynomial implementation.

**Table 46** High influential point identification

```
influence = model1.get_influence()
cooks_d, _ = influence.cooks_distance
high_influence_points = np.where(cooks_d > 4 / len(cooks_d))[0]
dates_to_drop = df.iloc[high_influence_points].index

print("High Influence Points Dates:")
print(dates_to_drop)

plt.figure(figsize = (10, 5))
plt.plot(df.index, df['CL_ExcessReturns'], label = 'CL Excess Returns')
plt.scatter(dates_to_drop, df.loc[dates_to_drop, 'CL_ExcessReturns'], color = 'red', label='High Influence
Points')
plt.axvspan(pd.Timestamp('2020-03-01'), pd.Timestamp('2021-03-01'), color = 'blue', alpha = 0.2, label =
'Pandemic Period')
plt.xlabel('Date')
plt.ylabel('CL Excess Returns')
plt.grid()
plt.legend()
plt.title('CL Excess Returns with High Influence Points')
plt.show()
```

```
High Influence Points Dates:
DatetimeIndex(['2020-04-01', '2020-05-01', '2020-06-01', '2021-02-01',
               '2021-03-01', '2021-11-01'],
              dtype='datetime64[ns]', name='Date', freq=None)
```

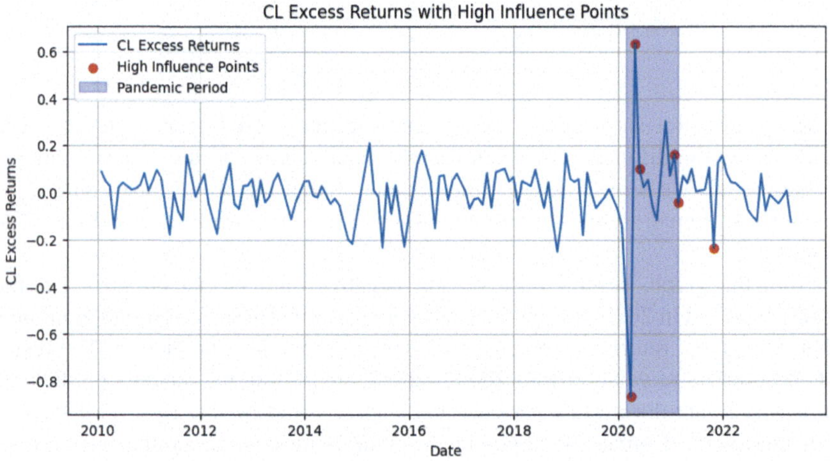

**Table 47** Residual plot

```
y_fitted = model1.fittedvalues
residuals = model1.resid


plt.plot(residuals, label='resid')
plt.plot(y_fitted, label = 'linear prediction')
plt.xlabel('Date')
plt.ylabel('Residuals')
plt.grid(True)
plt.legend()
plt.show()
```

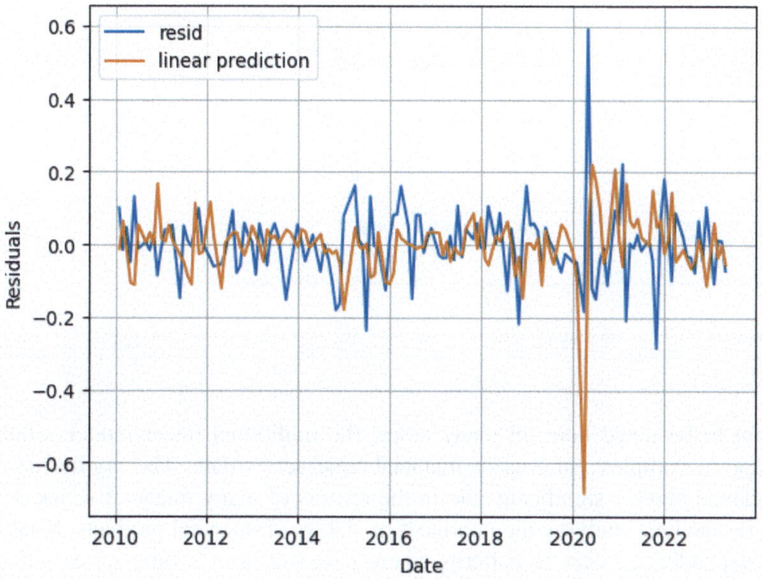


We can also experiment by including interaction terms to account for interactions between predictors. Table 49 shows the sample code.

Here we see the SP_ExcessReturns_inflation is −0.1629 ($p$-value: 0.826), SP_ExcessReturns_indpro is 0.5274 ($p$-value: 0.112), SP_ExcessReturns_termSpread is 16.7071 ($p$-value: 0.793), inflation_indpro is −0.0629 ($p$-value: 0.003), inflation_termSpread is 0.3785 ($p$-value: 0.974), and indpro_termSpread is −5.6151 ($p$-value: 0.161). The interaction terms show varying degrees of significance. inflation_indpro is significant, indicating a meaningful interaction effect.

We can also experiment by dropping high influential points as displayed in Table 50.

**Table 48** OLS with polynomial terms

```
formula = 'CL_ExcessReturns ~ SP_ExcessReturns + np.power(SP_ExcessReturns, 2) + inflation + indpro +
termSpread + yieldSpread + ConsumerCredit'
model4 = sm.formula.ols(formula, data = df).fit()
print(model4.summary())
```

```
                            OLS Regression Results
==============================================================================
Dep. Variable:       CL_ExcessReturns   R-squared:                       0.445
Model:                            OLS   Adj. R-squared:                  0.415
Method:                 Least Squares   F-statistic:                     14.76
Date:                Sat, 03 Aug 2024   Prob (F-statistic):           4.93e-14
Time:                        13:58:36   Log-Likelihood:                 122.98
No. Observations:                 137   AIC:                            -230.0
Df Residuals:                     129   BIC:                            -206.6
Df Model:                           7
Covariance Type:            nonrobust
=================================================================================================
                                    coef    std err          t      P>|t|      [0.025      0.975]
-------------------------------------------------------------------------------------------------
Intercept                        -0.0359      0.019     -1.900      0.060      -0.073       0.001
SP_ExcessReturns                  0.8734      0.206      4.244      0.000       0.466       1.281
np.power(SP_ExcessReturns, 2)     2.5241      3.187      0.792      0.430      -3.782       8.830
inflation                         0.0731      0.030      2.477      0.015       0.015       0.131
indpro                            0.0352      0.006      5.998      0.000       0.024       0.047
termSpread                        9.7090      3.650      2.660      0.009       2.487      16.931
yieldSpread                       0.0673      0.844      0.080      0.937      -1.603       1.737
ConsumerCredit                    0.6513      1.489      0.437      0.663      -2.295       3.598
==============================================================================
Omnibus:                       57.905   Durbin-Watson:                   2.274
Prob(Omnibus):                  0.000   Jarque-Bera (JB):              457.500
Skew:                           1.209   Prob(JB):                    4.52e-100
Kurtosis:                      11.620   Cond. No.                         727.
==============================================================================

Notes:
[1] Standard Errors assume that the covariance matrix of the errors is correctly specified.
```

Point to be noted here, in many cases, the traditional linear models often do not capture complex patterns in financial time series data. The nonlinear serial dependence plays a significant role in the returns of many financial series, which led to researchers studying the nonlinear modeling of financial products. Nonlinear serial dependence refers to patterns where past values of a time series influence future values in a nonlinear manner. This can include phenomena like volatility clustering, where periods of high volatility are followed by more high volatility, and vice versa. Nonlinear models can potentially offer better pricing of financial securities by capturing these intricate patterns and dependencies. For example, models like GARCH (Generalized Autoregressive Conditional Heteroscedasticity) account for changing volatility over time. The rise of machine learning and artificial intelligence has helped the development of advanced nonlinear models that can learn from complex patterns in data. Techniques like neural networks, support vector machines, and ensemble methods are increasingly used to model financial markets. Moreover, nonlinear Econometric models such as Smooth Transition Auto Regressive (STAR) models and Threshold Auto Regressive (TAR) models are used to capture regime changes and nonlinear relationships in financial data. However, nonlinearity is beyond the scope of this book. I shall address nonlinearity in financial modeling in a separate book soon.

**Table 49** OLS regression analysis with interaction terms

```
df['SP_ExcessReturns_inflation'] = df['SP_ExcessReturns'] * df['inflation']
df['SP_ExcessReturns_indpro'] = df['SP_ExcessReturns'] * df['indpro']
df['SP_ExcessReturns_termSpread'] = df['SP_ExcessReturns'] * df['termSpread']

df['inflation_indpro'] = df['inflation'] * df['indpro']
df['inflation_termSpread'] = df['inflation'] * df['termSpread']

df['indpro_termSpread'] = df['indpro'] * df['termSpread']

formula = (
  'CL_ExcessReturns ~ SP_ExcessReturns + inflation + indpro + termSpread + yieldSpread +
ConsumerCredit + '
  'SP_ExcessReturns_inflation + SP_ExcessReturns_indpro + SP_ExcessReturns_termSpread + '
  'inflation_indpro + inflation_termSpread + '
  'indpro_termSpread')
model5 = sm.formula.ols(formula, data=df).fit()
print(model5.summary())
```

```
                            OLS Regression Results
==============================================================================
Dep. Variable:       CL_ExcessReturns   R-squared:                       0.524
Model:                            OLS   Adj. R-squared:                  0.478
Method:                 Least Squares   F-statistic:                     11.39
Date:                Sat, 03 Aug 2024   Prob (F-statistic):           4.05e-15
Time:                        14:02:01   Log-Likelihood:                 133.58
No. Observations:                 137   AIC:                            -241.2
Df Residuals:                     124   BIC:                            -203.2
Df Model:                          12
Covariance Type:            nonrobust
===============================================================================================
                                  coef    std err          t      P>|t|      [0.025      0.975]
-----------------------------------------------------------------------------------------------
Intercept                      -0.0175      0.019     -0.944      0.347      -0.054       0.019
SP_ExcessReturns                0.8822      0.295      2.991      0.003       0.298       1.466
inflation                       0.0686      0.036      1.905      0.059      -0.003       0.140
indpro                          0.0191      0.012      1.529      0.129      -0.006       0.044
termSpread                     10.1299      5.080      1.994      0.048       0.075      20.185
yieldSpread                    -0.1072      0.819     -0.131      0.896      -1.729       1.514
ConsumerCredit                 -0.0480      1.434     -0.033      0.973      -2.886       2.790
SP_ExcessReturns_inflation     -0.1629      0.739     -0.220      0.826      -1.625       1.300
SP_ExcessReturns_indpro         0.5274      0.329      1.602      0.112      -0.124       1.179
SP_ExcessReturns_termSpread    16.7071     63.560      0.263      0.793    -109.095     142.509
inflation_indpro               -0.0629      0.020     -3.076      0.003      -0.103      -0.022
inflation_termSpread            0.3785     11.410      0.033      0.974     -22.206      22.963
indpro_termSpread              -5.6151      3.986     -1.409      0.161     -13.504       2.273
==============================================================================
Omnibus:                       57.869   Durbin-Watson:                   1.889
Prob(Omnibus):                  0.000   Jarque-Bera (JB):              498.531
Skew:                           1.173   Prob(JB):                    5.56e-109
Kurtosis:                      12.046   Cond. No.                     1.79e+04
==============================================================================

Notes:
[1] Standard Errors assume that the covariance matrix of the errors is correctly specified.
[2] The condition number is large, 1.79e+04. This might indicate that there are
strong multicollinearity or other numerical problems.
```

**Table 50** Model refit after removing high influential points

```
influence = model1.get_influence()
cooks_d, _ = influence.cooks_distance
high_influence_points = np.where(cooks_d > 4 / len(cooks_d))[0]
dates_to_drop = df.iloc[high_influence_points].index
df_cleaned = df.drop(index=dates_to_drop)
formula = 'CL_ExcessReturns ~ SP_ExcessReturns + inflation + indpro + termSpread + yieldSpread +
ConsumerCredit'

cleaned_model = sm.ols(formula, df_cleaned).fit()
print(cleaned_model.summary())
```

```
                            OLS Regression Results
==============================================================================
Dep. Variable:       CL_ExcessReturns   R-squared:                       0.384
Model:                            OLS   Adj. R-squared:                  0.353
Method:                 Least Squares   F-statistic:                     12.57
Date:                Sat, 03 Aug 2024   Prob (F-statistic):           5.54e-11
Time:                        14:03:00   Log-Likelihood:                 156.69
No. Observations:                 128   AIC:                            -299.4
Df Residuals:                     121   BIC:                            -279.4
Df Model:                           6
Covariance Type:            nonrobust
====================================================================================
                       coef    std err          t      P>|t|      [0.025      0.975]
------------------------------------------------------------------------------------
Intercept           -0.0272      0.014     -1.880      0.063      -0.056       0.001
SP_ExcessReturns     0.8096      0.150      5.410      0.000       0.513       1.106
inflation            0.1045      0.023      4.612      0.000       0.060       0.149
indpro              -0.0020      0.011     -0.173      0.863      -0.025       0.021
termSpread           8.7842      2.755      3.188      0.002       3.329      14.239
yieldSpread          0.5866      0.620      0.947      0.346      -0.640       1.813
ConsumerCredit      -1.6370      1.742     -0.940      0.349      -5.085       1.811
==============================================================================
Omnibus:                        4.611   Durbin-Watson:                   2.052
Prob(Omnibus):                  0.100   Jarque-Bera (JB):                4.104
Skew:                          -0.355   Prob(JB):                        0.128
Kurtosis:                       3.516   Cond. No.                         454.
==============================================================================

Notes:
[1] Standard Errors assume that the covariance matrix of the errors is correctly specified.
```

### 5.2.7 Dummy Variable Construction

Now we go back to the histogram of the residual plot; we see a large positive outlier (6.0). These data point may be outlier or other characteristics (such as pandemic during 2021) may have distorted the predictive power of the model. To show the exact dates, we examine a table of smallest and largest residuals as shown in Table 51 and incorporate those values as dummy variables in the regression model.

The two extreme residuals were during Nov 2021 (–0.28) and May 2020 (0.59). To remove these outliers, we construct two separate dummy variables and add those in our model as shown in Table 52.

**Table 51** Code snippet for dummy variable

```
y_fitted = model1.fittedvalues
residuals = model1.resid
print(residuals.nsmallest(1))
print(residuals.nlargest(1))
```

```
Date
2021-11-01   -0.284146
dtype: float64
Date
2020-05-01    0.593049
dtype: float64
```

**Table 52** Dummy variable creation

```
df['nov2021'] = np.where(df.index == '2021-11-01', 1, 0)
df['may2020'] = np.where(df.index == '2020-05-01', 1, 0)
formula = 'CL_ExcessReturns ~ SP_ExcessReturns + inflation + indpro + termSpread + yieldSpread + ConsumerCredit + termSpread + nov2021 + may2020'
model6 = sm.ols(formula, df).fit()
print(model6.summary())
```

```
                            OLS Regression Results
==============================================================================
Dep. Variable:       CL_ExcessReturns   R-squared:                       0.633
Model:                            OLS   Adj. R-squared:                  0.610
Method:                 Least Squares   F-statistic:                     27.55
Date:                Sat, 03 Aug 2024   Prob (F-statistic):           1.83e-24
Time:                        14:04:30   Log-Likelihood:                 151.28
No. Observations:                 137   AIC:                            -284.6
Df Residuals:                     128   BIC:                            -258.3
Df Model:                           8
Covariance Type:            nonrobust
====================================================================================
                       coef    std err          t      P>|t|      [0.025      0.975]
------------------------------------------------------------------------------------
Intercept           -0.0507      0.015     -3.424      0.001      -0.080      -0.021
SP_ExcessReturns     0.7636      0.169      4.531      0.000       0.430       1.097
inflation            0.1053      0.024      4.319      0.000       0.057       0.153
indpro               0.0306      0.005      6.344      0.000       0.021       0.040
termSpread           8.4652      2.973      2.848      0.005       2.584      14.347
yieldSpread          0.5119      0.690      0.742      0.460      -0.854       1.877
ConsumerCredit       1.4428      1.227      1.176      0.242      -0.984       3.870
nov2021             -0.2984      0.085     -3.529      0.001      -0.466      -0.131
may2020              0.6280      0.085      7.364      0.000       0.459       0.797
==============================================================================
Omnibus:                        2.874   Durbin-Watson:                   2.044
Prob(Omnibus):                  0.238   Jarque-Bera (JB):                2.346
Skew:                          -0.270   Prob(JB):                        0.309
Kurtosis:                       3.347   Cond. No.                         718.
==============================================================================

Notes:
[1] Standard Errors assume that the covariance matrix of the errors is correctly specified.
```

**Table 53** Ramsey's regression specification error test

```
print(reset_ramsey(model1, degree = 4))
```

```
<F test: F=4.857980021437261, p=0.0031161687425688644, df_denom=127, df_num=3>
```

The dummy variable parameters turned out to be significant, and the Adjusted $R^2$ values increased from 0.41 to 0.61, showing a better fit and a more explanatory model compared to the original. The updated model shows improved normality of residuals, as indicated by the Omnibus and Jarque–Bera tests. In summary, 'model6' provides a better fit for the data and includes additional significant variables (dummy variables), showing that it explains the variation in Crude-Oil returns more effectively.

### 5.2.8 Functional Form Misspecification

Even if a model has all the necessary explanatory variables included, it may suffer from functional misspecification. We use RESET (Regression Specification Error Test). Table 53 displays the code snippet.

With a *p*-value of $0.003 < 0.05$, we reject the null hypothesis. This suggests there is evidence of specification error in the model, which means that the model may have some omitted variables. The model might be missing nonlinear relationships or interactions.

### 5.2.9 Stability Check

Stability check is crucial to ensure that the model's coefficients remain consistent over time. Here are some common practices for performing stability checks on the model:

- Recursive Estimates (CUSUM and CUSUMSQ Tests)
- Chow Test
- Rolling Regression
- Structural Break Tests (Bai-Perron Test)

Both the tests from Table 54 display the test statistic (0.433) < critical *p*-value (0.992). Both tests show a high *p*-value (close to 1), suggesting there is no significant evidence of structural breaks in the model. Since the test statistics are well below the critical values at 1%, 5%, and 10% levels, this shows that the model coefficients are stable over time.

Rolling regression involves estimating the model over different rolling windows and observing how the coefficients change over time. Table 55 shows the rolling regression test procedure. This generated plot helps to analyze the temporal stability of each coefficient, potentially uncovering insights about how different variables impact the model over time and identifying periods of instability that might require further investigation.

**Table 54** CUMSUM and CUMSUMSQ tests

```
cusum_test = breaks_cusumolsresid(model1.resid)
cusum_test_summary = breaks_cusumolsresid(model1.resid, ddof=0)

print("CUSUM Test Summary:", cusum_test)
print("CUSUMSQ Test Summary:", cusum_test_summary
```

```
CUSUM Test Summary: (0.4328404995510638, 0.9920026751962366, [(1, 1.63), (5, 1.36), (10, 1.22)])
CUSUMSQ Test Summary: (0.4328404995510638, 0.9920026751962366, [(1, 1.63), (5, 1.36), (10, 1.22)])
```

Here, the x-axis is the time periods or sliding window positions. As the window moves forward, the coefficients are recalculated, giving a sense of each variable's coefficient over time. For example, at each step along the x-axis, the model was trained on a subset of data, and coefficients were recalculated for that subset.

The *y*-axis shows the magnitude and direction of each coefficient value. Positive values indicate a positive relationship with the dependent variable, while negative values indicate a negative relationship. Large fluctuations in a coefficient indicate that the influence of that predictor variable changes significantly over time.

If the coefficients are relatively stable (remaining close to a fixed level) across the window range, it suggests the relationship between the predictor and response variable is consistent over time. Conversely, significant volatility, as seen with yieldSpread and ConsumerCredit(significant drops and spikes). The large spike and dip in yieldSpread around the 100th observation could suggest an economic event or regime change affecting this variable's relationship with the dependent variable.

The BDS (Brock, Dechert, Scheinkman) (Brock et al., 1996) test is used to detect nonlinearity, chaos, or other deviations from the independent and identically distributed (IID) assumption in time series data. Table 56 displays the test script.

The *p*-value of 0.0651 is just above the conventional significance level of 0.05. This result suggests there is some evidence of nonlinearity in the residuals, but it is not strong enough to reject the null hypothesis at the 0.05 level (Table 57).

The *p*-value of 0.41 > 0.05 shows there is no statistical evidence of a structural break at the specified breakpoint in the data. This aligns with the CUSUM test performed in Table 54. The lack of a structural break means, the model can be used to make inferences or predictions over the entire sample period without needing adjustments for different time periods.

## 6 January Effect

The idea that stock market values often increase more in January than in any other month is known as the "January effect." In 1942, an investment banker (Sidney B. Wachtel), made the first observation of the January Effect. Using data dating back to 1925, he found that during the first half of January, small-cap companies often

**Table 55** Rolling regression test

```
formula = 'CL_ExcessReturns ~ SP_ExcessReturns + inflation + indpro + termSpread + yieldSpread +
ConsumerCredit'

window = 12
rolling_params = []
for i in range(window, len(df)):
    rolling_model = sm.ols(formula, data=df.iloc[i-window:i]).fit()
    rolling_params.append(rolling_model.params.values)

rolling_params = np.array(rolling_params)
param_names = rolling_model.params.index

rolling_df = pd.DataFrame(rolling_params, columns=param_names)

rolling_df.plot(title="Rolling Coefficients", figsize=(10, 6))
plt.grid()
plt.show()
```

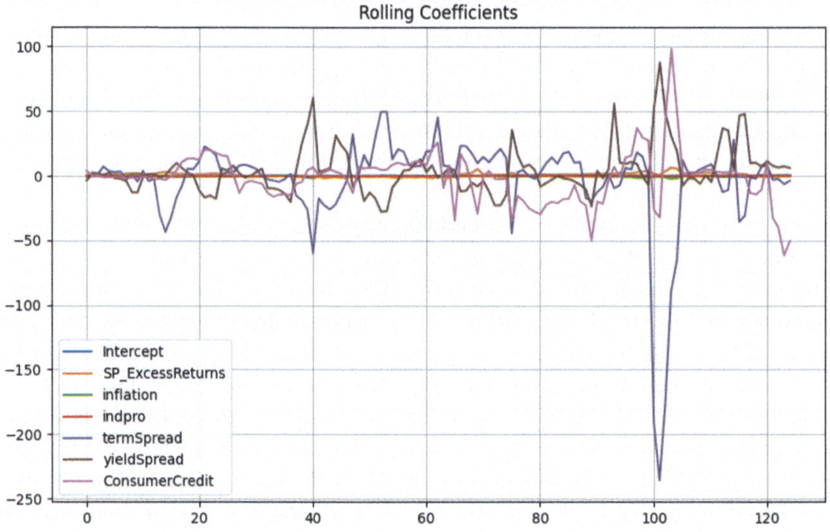


performed better than large-cap corporations. Since then, a lot of researchers have tried to find the evidence of the stronger effect of January over time. According to one study that examined data from 1904 to 1974, January stock returns were five times more than the norm. Salomon Smith Barney found an average January outperformance of 0.82% when comparing the returns of small-cap stocks and large-cap stocks from 1972 to 2002.

**Table 56** BrockDechertScheinkman test

```
bds_stat, p_value = bds(model1.resid)

print("BDS Test statistic:", bds_stat)
print("BDS Test p-value:", p_value)

if p_value < 0.05:
    print("BDS indicates nonlinearity in the residuals.")
else:
    print("BDS indicates linearity in the residuals.")
```

```
BDS Test statistic: 1.8444283825428507
BDS Test p-value: 0.06512073412720783
BDS indicates linearity in the residuals.
```

In the USA, tax planning is a major driver of the January effect. According to this hypothesis, investors sell off underperforming stocks in December to lock in a capital loss for the year, thereby reducing their tax bill, which causes a temporary dip in prices. In January, prices recovered when buying picks up again. Another potential driver of the January Effect stock market anomalies is the year-end bonus. With extra cash availability, investors often plow money into the markets and drive stock prices higher. There is also a possibility that investor psychology drives much of the phenomenon. Many people tend to start new things at the beginning of the year, and taking a run at the stock market might be one of them. We test the existence of a January effect by creating a dummy variable that takes the value of 1 only in January across both years in the dataset, and 0 for other months (Table 58). By incorporating this variable, it is possible to determine whether January returns deviate significantly from returns in other months. This could help find the influence of seasonal factors or investor behavior connected to new-year investing or tax-loss harvesting. The nov2021 and may2020 variables we have from Table 51.

We can see that the jan coefficient 0.05 ($p$-value: 0.0.04 < 0.05) is significant, suggesting a meaningful effect of January on *CL_ExcessReturns*. The inclusion of the Jan variable marginally improves the model's explanatory power (0.64 compared to 0.63), suggesting better model for explaining Crude-Oil returns.

## 7 Key Takeaways

In this chapter, we implemented the theoretical constructs discussed in previous chapters by developing and testing regression models. Each model was rigorously examined through various assumptions and statistical tests to ensure robustness such as Multicollinearity check, Linearity check, Residuals vs. Fitted Plot, Homoscedasticity, Independence of errors, etc. This process included parameter estimation and diagnostic tests to confirm the reliability and robustness of

**Table 57** Chow test

```
breakpoint = len(df)//2

Y = df['CL_ExcessReturns']
X = sm.add_constant(df[['SP_ExcessReturns', 'inflation', 'indpro', 'termSpread', 'yieldSpread',
'ConsumerCredit']])

full_model = sm.OLS(Y, X).fit()
X1 = sm.add_constant(df[['SP_ExcessReturns', 'inflation', 'indpro', 'termSpread', 'yieldSpread',
'ConsumerCredit']].iloc[:breakpoint])
Y1 = df['CL_ExcessReturns'].iloc[:breakpoint]
X2 = sm.add_constant(df[['SP_ExcessReturns', 'inflation', 'indpro', 'termSpread', 'yieldSpread',
'ConsumerCredit']].iloc[breakpoint:])
Y2 = df['CL_ExcessReturns'].iloc[breakpoint:]

model7 = sm.OLS(Y1, X1).fit()
model8 = sm.OLS(Y2, X2).fit()

ssr_full = full_model.ssr
ssr1 = model7.ssr
ssr2 = model8.ssr

num_restrictions = X.shape[1]
num_params = num_restrictions - 1

f_stat = ((ssr_full - (ssr1 + ssr2)) / num_restrictions) / ((ssr1 + ssr2) / (len(Y) - 2 * num_restrictions))
print("Chow Test F-statistic:", f_stat)

df_num = num_restrictions
df_denom = len(Y) - 2 * num_restrictions

p_value = stats.f.sf(f_stat, df_num, df_denom)
print("Chow Test p-value:", p_value)

if p_value < 0.05:
    print("The Chow Test indicates a significant structural break.")
else:
    print("The Chow Test does not indicate a significant structural break.")
```

```
Chow Test F-statistic: 1.0235239348641676
Chow Test p-value: 0.41815394391584504
The Chow Test does not indicate a significant structural break.
```

**Table 58** Implementation of January effect

```
df['nov2021'] = np.where(df.index == '2021-11-01', 1, 0)
df['may2020'] = np.where(df.index == '2020-05-01', 1, 0)
df['jan'] = np.where(df.index.month == 1, 1, 0)
formula = 'CL_ExcessReturns ~ SP_ExcessReturns + inflation + indpro + termSpread + yieldSpread +
ConsumerCredit +\
 nov2021 + may2020 + jan'
model9 = sm.ols(formula, df).fit()
print(model9.summary())
```

```
==============================================================================
Dep. Variable:       CL_ExcessReturns   R-squared:                       0.644
Model:                            OLS   Adj. R-squared:                  0.619
Method:                 Least Squares   F-statistic:                     25.55
Date:                Sat, 03 Aug 2024   Prob (F-statistic):           1.38e-24
Time:                        14:09:44   Log-Likelihood:                 153.48
No. Observations:                 137   AIC:                            -287.0
Df Residuals:                     127   BIC:                            -257.8
Df Model:                           9
Covariance Type:            nonrobust
====================================================================================
                       coef    std err          t      P>|t|      [0.025      0.975]
------------------------------------------------------------------------------------
Intercept           -0.0545      0.015     -3.699      0.000      -0.084      -0.025
SP_ExcessReturns     0.7698      0.167      4.623      0.000       0.440       1.099
inflation            0.1078      0.024      4.470      0.000       0.060       0.155
indpro               0.0310      0.005      6.489      0.000       0.022       0.040
termSpread           8.5231      2.937      2.902      0.004       2.712      14.334
yieldSpread          0.5028      0.682      0.738      0.462      -0.846       1.852
ConsumerCredit       1.2902      1.214      1.063      0.290      -1.112       3.693
nov2021             -0.2960      0.084     -3.543      0.001      -0.461      -0.131
may2020              0.6308      0.084      7.486      0.000       0.464       0.798
jan                  0.0551      0.027      2.037      0.044       0.002       0.109
==============================================================================
Omnibus:                        2.389   Durbin-Watson:                   2.092
Prob(Omnibus):                  0.303   Jarque-Bera (JB):                1.937
Skew:                          -0.273   Prob(JB):                        0.380
Kurtosis:                       3.205   Cond. No.                         718.
==============================================================================

Notes:
[1] Standard Errors assume that the covariance matrix of the errors is correctly specified.
```

the models developed. Finally, we explored the January effect (or turn-of-the-year effect), a phenomenon where securities tend to increase in value more rapidly in January compared to other months.

## References


Breusch, T. S., & Pagan, A. R. (1979). A simple test for heteroscedasticity and random coefficient variation. *Econometrica, 47*(5), 1287. https://doi.org/10.2307/1911963

Brock, W. A., Scheinkman, J. A., Dechert, W. D., & LeBaron, B. (1996). A test for independence based on the correlation dimension. *Econometric Reviews, 15*(3), 197–235. https://doi.org/10.1080/07474939608800353

Cook, R. D. (1979). Influential observations in linear regression. *Journal of the American Statistical Association, 74*(365), 169–174. https://doi.org/10.1080/01621459.1979.10481634

Durbin, J., & Watson, G. S. (1971). Testing for serial correlation in least squares regression. III. *Biometrika, 58*(1), 1–19. https://doi.org/10.1093/biomet/58.1.1

Koenker, R., & Bassett Jr, G. (1978). Regression quantiles. *Econometrica: Journal of the Econometric Society*, 33–50.

MacKinnon, J. G., & White, H. (1985). Some heteroskedasticity-consistent covariance matrix estimators with improved finite sample properties. *Journal of Econometrics, 29*(3), 305–325. https://doi.org/10.1016/0304-4076(85)90158-7

Scholes, M., & Williams, J. (1977). Estimating betas from nonsynchronous data. *Journal of Financial Economics, 5*(3), 309–327.

White, H. (1980). A heteroskedasticity-consistent covariance matrix estimator and a direct test for heteroskedasticity. *Econometrica, 48*(4), 817. https://doi.org/10.2307/1912934

# Dynamic Model Implementation 6

In this chapter, we will use Two-Stage Least Squares (2SLS) estimation, causality testing, and dynamic modeling techniques. Together, these methods help achieve a deeper, more reliable analysis, especially in complex environments where variables influence each other over time. All the source code[1] can be found at the footnote.

## 1 Two-Stage Least Squares (2SLS) Estimation

Dynamic models often involve endogenous regressors due to feedback effects and lagged relationships. 2SLS offers a robust way to address these issues by using external instruments.

Endogeneity arises when an explanatory variable ($X$) is correlated with the error term or is jointly determined with the dependent variable ($Y$). This violates a key assumption of OLS regression where one or more explanatory variables (such as price or income) are jointly determined with the dependent variable (like quantity demanded or consumption).

Let us form a simple mathematical intuition to explain this: $y = \beta_1 * 1 + \beta_2 x_2 + \beta_3 x_3 + \cdots + \varepsilon.$ . In this equation we assume that all explanatory variables ($x_2$ and $x_3$) are not correlated with the error term $\varepsilon$. However, if one or more of these variables are correlated with the error term, the OLS estimator becomes inconsistent and provide biased estimation. This bias is due to Omitted Variable Bias, which occurs because part of the variance in $y$ is wrongly attributed to the endogenous variable instead of being captured by the error term.

[1] PracticalGuideEconometrics/Chapter_6.ipynb at main · saritmaitra/PracticalGuideEconometrics.



S. Maitra, *A Practical Guide to Static and Dynamic Econometric Modelling*, Contributions to Economics, https://doi.org/10.1007/978-3-031-86862-7_6

To simplify, endogeneity can lead to biased estimates in OLS regression. To address endogeneity, Instrumental Variables (IV) estimation is normally used. IV estimation helps address endogeneity by using an instrument that is correlated with the endogenous variable but uncorrelated with the error term.

Two-Stage Least Squares (2SLS) is a common IV that involves two stages. In stage 1 we regress the endogenous variable on the instrument and other exogenous variables to obtain predicted values. In stage 2, we regress the dependent variable on the predicted values from stage 1 and the other exogenous variables. It is crucial to choose a valid instrument that meets the assumptions mentioned earlier (correlated with the endogenous variable and uncorrelated with the error term). After performing 2SLS, it is important to check the model diagnostics to ensure the validity of the results.

Let us consider a use case. Here the background is that, studying the impact of monetary policy on economic output often involves analyzing the effect of interest rates (a key tool of monetary policy) on GDP (a primary measure of economic output). When the central bank changes interest rates, it affects borrowing costs for businesses and consumers. Lower interest rates generally encourage borrowing and spending, boosting investment and economic activity, leading to higher GDP growth. Conversely, higher interest rates tend to discourage borrowing and spending, slowing down economic growth. These changes in investment and spending ultimately influence the overall economic output, or GDP.

*"The Impact of Monetary Policy on Economic Output". Here the problem is, studying the effect of monetary policy (e.g., interest rates set by the central bank) on economic output is a common challenge.*

We will model the relationship as $\text{GDP}_t = \alpha + \beta * \text{InterestRate}_t + \varepsilon_t$, where, InterestRate is endogenous due to (1) Reverse causality—Interest rates are often adjusted in response to changes in GDP and (2) Omitted variables—Other macroeconomic factors, like inflation or global demand, influence both GDP and interest rates.

Let us try to solve this by using 2SLS to address endogeneity by finding an instrumental variable that, (1) is strongly correlated with interest rates, and (2) is uncorrelated with the error term $\varepsilon_t$ and does not directly affect GDP. We know that 2SLS consists of 2 stages wherein at the first stage we regress $\text{InterestRate}_t$ on the IV (e.g., money supply and other exogenous variables) to get predicted values: $\text{InterestRate}_t = \pi_0 + \pi_1 * \text{MoneySupply}_{t-1} + v_t$ and in the second stage we will use the predicted $\text{InterestRate}_t$ from the first stage to estimate the effect on GDP: $\text{GDP}_t = \alpha + \beta$ * InterestRate^t $+ \epsilon_t$.

This use case is relevant for:

- Evaluating the effectiveness of central bank policies.
- Analyzing policy-driven interventions in macroeconomic modeling.

- Understanding the causal relationships between monetary policy tools and economic performance.

Table 1 displays data ingestion from the United States Federal Reserve Economic Data (FRED). Notice that we have considered crude oil Futures prices (CL = $F$) instead of spot price. For an economic model analyzing relationships with inflation, stock returns, and macroeconomic indicators, WTI Futures prices (CL = $F$) are often preferable because they are forward-looking and more closely aligned with financial market activities, which are often interlinked with macroeconomic variables.

We have ingested multiple economic series here which we will use throughout this chapter. GDP is usually non-stationary (exhibits trends over time). Economic relationships often use growth rates rather than absolute levels (e.g., quarterly growth). So, we apply data transformation by taking the logarithm of GDP to interpret changes in percentage terms and using differencing to remove trends and ensure stationarity. Interest rates are often stationary but could show small trends or structural breaks over time. No log transform is needed because interest rates are already in percentage form. Money supply is usually non-stationary and shows growth over time. Log transformation helps interpret changes as percentages and stabilize the variance and differencing can help remove non-stationary trends. So, we take logarithm and difference to calculate growth rates. Table 2 displays the transformation techniques.

These transformations are quite important to understand. We will use many of these variables in this chapter for different modeling purpose. Here, it can be noticed that wti_ExcessReturns is not lagged, it is directly computed as the difference in log returns of CL = $F$ minus DGS3MO. SP_ExcessReturns is also not lagged and is computed as the difference in log returns of ^GSPC minus DGS3MO. Inflation is not lagged and calculated as the percentage change in CPIAUCSL over time. ConsumerCredit is not lagged and this is the change in TOTALSL between consecutive periods. yieldSpread is not lagged and directly calculated as the difference between DGS10 and DGS3MO for the same period. GDP is also not lagged and calculated as the difference in the log of GDP over time. InterestRate is not lagged and directly takes the values of FEDFUNDS for the same period. Lagged_MoneySupply is not lagged as calculated. We are calculating it as the difference in the log of Lagged_MoneySupply. Unemployment_rate is lagged and we explicitly shift UNRATE by 1 period (shift(1)), making this a lagged variable.

Before going for implementation, we must do a stationarity check and resolve any issues related to data stationarity. Tables 3 and 4 display the ADF test procedures on the related variables.

Now that we have the stationary dataset, we will implement Two Stage least Square (2SLS) in two stages as displayed in Table 5. Here, during first stage we will address endogeneity in the **InterestRate_diff** variable by using the **Lagged_MoneySupply** as an instrument. After obtaining the predicted values for the interest rate, we will use OLS to estimate the relationship between GDP and the

**Table 1** Data ingestion from FRED

```
import yfinance as yf
import pandas as pd
import numpy as np
import datetime as dt
import pandas_datareader as pdr

stocks = ['CL=F']
market_index = '^GSPC'

start = dt.datetime(2010, 1, 1)
end = dt.datetime(2024,1,1)

data = yf.download(stocks + [market_index], start='2010-01-01', end='2024-01-01', interval='1mo')['Adj
Close']

data.index = pd.to_datetime(data.index)
data.reset_index(inplace=True)

# Total Consumer Credit Owned and Securitized
cpiaucsl = pdr.get_data_fred('CPIAUCSL', start=start, end=end)
cpiaucsl.reset_index(inplace=True)

# 3-month Treasury Bill rate (risk-free rate)
dgs3mo = pdr.get_data_fred('DGS3MO', start=start, end=end)
# Convert to monthly frequency and from percentage to decimal
dgs3mo = dgs3mo.resample('ME').last() / 100
dgs3mo.reset_index(inplace=True)

# 10-year Treasury Bill rate (risk-free rate)
DGS10 = pdr.get_data_fred('DGS10', start=start, end=end)
# Convert to monthly frequency and from percentage to decimal
DGS10 = DGS10.resample('ME').last() / 100
DGS10.reset_index(inplace=True)

# GDP
gdp = pdr.get_data_fred('GDP', start=start, end=end)
gdp = gdp.resample('ME').bfill().ffill()
gdp.reset_index(inplace=True)

# Federal Funds Rate
interest_rate = pdr.get_data_fred('FEDFUNDS', start=start, end=end)
interest_rate = interest_rate.resample('M').last()
interest_rate.reset_index(inplace=True)

# industrial production
indpro = pdr.get_data_fred('INDPRO', start=start, end=end)
indpro.reset_index(inplace=True)
```

(continued)

**Table 1** (continued)

```
# Total Consumer Credit Owned and Securitized
totalsl = pdr.get_data_fred('TOTALSL', start=start, end=end)
totalsl.reset_index(inplace=True)

# Money supply
money_supply = pdr.get_data_fred('M2SL', start=start, end=end)
money_supply['Lagged_MoneySupply'] = money_supply['M2SL'].shift(1)
money_supply.reset_index(inplace=True)

# unemployment rate
unemployment_rate = pdr.get_data_fred('UNRATE', start, end)
unemployment_rate.reset_index(inplace=True)

data = pd.concat([data, cpiaucsl['CPIAUCSL'], dgs3mo['DGS3MO'], DGS10['DGS10'], gdp['GDP'],
        indpro['INDPRO'], totalsl['TOTALSL'], money_supply['Lagged_MoneySupply'],
            interest_rate['FEDFUNDS'], unemployment_rate['UNRATE']], axis=1)
data = data.set_index('Date')
print(data.head())
```

```
[*********************100%***********************]  2 of 2 completed
                CL=F        ^GSPC  CPIAUCSL  DGS3MO  DGS10        GDP  \
Date
2010-01-01  72.889999  1073.869995   217.488  0.0008  0.0363  14980.193
2010-02-01  79.660004  1104.489990   217.281  0.0013  0.0361  14980.193
2010-03-01  83.760002  1169.430054   217.353  0.0016  0.0384  14980.193
2010-04-01  86.150002  1186.689941   217.403  0.0016  0.0369  15141.607
2010-05-01  73.970001  1089.410034   217.290  0.0016  0.0331  15141.607

             INDPRO    TOTALSL  Lagged_MoneySupply  FEDFUNDS  UNRATE
Date
2010-01-01  89.1897  2543.50802                 NaN      0.11     9.8
2010-02-01  89.5046  2530.02428              8478.0      0.13     9.8
2010-03-01  90.1356  2536.55195              8527.6      0.16     9.9
2010-04-01  90.4607  2532.76479              8523.7      0.20     9.9
2010-05-01  91.7014  2521.68794              8555.1      0.20     9.6
```

instrumented interest rate. This process resolves the endogeneity issue in the first stage and proceeds with standard regression in the second stage.

The first stage shows that Lagged_MoneySupply is a moderately strong instrument for InterestRate_diff. The $F$-statistic > 10 is a good sign, meeting the general threshold for a valid instrument. Despite having a moderately strong instrument, the second stage shows no meaningful relationship between InterestRate_diff and GDP_diff. This suggests that changes in interest rates (instrumented by lagged money supply) do not explain variations in GDP growth.

The lack of significance in the second stage implies that either the hypothesized relationship between interest rates and GDP growth is weak or non-existent or there are omitted variables or nonlinear effects that this linear model cannot capture. With only 118 observations, the obtained results are likely to be sensitive to sample variability. A larger dataset could provide more robust findings.

**Table 2** Data transformation

```
df = pd.DataFrame()
df['wti_ExcessReturns'] = np.log(data['CL = F']).diff() - data['DGS3MO']
df['SP_ExcessReturns'] = np.log(data['^GSPC']).diff() - data['DGS3MO']
df['inflation'] = (data['CPIAUCSL'].diff() / data['CPIAUCSL'].shift(1)) * 100
df['ConsumerCredit'] = data['TOTALSL'] - data['TOTALSL'].shift(1)
df['yieldSpread'] = data['DGS10'] - data['DGS3MO']
df['GDP'] = np.log(data['GDP']).diff()
df['InterestRate'] = data['FEDFUNDS']
df['Lagged_MoneySupply'] = np.log(data['Lagged_MoneySupply']).diff()
df['unemployment_rate'] = data['UNRATE'].shift(1)
df.dropna(inplace = True)
print(df.head())
```

```
            wti_ExcessReturns  SP_ExcessReturns  inflation  ConsumerCredit
Date
2010-03-01           0.048588          0.055533   0.033137         6.52767
2010-04-01           0.026534          0.013051   0.023004        -3.78716
2010-05-01          -0.154030         -0.087132  -0.051977       -11.07685
2010-06-01           0.020393         -0.057188  -0.041880        -3.27153
2010-07-01           0.041462          0.065016   0.186925         2.68839

            yieldSpread       GDP  InterestRate  Lagged_MoneySupply  \
Date
2010-03-01       0.0368  0.000000          0.16            0.005833
2010-04-01       0.0353  0.010718          0.20           -0.000457
2010-05-01       0.0315  0.000000          0.20            0.003677
2010-06-01       0.0279  0.000000          0.18            0.006315
2010-07-01       0.0279  0.011025          0.18            0.002216

            unemployment_rate
Date
2010-03-01                9.8
2010-04-01                9.9
2010-05-01                9.9
2010-06-01                9.6
2010-07-01                9.4
```

## 1.1 Relationship Between 'Inflation' and 'Stock Returns'

Let us discuss the complex relationship between inflation and how does it affect stock trading. In the short term, rising inflation can reduce purchasing power and raise uncertainty, potentially resulting in lower stock returns. However, in the long term, businesses may adjust their prices to reflect inflation and try to neutralize its effect on returns.

The relationship between inflation and excess returns of crude oil stock is multifaceted and influenced by various economic factors, including market returns and consumer credit, etc. Understanding these relationships requires considering the broader economic context, including interest rates, economic growth, geopolitical events, and supply–demand dynamics. Statistical modeling, historical data analysis, and scenario analysis can offer valuable insights into these complex dynamics.

**Table 3** Stationarity check using ADF test

```
variables = ['GDP', 'InterestRate', 'Lagged_MoneySupply']

# ADF Test
adf_results = []
for var in variables:
    adf_result = adfuller(df[var])
    adf_results.append([var, adf_result[0], adf_result[1], adf_result[4]['1%'],
                 adf_result[4]['5%'], adf_result[4]['10%'],
                 'Yes' if adf_result[1] < 0.05 else 'No'])

adf_table = pd.DataFrame(adf_results, columns=['Variable', 'Statistic', 'p-value',
                          'Critical Value (1%)', 'Critical Value (5%)',
                          'Critical Value (10%)', 'Stationary (ADF)'])

print("ADF Test Results")
display(adf_table)
```

ADF Test Results

| | Variable | Statistic | p-value | Critical Value (1%) | Critical Value (5%) | Critical Value (10%) | Stationary (ADF) |
|---|---|---|---|---|---|---|---|
| 0 | GDP | -2.216898 | 0.200170 | -3.491818 | -2.888444 | -2.581120 | No |
| 1 | InterestRate | -1.331398 | 0.614688 | -3.488535 | -2.887020 | -2.580360 | No |
| 2 | Lagged_MoneySupply | -5.545198 | 0.000002 | -3.487022 | -2.886363 | -2.580009 | Yes |

**Table 4** Data transformation and recheck stationarity on the transformed variables

```
variables = ['GDP', 'InterestRate']

for var in variables:
    df[f'{var}_diff'] = df[var].diff()
df.dropna(inplace=True)

adf_results = []
for var in variables:
    adf_result = adfuller(df[f'{var}_diff'])
    adf_results.append([var, adf_result[0], adf_result[1], adf_result[4]['1%'],
                 adf_result[4]['5%'], adf_result[4]['10%'],
                 'Yes' if adf_result[1] < 0.05 else 'No'])

adf_table = pd.DataFrame(adf_results, columns=['Variable', 'Statistic', 'p-value',
                          'Critical Value (1%)', 'Critical Value (5%)',
                          'Critical Value (10%)', 'Stationary (ADF)'])

print("ADF Test Results (After Stationarizing)")
display(adf_table)
```

ADF Test Results (After Stationarizing)

| | Variable | Statistic | p-value | Critical Value (1%) | Critical Value (5%) | Critical Value (10%) | Stationary (ADF) |
|---|---|---|---|---|---|---|---|
| 0 | GDP | -4.767404 | 0.000063 | -3.491818 | -2.888444 | -2.58112 | Yes |
| 1 | InterestRate | -3.377035 | 0.011767 | -3.488535 | -2.887020 | -2.58036 | Yes |

Here the use case is:

**Table 5** 2SLS implementation

```
print("Step 1: Regress InterestRate_diff on Lagged_MoneySupply (Instrument)")
print()
X_stage1 = sm.add_constant(df[['Lagged_MoneySupply']])
stage1_model = sm.OLS(df['InterestRate_diff'], X_stage1).fit()
print(stage1_model.summary())

# Predicted values (fitted values for InterestRate_diff)
df['InterestRate_pred'] = stage1_model.predict(X_stage1)

print()
print()

print("Step 2: Regress GDP_diff on the predicted InterestRate_diff (instrumented) and exogenous
variables")
print()
X_stage2 = sm.add_constant(df[['InterestRate_pred', 'inflation']])
stage2_model = sm.OLS(df['GDP_diff'], X_stage2).fit()
print(stage2_model.summary())
```

```
Step 1: Regress InterestRate_diff on Lagged_MoneySupply (Instrument)

                            OLS Regression Results
==============================================================================
Dep. Variable:      InterestRate_diff   R-squared:                       0.355
Model:                            OLS   Adj. R-squared:                  0.350
Method:                 Least Squares   F-statistic:                     63.90
Date:                Mon, 16 Dec 2024   Prob (F-statistic):           1.08e-12
Time:                        08:29:25   Log-Likelihood:                 28.776
No. Observations:                 118   AIC:                            -53.55
Df Residuals:                     116   BIC:                            -48.01
Df Model:                           1
Covariance Type:            nonrobust
======================================================================================
                         coef    std err          t      P>|t|      [0.025      0.975]
--------------------------------------------------------------------------------------
const                  0.1402      0.021      6.570      0.000       0.098       0.182
Lagged_MoneySupply   -17.4773      2.186     -7.994      0.000     -21.808     -13.147
==============================================================================
Omnibus:                       92.953   Durbin-Watson:                   1.498
Prob(Omnibus):                  0.000   Jarque-Bera (JB):             1120.581
Skew:                           2.463   Prob(JB):                    4.67e-244
Kurtosis:                      17.271   Cond. No.                         124.
==============================================================================

Notes:
[1] Standard Errors assume that the covariance matrix of the errors is correctly specified.
```

(continued)

**Table 5** (continued)

```
Step 2: Regress GDP_diff on the predicted InterestRate_diff (instrumented) and exogenous variables

                            OLS Regression Results
==============================================================================
Dep. Variable:               GDP_diff   R-squared:                       0.000
Model:                            OLS   Adj. R-squared:                 -0.009
Method:                 Least Squares   F-statistic:                  0.003353
Date:                Mon, 16 Dec 2024   Prob (F-statistic):              0.954
Time:                        08:29:25   Log-Likelihood:                 362.21
No. Observations:                 118   AIC:                            -720.4
Df Residuals:                     116   BIC:                            -714.9
Df Model:                           1
Covariance Type:            nonrobust
=====================================================================================
                        coef    std err          t      P>|t|      [0.025      0.975]
-------------------------------------------------------------------------------------
const             -1.881e-05      0.001     -0.017      0.986      -0.002       0.002
InterestRate_pred     0.0004      0.007      0.058      0.954      -0.014       0.015
==============================================================================
Omnibus:                        1.180   Durbin-Watson:                   2.724
Prob(Omnibus):                  0.554   Jarque-Bera (JB):                0.721
Skew:                           0.118   Prob(JB):                        0.697
Kurtosis:                       3.301   Cond. No.                         7.12
==============================================================================

Notes:
[1] Standard Errors assume that the covariance matrix of the errors is correctly specified.
```

*Investigating the interplay between inflation and crude oil stock returns. The goal is to understand the complex relationship between inflation and excess returns of crude oil stock, considering the influence of other economic factors, specifically the market returns and consumer credit.*

We will examine the simultaneous relationship between inflation and crude oil stock returns, as well as their dependence on other economic factors like market returns (S&P Excess Returns) and consumer credit. To model these relationships, we will investigate Two-Stage Least Squares (2SLS) to address the endogeneity between inflation and CL_ExcessReturns. Let us form the equations for 2SLS procedure.

- Inflation equation $\rightarrow$ $\text{Inflation}_t = \alpha_0 + \alpha_1 \text{CL\_ExcessReturns}_t + \alpha_2 \text{ConsumerCredit}_t + \varepsilon_1 t$. CL_ExcessReturns is endogenous here because it can be influenced by inflation and other factors (like market returns and consumer credit). We exclude S&P Excess Returns from this equation to make it over-identified.
- CL_ExcessReturns equation $\rightarrow$ $\text{CL\_ExcessReturns}_t = \beta_0 + \beta_1 \text{SP\_ExcessReturns}_t + \beta_2 \text{Inflation}_\text{t} + \beta_3 \text{ConsumerCredit}_\text{t} + \varepsilon_2 t$. Inflation is endogenous in this equation because it can be influenced by economic and market factors, including stock returns. We exclude Consumer Credit from this equation to make it over-identified.

Two-Stage Least Squares (2SLS) procedure includes of two stages.

In the first stage of inflation equation, since CL_ExcessReturns is endogenous, we use the exogenous variables SP_ExcessReturns and ConsumerCredit as instruments to predict CL_ExcessReturns. The first stage regression becomes CL_ExcessReturns$_t$ = $\gamma_0 + \gamma_1$SP_ExcessReturns$_t$ + $\gamma_2$ConsumerCredit$_t$ + $\varepsilon_3 t$. After running this regression, we will obtain the predicted values of CL_ExcessReturns as CL_ExcessReturns^.

Likewise, the first stage for CL_ExcessReturns equation, since inflation is endogenous, we use the exogenous variables SP_ExcessReturns and ConsumerCredit as instruments to predict inflation. The first stage regression becomes Inflation$_t$ = $\delta_0 + \delta_1 SP\_ExcessReturns_t + \delta_2 ConsumerCredit_t + \varepsilon_4 t$. After running this regression, we will obtain the predicted values of Inflation as Inflation^.

Above equations are part of first stage. Now in the second stage, we substitute the predicted values of the endogenous variables into their respective equations.

- Inflation$_t$ = $\alpha_0 + \alpha_1$ CL_ExcessReturns^$_t$ + $\alpha_2$ConsumerCredit$_t$ + $\varepsilon_1$ $t$. We will estimate this equation using OLS to get the values of $\alpha_0$, $\alpha_1$, $\alpha_2$.
- CL_ExcessReturns$_t$ = $\beta_0 + \beta_1$ SP_ExcessReturns$_t$ + $\beta_2$ Inflation^$_t$ + $\beta 3$ ConsumerCredit$_t$ + $\varepsilon_2 t$ to estimate this equation using OLS to get the values of $\beta_0$, $\beta_1$, $\beta_2$, $\beta_3$.

Like before, we follow the similar procedures to perform the stationarity tests followed by Pearson's correlation check displayed in Tables 6, 7, and 8.

The strongest correlation here is between S&P 500 excess returns and WTI (crude oil) excess returns (0.408140) but not strong enough to eliminate any of these variables. So, we move ahead with the 2SLS model displayed in Table 9.

Considering the Inflation Equation, the relationship between inflation_diff and the independent variables (CL_ExcessReturns and ConsumerCredit) is weak and not statistically significant, with low explanatory power ($R$-squared = 0.029). The model is not significant ($p$-value = 0.183). Now, considering CL_ExcessReturns Equation, this model explains about 16.7% of the variation in wti_ExcessReturns, with SP_ExcessReturns being the only statistically significant predictor ($p$-value = 0.039). However, the Inflation variable has no significant impact on wti_ExcessReturns. We can explore model improvements such as addressing adding more data, adding more variables, or using robust standard errors to account for heteroscedasticity and non-normality.

## 1.2 Causality Test Implementation

We talked about the traditional approaches to time series forecasting, both univariate and multivariate. Now, we present the concept of causality and how it affects time series analysis in general.

Regression analysis cannot establish causation. Therefore, to perform causation analysis on the data with the formula wti_ExcessReturns ~ SP_ExcessReturns +

**Table 6** Stationarity test on relevant variables ('wti_ExcessReturns', 'SP_ExcessReturns', 'ConsumerCredit', 'inflation')

```
variables = ['wti_ExcessReturns', 'SP_ExcessReturns', 'ConsumerCredit','inflation']

results = {}
for var in variables:
    series = df[var].dropna()
    adf_test = adfuller(series, autolag='AIC')
    results[var] = {
        'ADF Statistic': adf_test[0],
        'p-value': adf_test[1],
        'Critical Values': adf_test[4],
        'Stationary': 'Yes' if adf_test[1] <= 0.05 else 'No'}

table_data = []
for var, result in results.items():
    table_data.append([
        var,
        result['ADF Statistic'],
        result['p-value'],
        result['Stationary']])

headers = ['Variable', 'ADF Statistic', 'p-value', 'Stationary']
table = tabulate(table_data, headers=headers, tablefmt='fancy_grid')
print(table)
```

| Variable | ADF Statistic | p-value | Stationary |
|---|---|---|---|
| wti_ExcessReturns | -10.0229 | 1.66077e-17 | Yes |
| SP_ExcessReturns | -2.92714 | 0.0422823 | Yes |
| ConsumerCredit | -9.82053 | 5.35322e-17 | Yes |
| inflation | -2.6804 | 0.0774924 | No |

inflation + ConsumerCredit + yieldSpread, we use Granger causality test (https://en.wikipedia.org/wiki/Granger_causality). It tests whether past values of one time series ($X$) can help predict future values of another time series ($Y$), beyond what can be predicted using only past values of $Y$. Null hypothesis is $X$ does not Granger-cause $Y$, alternative Hypothesis is $X$ does Granger-cause $Y$.

If the $p$-value < significance level (0.05), we reject the null hypothesis. This means there is evidence to suggest that $X$ Granger-causes $Y$. Alternately, we do not reject the null hypothesis. This means there is not enough evidence to say that $X$ Granger-causes $Y$. Table 10 shows the test procedure.

We can see that none of the variables Granger-cause the dependent variable at the 5% level (since all $p$-values > 0.05). Therefore, we can infer from here that, none of the variables (SP_ExcessReturns, inflation_diff, ConsumerCredit, or wti_ExcessReturns) show evidence of Granger causality with the dependent variable at any of the tested lags (1 to 6).

**Table 7** Transform non-stationary variables and retest to ensure stationarity

```
non_stationary_vars = ["inflation']

for var in non_stationary_vars:
    df[f'{var}_diff'] = df[var].diff()

results_diff = {}
for var in non_stationary_vars:
    series = df[f'{var}_diff'].dropna()
    adf_test = adfuller(series, autolag='AIC')
    results_diff[var] = {
        'ADF Statistic': adf_test[0],
        'p-value': adf_test[1],
        'Critical Values': adf_test[4],
        'Stationary': 'Yes' if adf_test[1] <= 0.05 else 'No'}

table_data_diff = []
for var, result in results_diff.items():
    table_data_diff.append([
        var + '_diff',
        result['ADF Statistic'],
        result['p-value'],
        result['Stationary']])

headers_diff = ['Variable', 'ADF Statistic', 'p-value', 'Stationary']
colalign = ["left", "decimal", "decimal", "center"]
table_diff = tabulate(table_data_diff, headers=headers_diff, tablefmt='fancy_grid', colalign=colalign)

print(table_diff)
```

| Variable | ADF Statistic | p-value | Stationary |
|---|---|---|---|
| inflation_diff | -8.58474 | 7.56074e-14 | Yes |

**Table 8** Pearson's correlation test

```
df[['SP_ExcessReturns', 'ConsumerCredit', 'inflation_diff', 'wti_ExcessReturns']].corr()
```

| | SP_ExcessReturns | ConsumerCredit | inflation | wti_ExcessReturns |
|---|---|---|---|---|
| **SP_ExcessReturns** | 1.000000 | 0.119047 | 0.110783 | 0.408140 |
| **ConsumerCredit** | 0.119047 | 1.000000 | 0.288494 | 0.027843 |
| **inflation** | 0.110783 | 0.288494 | 1.000000 | 0.229756 |
| **wti_ExcessReturns** | 0.408140 | 0.027843 | 0.229756 | 1.000000 |

## 2 AR Model Implementation

Using SP 500 series, let us fit an AR model of order 1, an AR(1). Autoregressive models assume that the relationship between a variable and its lagged values stays constant over time. This requires that the mean, variance, and autocovariances

**Table 9** Two Stage Least Squares using $\text{Inflation}_t = \alpha_0 + \alpha_1\text{CL\_ExcessReturns}_t + \alpha_2\text{ConsumerCredit}_t + \varepsilon_1 t$ and $\text{CL\_ExcessReturns}_t = \beta_0 + \beta_1\text{SP\_ExcessReturns}_t + \beta_2\text{Inflation}_t + \beta_3\text{ConsumerCredit}_t + \varepsilon_2 t$

```
df.dropna(inplace=True)


endog1 = df['inflation_diff']
endog2 = df['wti_ExcessReturns']
exog1 = df[['ConsumerCredit']]
exog2 = df[['SP_ExcessReturns']]


instr1 = df[['SP_ExcessReturns', 'ConsumerCredit']]
instr2 = df[['SP_ExcessReturns', 'ConsumerCredit']]


# First Stage: Predict endogenous variables
model1_stage1 = sm.OLS(endog2, sm.add_constant(instr1)).fit()
predicted_cl_excess_returns = model1_stage1.predict(sm.add_constant(instr1))
model2_stage1 = sm.OLS(endog1, sm.add_constant(instr2)).fit()
# Predict Inflation
predicted_inflation = model2_stage1.predict(sm.add_constant(instr2))


# Second Stage: Use predicted values in original equations")
# Inflation Equation
model1_stage2 = sm.OLS(endog1, sm.add_constant(pd.concat([pd.Series(predicted_cl_excess_returns,
                                    name='CL_ExcessReturns'), exog1], axis=1))).fit()
# CL_ExcessReturns Equation
model2_stage2 = sm.OLS(endog2, sm.add_constant(pd.concat([pd.Series(predicted_inflation,
                                    name='Inflation'), exog2], axis=1))).fit()
print("Inflation Equation Results:")
print(model1_stage2.summary())


print("\nCL_ExcessReturns Equation Results:")
print(model2_stage2.summary())
```

(continued)

**Table 9** (continued)

Inflation Equation Results:

OLS Regression Results

| | | | |
|---|---|---|---|
| Dep. Variable: | inflation_diff | R-squared: | 0.029 |
| Model: | OLS | Adj. R-squared: | 0.012 |
| Method: | Least Squares | F-statistic: | 1.726 |
| Date: | Mon, 16 Dec 2024 | Prob (F-statistic): | 0.183 |
| Time: | 10:18:09 | Log-Likelihood: | -0.72298 |
| No. Observations: | 117 | AIC: | 7.446 |
| Df Residuals: | 114 | BIC: | 15.73 |
| Df Model: | 2 | | |
| Covariance Type: | nonrobust | | |

| | coef | std err | t | P>\|t\| | [0.025 | 0.975] |
|---|---|---|---|---|---|---|
| const | -0.0126 | 0.031 | -0.402 | 0.688 | -0.075 | 0.050 |
| CL_ExcessReturns | 0.8249 | 0.512 | 1.611 | 0.110 | -0.189 | 1.839 |
| ConsumerCredit | 0.0010 | 0.001 | 0.813 | 0.418 | -0.001 | 0.004 |

| | | | |
|---|---|---|---|
| Omnibus: | 9.799 | Durbin-Watson: | 2.464 |
| Prob(Omnibus): | 0.007 | Jarque-Bera (JB): | 21.351 |
| Skew: | 0.172 | Prob(JB): | 2.31e-05 |
| Kurtosis: | 5.064 | Cond. No. | 556. |

Notes:
[1] Standard Errors assume that the covariance matrix of the errors is correctly specified.

CL_ExcessReturns Equation Results:

OLS Regression Results

| | | | |
|---|---|---|---|
| Dep. Variable: | wti_ExcessReturns | R-squared: | 0.167 |
| Model: | OLS | Adj. R-squared: | 0.152 |
| Method: | Least Squares | F-statistic: | 11.43 |
| Date: | Mon, 16 Dec 2024 | Prob (F-statistic): | 2.99e-05 |
| Time: | 10:18:09 | Log-Likelihood: | 103.73 |
| No. Observations: | 117 | AIC: | -201.5 |
| Df Residuals: | 114 | BIC: | -193.2 |
| Df Model: | 2 | | |
| Covariance Type: | nonrobust | | |

| | coef | std err | t | P>\|t\| | [0.025 | 0.975] |
|---|---|---|---|---|---|---|
| const | -0.0002 | 0.010 | -0.024 | 0.981 | -0.019 | 0.019 |
| Inflation | -0.1378 | 0.564 | -0.244 | 0.807 | -1.255 | 0.979 |
| SP_ExcessReturns | 1.1081 | 0.530 | 2.092 | 0.039 | 0.059 | 2.158 |

| | | | |
|---|---|---|---|
| Omnibus: | 54.649 | Durbin-Watson: | 1.869 |
| Prob(Omnibus): | 0.000 | Jarque-Bera (JB): | 452.043 |
| Skew: | 1.274 | Prob(JB): | 6.92e-99 |
| Kurtosis: | 12.286 | Cond. No. | 81.2 |

Notes:
[1] Standard Errors assume that the covariance matrix of the errors is correctly specified.

**Table 10** Granger causality test

```
max_lag = 6
variables = ['SP_ExcessReturns', 'inflation_diff', 'ConsumerCredit', 'wti_ExcessReturns']

p_values = {}
for var in variables:
    test_result = grangercausalitytests(df[['wti_ExcessReturns', var]], maxlag=max_lag)
    p_values[var] = [round(test_result[i+1][0]['ssr_ftest'][1], 4) for i in range(max_lag)]
granger_summary = pd.DataFrame(p_values, index=[f'lag_{i+1}' for i in range(max_lag)])
granger_summary
```

| | SP_ExcessReturns | inflation_diff | ConsumerCredit | wti_ExcessReturns |
|---|---|---|---|---|
| **lag_1** | 0.2381 | 0.6978 | 0.7969 | 1.0 |
| **lag_2** | 0.4998 | 0.9193 | 0.9728 | 1.0 |
| **lag_3** | 0.4372 | 0.9498 | 0.5121 | 1.0 |
| **lag_4** | 0.4447 | 0.9426 | 0.5959 | 1.0 |
| **lag_5** | 0.3774 | 0.7186 | 0.6725 | 1.0 |
| **lag_6** | 0.3538 | 0.6938 | 0.7209 | 1.0 |

of the time series are constant over time, thus, stationarity is a key assumption. Table 11 performs stationarity test on GDP dataset.

The *p*-value (0.974593) is much greater than the typical significance levels (0.01, 0.05, 0.10). This means we do not reject the null hypothesis of the ADF test. The null hypothesis of the ADF test is that the time series data has a unit root, which means it is non-stationary (Table 12).

The *p*-value (4.0979e−24) is less than the common significance levels (0.01, 0.05, 0.10). This means we reject the null hypothesis of the ADF test; we have statistical evidence to suggest that the series is stationary.

Table 13 displays how to apply an automatic method to determine the optimal lag order ($p$) which is important for AR model. Statsmodels API automates the process of lag selection by evaluating models with different lag lengths and selecting the best one based on an information criterion like AIC or BIC.

The output is [1, 2, 3, 4, 5, 6, 7, 8, 9, 10]. Here it takes the time series and tries different lag orders up to maxlag. This suggests that the current value of ^GSPC is best predicted by using the values of ^GSPC from the previous 1, 2, … 10 periods. These past values have a statistically significant relationship with the current GDP value. Based on this output, we should build an AR(3) model. This means your model equation will look something like this: $\mathrm{SP}_{(t)} = c + \alpha_1 \mathrm{SP}_{(t-1)} + \alpha_2 \mathrm{SP}_{(t-2)} + \alpha_3 \mathrm{SP}_{(t-3)} + \cdots + \alpha_{10} \mathrm{SP}_{(t-10)} + \varepsilon_t$, where $\mathrm{SP}_{(t)}$ is the SP value at time $t$, $c$ is a constant term, $\alpha_1, \alpha_2, \alpha_3 \ldots$ are the coefficients for the lagged SP values, $\varepsilon_t$ is the random error term. Now let us refit the model with the identified lag (Table 14).

**Table 11** Augmented Dicky-Fuller test of stationarity on ^GSPC daily series

```
adf_result = adfuller(data['^GSPC'].dropna())
ticker = "^GSPC"
start_date = "2010-01-01"
end_date = "2024-01-01"

sp_data= yf.download(ticker, start=start_date, end=end_date)['Adj Close']

adf_result = adfuller(sp_data)

table_data = []
stationary = 'Yes' if adf_result[1] <= 0.05 else 'No'
table_data.append([
    'sp',
    adf_result[0],
    adf_result[1],
    stationary])

headers = ['Variable', 'ADF Statistic', 'p-value', 'Stationary']
table = tabulate(table_data, headers=headers, tablefmt = 'fancy_grid')
print(table)
```

| Variable | ADF Statistic | p-value | Stationary |
|---|---|---|---|
| sp | 0.243395 | 0.974593 | No |

**Table 12** SP 500 data differencing and retest for stationarity

```
sp = np.log(sp_data).diff().dropna()
adf_result = adfuller(sp)

table_data = []
stationary = 'Yes' if adf_result[1] <= 0.05 else 'No'
table_data.append([
    'sp',
    adf_result[0],
    adf_result[1],
    stationary])

headers = ['Variable', 'ADF Statistic', 'p-value', 'Stationary']
table = tabulate(table_data, headers = headers, tablefmt = 'fancy_grid')
print(table)
```

| Variable | ADF Statistic | p-value | Stationary |
|---|---|---|---|
| sp | -12.9088 | 4.09798e-24 | Yes |

| | ADF Statistic | p-value | No. of lags used | No. of observations | Critical Value (1%) | Critical Value (5%) | Critical Value (10%) |
|---|---|---|---|---|---|---|---|
| 0 | -12.908829 | 4.097977e-24 | 26 | 3494 | -3.432223 | -2.862368 | -2.567211 |

**Table 13** Optimal AR lag order (p) identification

```
select_model = ar_select_order(sp_data, maxlag = 12)
print(select_model.ar_lags)
```

**Table 14** Autoregressive model refit AutoReg([1, 2, 3, 4, 5, 6, 7, 8, 9, 10])

```
optimal_lags = select_model.ar_lags
ar_model = AutoReg(sp, lags=optimal_lags)
results = ar_model.fit()
print(results.summary())
```

```
                            AutoReg Model Results
==============================================================================
Dep. Variable:                  ^GSPC   No. Observations:                 3521
Model:                    AutoReg(10)   Log Likelihood               10905.209
Method:               Conditional MLE   S.D. of innovations              0.011
Date:                Mon, 16 Dec 2024   AIC                         -21786.418
Time:                        15:00:27   BIC                         -21712.454
Sample:                            10   HQIC                        -21760.025
                                 3521
==============================================================================
                 coef    std err          z      P>|z|      [0.025      0.975]
------------------------------------------------------------------------------
const          0.0004      0.000      2.426      0.015    8.6e-05       0.001
^GSPC.L1      -0.0945      0.017     -5.601      0.000     -0.128      -0.061
^GSPC.L2       0.0504      0.017      2.982      0.003      0.017       0.084
^GSPC.L3      -0.0185      0.017     -1.093      0.274     -0.052       0.015
^GSPC.L4      -0.0439      0.017     -2.608      0.009     -0.077      -0.011
^GSPC.L5      -0.0139      0.017     -0.826      0.409     -0.047       0.019
^GSPC.L6      -0.0616      0.017     -3.660      0.000     -0.095      -0.029
^GSPC.L7       0.0798      0.017      4.735      0.000      0.047       0.113
^GSPC.L8      -0.0619      0.017     -3.659      0.000     -0.095      -0.029
^GSPC.L9       0.0627      0.017      3.705      0.000      0.030       0.096
^GSPC.L10     -0.0026      0.017     -0.155      0.877     -0.036       0.030
                                    Roots
==============================================================================
                   Real          Imaginary           Modulus         Frequency
------------------------------------------------------------------------------
AR.1            -1.0872           -0.4568j            1.1792           -0.4367
AR.2            -1.0872           +0.4568j            1.1792            0.4367
AR.3            -0.5576           -1.2221j            1.3433           -0.3181
AR.4            -0.5576           +1.2221j            1.3433            0.3181
AR.5             1.5107           -0.0000j            1.5107           -0.0000
AR.6             1.0658           -0.8853j            1.3856           -0.1103
AR.7             1.0658           +0.8853j            1.3856            0.1103
AR.8             0.3100           -1.4795j            1.5116           -0.2171
AR.9             0.3100           +1.4795j            1.5116            0.2171
AR.10           23.0407           -0.0000j           23.0407           -0.0000
------------------------------------------------------------------------------
```

We can observe the statistically significant lags ($p$-value < 0.05) from L1, L2, L4, L6, L7, L8, L9 showing a combination of positive and negative influences. L7 (positive), L8 (negative), and L9 (positive) showing significant and alternating in sign, suggesting complex oscillatory or cyclical dynamics. Lags L3, L5, L10 are not statically significant. These lags do not contribute to explain the dependent variable.

A basic AR model (AutoReg) in statsmodels is designed for univariate time series analysis. This means it works with a single dependent variable and its lagged values. Let us estimate a model that includes lagged variables. We will consider Unemployment Rate (UNRATE) and the Consumer Price Index (CPI).

## 2.1 Koyck Transformation

We know that the Distributed Lag models capture the effect of a variable across time. Distributed Lag models can imply either a finite or infinite lag structure, depending on how we specify them and the nature of the effect we are trying to capture.

Let us understand how this works:

- In finite distributed lag (FDL) models, we specify a set number of lags, meaning only a limited number of past values of the independent variable affect the dependent variable. For example, if we limit the lag to three periods, only the current and last three values of the independent variable are considered. This makes the model finite and more manageable in practice.
- In some cases, the effect of an independent variable is believed to persist indefinitely, diminishing gradually but never truly reaching zero. For example, economic shocks may have long-lasting effects that decrease over time. This can lead to an infinite distributed lag model, where theoretically, every past value of the independent variable influences the current value of the dependent variable.

Koyck Transformation (Johansen & Juselius, 1990) can be used to simplify the estimation of Infinite Distributed Lag (IDL) models, which capture the effects of an independent variable over multiple time periods.

Let us understand the mathematical intuition behind Koyck transformation. In Distributed Lag models, the goal is to capture the effects of an independent variable ($X_t$) on a dependent variable ($Y_t$) over multiple periods. For example, if an increase in $X$ affects $Y$ not only immediately but also over the next several periods. We can formulate this as $Y_t = \beta_0 + \beta_1 X_t + \beta_2 X_{t-1} + \beta_3 X_{t-1} + \cdots + \varepsilon_t$. Here, $\beta_1$, $\beta_2$, $\beta_3$,... are the coefficients that capture how past values of $X$ affect $Y$ over time.

In finite distributed lag (FDL) models, we include only a limited number of lags. For instance, if we set three lags, the model stops at $X_{t-1}$. In the Infinite Distributed Lag (IDL) models, the effects of $X$ continue indefinitely but decrease gradually. Estimating all the lagged coefficients in an IDL model is practically impossible. The Koyck Transformation simplifies the estimation of IDL models by assuming that the effects of $X$ on $Y$ decline geometrically over time. This means: the effect of $X_{t-1}$ is smaller than $X_t$ and the effect of $X_{t-1}$ is even smaller than $X_{t-1}$, and so on.

We present this assumption as $Y_t = \beta_0 + \beta X_t + \beta\lambda X_{(t-1)} + \beta\lambda^2 X_{(t-2)} + \cdots + \varepsilon_t$, where $\beta$ is the immediate effect of $X$ on $Y$ and $\lambda$ is the decay factor ($0 < \lambda < 1$), which determines how quickly the effect diminishes over time.

To understand how the transformation lets us take the original equation $Y_t = \beta_0 + \beta_1 X_t + \beta_2 X_{t-1} + \beta_3 X_{t-1} + \cdots + \varepsilon_t$ and re-write $Y_{(t-1)}$ (the lagged dependent variable) $Y_{t-1} = \beta_0 + \beta X_{t-1} + \beta\lambda X_{t-1} + \beta\lambda^2 X_{t-3} + \cdots + \varepsilon_{t-1}$. Now if we subtract from $Y_t$ we get $Y_t - \lambda Y_{t-1} = \beta_0(1-\lambda) + \beta X_t + (\varepsilon_t - \lambda\varepsilon_{t-1})$ which can be further simplified to $Y_t = \alpha_0 + \alpha_1 Y_{t-1} + \beta X_t + \varepsilon_t$ where, $\alpha_0 = \beta_0(1-\lambda)$ is the adjusted intercept and $\alpha_1 = \lambda$ is the persistence parameter showing how much of $Y_{(t-1)}$ influences $Y_t$.

Koyck Transformation is often associated with univariate Infinite Distributed Lag (IDL) models because it simplifies lagged effects of a single independent variable (e.g., $X_t$) on a dependent variable ($Y_y$). The transformation uses geometric decay to reduce the complexity of handling an infinite series of lags. Let us start with an example where we use univariate Koyck model to capture the persistence in $\text{UNRATE}_t$ due to its lagged value $\text{UNRATE}_t = \alpha_0 + \lambda\text{UNRATE}_{t-1} + \varepsilon_t$.

As always, before fitting the model, we must confirm that the data is free of unit roots; if not, we must perform the necessary transformation to stationarize the data. Table 15 implements the unit root check.

Applying lags to differenced inflation and unemployment data is crucial in modeling the Phillips curve relationship. The Phillips curve theory suggests that changes in inflation precede changes in unemployment. By applying a lag to the inflation variable, we are aligning the data to reflect this causal relationship. We are essentially examining how past inflation changes influence current unemployment changes. Moreover, in a univariate context, the unemployment rate often shows autocorrelation, meaning that its current value is correlated with its past values. Including a lagged unemployment term in helps capture this autocorrelation and can improve the accuracy of model.

**Table 15** Unit root testing

```
columns_to_test = ['inflation', 'unemployment_rate']

table_data = []
for column in columns_to_test:
    result = adfuller(df[column])
    stationary = 'Yes' if result[1] <= 0.05 else 'No'
    table_data.append([column, result[0], result[1], stationary])

headers = ['Variable', 'ADF Statistic', 'p-value', 'Stationary']
table = tabulate(table_data, headers=headers, tablefmt='fancy_grid')
print(table)
```

| Variable | ADF Statistic | p-value | Stationary |
|---|---|---|---|
| inflation | -2.6804 | 0.0774924 | No |
| unemployment_rate | -2.8357 | 0.0533528 | No |

Koyck Transformation Logic: The Koyck transformation itself is based on the idea of distributed lags, meaning that the impact of an independent variable is spread out over time. Applying a lag to the independent variable is a key part of setting up the Koyck model structure. Table 16 displays the necessary transformation to stationarize the series and introduce lag.

Now since all variables are stationary, let us apply the Koyck transformation to model the unemployment rate (UNRATE) using its lagged value and extract the Koyck parameters as displayed in Table 17.

We obtain Alpha (long-run equilibrium) as 9.8654 and Lambda (decay parameter) as 0.4044. Alpha suggests that, in the long run, the unemployment rate tends to stabilize around 9.86 or around 10 months considering the data is in monthly

**Table 16** Data stationarize and apply lag

```
df['inflation_diff'] = df['inflation'].diff()
df['unemployment_rate_diff'] = df['unemployment_rate'].diff()
df['inflation_diff_lag'] = df['inflation_diff'].shift(1)
df['unemployment_rate_lag'] = df['unemployment_rate_diff'].shift(1)
df.dropna(inplace=True)

columns_to_test = ['inflation_diff', 'unemployment_rate_diff', 'inflation_diff_lag', 'unemployment_rate_lag']

table_data = []
for column in columns_to_test:
    result = adfuller(df[column])
    stationary = 'Yes' if result[1] <= 0.05 else 'No'
    table_data.append([column, result[0], result[1], stationary])

headers = ['Variable', 'ADF Statistic', 'p-value', 'Stationary']
table = tabulate(table_data, headers=headers, tablefmt='fancy_grid')
print(table)
```

| Variable | ADF Statistic | p-value | Stationary |
|---|---|---|---|
| inflation_diff | -8.59065 | 7.30188e-14 | Yes |
| unemployment_rate_diff | -11.2361 | 1.85594e-20 | Yes |
| inflation_diff_lag | -8.59917 | 6.94422e-14 | Yes |
| unemployment_rate_lag | -11.2322 | 1.89567e-20 | Yes |

**Table 17** Koyck model fit and extract Koyck parameters

```
Y = df['unemployment_rate']
X = sm.add_constant(df['unemployment_rate_lag'])
model = sm.OLS(Y, X).fit()

alpha = model.params[0] / (1 - model.params[1])
lamda = model.params[1]

print(f"Alpha (long-run equilibrium): {alpha:.4f}")
print(f"Lambda (decay parameter): {lamda:.4f}")
```

frequency. Lambda (0.4044) shows that previous unemployment has a significant impact on the current rate. The unemployment rate adjusts relatively slowly toward its long-run equilibrium. Each period, about 40.44% of the deviation from the long-run equilibrium persists. Table 18 displays the geometric decay of lagged effects.

We can see that the effects decrease exponentially (or geometrically), following the $\lambda^t$ relationship. This confirms the model assumption. Lagged impact is limited and after 5–6 periods (lags), the effect approaches zero, showing that the initial impact has almost completely dissipated. The previous period's unemployment rate has a strong immediate impact, but its influence diminishes significantly in subsequent periods. The decay rate ($0 < \lambda < 1$) determines how persistent the effects are. If $\lambda$ is close to 1, the effects decay slowly, if $\lambda$ is close to 0, the effects decay very quickly, as seen in this plot.

**Table 18** Geometric decay of lagged effects

```
lags = np.arange(12)

def koyck_decay(lags, alpha, lamda):
    return alpha * (lamda ** lags)

plt.figure(figsize=(8, 4))
plt.plot(lags, koyck_decay(lags, alpha, lamda), marker='o', linestyle='-')
plt.title('Geometric Decay of Lagged Effects (Koyck Transformation)')
plt.xlabel('Lag')
plt.ylabel('Effect')
plt.grid(True)
plt.show()
```

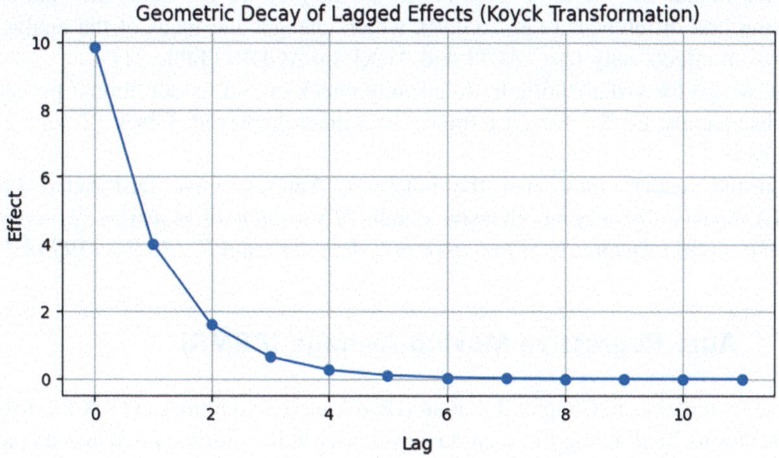

## 2.2 Auto Regressive Distributed Lag (ARDL)

The ARDL model includes lagged values of the dependent variables and/or lagged values of the independent variables to capture the temporal dependencies and relationships in the data over time. Let us define our use case for modeling:

*We want to analyze how Government Expenditure (EXP), Consumer Price Index (CPI), and their lagged effects influence GDP over time. Specifically, we hypothesize that current and lagged values of EXP and CPI affect GDP, while also accounting for GDP's own past values.*

Table 19 displays relevant data (GDP, CPI, and Government expenditure) ingestion from FRED and visualization.

Table 20 examines the stationarity by employing ADF test as shown in:

Let us understand the data handling process here. The advantage of ARDL is that it works with a mix of levels and differences. If the GDP is non-stationary but not differenced, the model implicitly accounts for its level. If we difference the GDP, the interpretation shifts from modeling levels to modeling changes. For the independent variables (CPI and EXP), the ARDL framework allows for a mix of I(0) and I(1) variables. Therefore, we do not need to difference the CPI and EXP if they are I(0) or I(1). We will keep GDP in levels, and ARDL will estimate the short- and long-run relationships appropriately.

Differencing may only be necessary for preprocessing before testing a more restrictive model like VAR or if variables are I(2). If we use data_diff, and we model the first differences (e.g., ΔGDP), which changes the focus of the analysis to short-run effects only (e.g., ΔCPI and ΔEXP on ΔGDP) (Table 21).

Now we go for visualization to do a sanity check on out model fitment process and subsequently go for forecast future 10 values displayed Tables 22 and 23, respectively.

Interested readers may visit the notebook Autoregressive Distributed Lag (ARDL) models[2] for a comprehensive detail. "*This notebook makes use of money demand data from Denmark, as first used in S. Johansen and K. Juselius (1990)[2]*".

# 3 Auto Regressive Moving Average (ARMA)

We have seen earlier in Chapter 3 that an ARMA model combines (1) AR (Autoregressive) terms by drawing the relationships between the current value and its past values ($y_t$) as a function of ($y_{t-1}, y_{t-1}, \ldots, y_{t-p}$) and (2) MA (Moving Average)

[2] https://www.statsmodels.org/dev/examples/notebooks/generated/autoregressive_distributed_lag.html.

**Table 19** GDP, CPI, and Government expenditure data ingestion and visualization

```
start_date = '2000-01-01'
end_date = '2023-12-31'

gdp = web.DataReader('GDP', 'fred', start_date, end_date)
cpi = web.DataReader('CPIAUCSL', 'fred', start_date, end_date)  # Consumer Price Index
exp = web.DataReader('W068RCQ027SBEA', 'fred', start_date, end_date)  # Government Expenditure

data = pd.concat([gdp, cpi, exp], axis=1)
data.columns = ['GDP', 'CPI', 'EXP']
data = data.dropna()

fig, ax = plt.subplots(figsize=(10, 5))

ax.plot(data.index, data['GDP'], label='GDP')
ax.plot(data.index, data['CPI'], label='CPI')
ax.plot(data.index, data['EXP'], label='Government Expenditure')
ax.set_xlabel('Date')
ax.set_ylabel('Values')
ax.set_title('Time Series of GDP, CPI, and Government Expenditure')
ax.legend()
ax.grid(True)
plt.show()
```

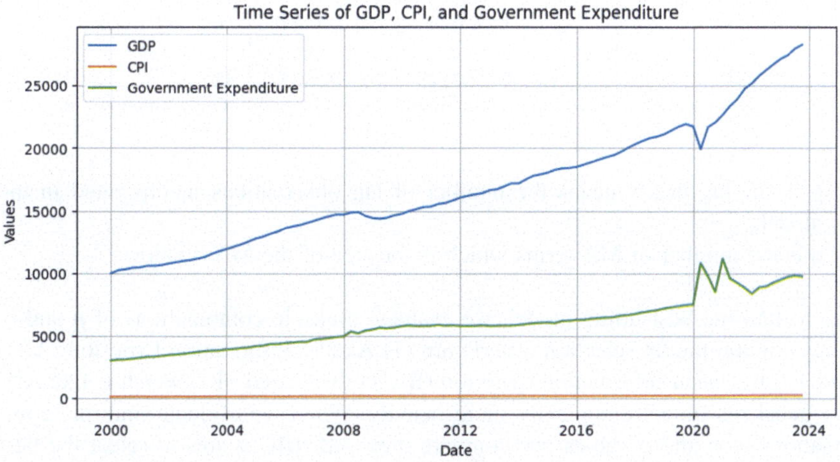


terms which explain the relationships between the current value and past error terms ($y_t$) as a function of ($\varepsilon_{t-1}, \varepsilon_{t-1} \ldots \varepsilon_{t-q}$).

The challenge with MA terms is that the lagged error terms ($\varepsilon_{t-1}, \varepsilon_{t-1} \ldots \varepsilon_{t-q}$) are unobservable because they depend on residuals or errors. But we know that residuals are only available after fitting the model. Because of this, ARMA models cannot be estimated using OLS, which assumes all variables are observable. To estimate the parameters of an ARMA model, Maximum Likelihood Estimation (MLE) is typically used.

In ARMA modeling, we must determine the $p$ (the number of AR terms) and $q$ (the number of MA terms).

**Table 20** ADF tests on GDP, CPI, and Government expenditure series

```
adf_results = []
for column in data.columns:
    result = adfuller(data[column].dropna())
    adf_results.append([column, result[0], result[1], result[4]['1%'], result[4]['5%'], result[4]['10%']])

adf_table = pd.DataFrame(adf_results, columns=['Variable', 'ADF Statistic', 'p-value', 'Critical Value (1%)',
                         'Critical Value (5%)', 'Critical Value (10%)'])

adf_table['Stationary'] = adf_table['p-value'].apply(lambda p: 'Yes' if p <= 0.05 else 'No')

table_data = []
for index, row in adf_table.iterrows():
    table_data.append([row['Variable'], row['ADF Statistic'], row['p-value'], row['Stationary']])

headers = ['Variable', 'ADF Statistic', 'p-value', 'Stationary']
table = tabulate(table_data, headers=headers, tablefmt='fancy_grid')
print(table)
```

| Variable | ADF Statistic | p-value | Stationary |
|---|---|---|---|
| GDP | 2.78808 | 1 | No |
| CPI | 1.91026 | 0.998544 | No |
| EXP | 0.564125 | 0.986697 | No |

- p is the lag order means the number of lag observations incorporated in the model.
- q is the number of MA terms which is the size of the MA window.

So, to find the best-fitting model, we evaluate multiple combinations of $p$ and $q$. The common model selection criteria are (1) Akaike Information Criterion (AIC) and, (2) Bayesian Information Criterion (BIC) (also called SIC) which is like AIC but penalizes model complexity more heavily. When we evaluate multiple combinations of $p$ and $q$ values, we compare their AIC/BIC scores to select the best model. Below workflow provides the steps required to estimate an ARMA Model.

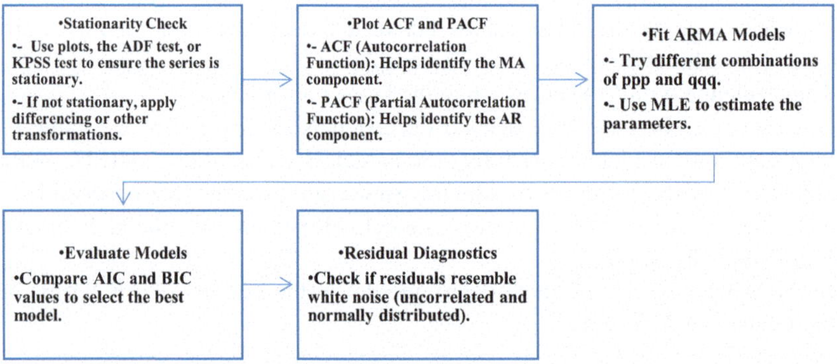

**Table 21** Select optimal lag order and fit ARDL model

```
lag_selection = ardl_select_order(data['GDP'],
                    exog=data[['CPI', 'EXP']],
                    maxlag=4,
                    maxorder=4)

ardl_model = lag_selection.model.fit()
print(ardl_model.summary())
```

```
                              ARDL Model Results
==============================================================================
Dep. Variable:                    GDP   No. Observations:                   96
Model:                  ARDL(4, 1, 1)   Log Likelihood                -584.915
Method:               Conditional MLE   S.D. of innovations            139.608
Date:                Tue, 17 Dec 2024   AIC                           1189.831
Time:                        14:54:33   BIC                           1215.049
Sample:                    01-01-2001   HQIC                          1200.009
                         - 10-01-2023
==============================================================================
                 coef    std err          z      P>|z|      [0.025      0.975]
------------------------------------------------------------------------------
const        787.1769    424.923      1.853      0.068     -57.978    1632.332
GDP.L1         0.7905      0.056     14.024      0.000       0.678       0.903
GDP.L2         0.6803      0.079      8.664      0.000       0.524       0.837
GDP.L3        -0.8753      0.094     -9.319      0.000      -1.062      -0.688
GDP.L4         0.4672      0.064      7.291      0.000       0.340       0.595
CPI.L0        35.2020     11.653      3.021      0.003      12.024      58.380
CPI.L1       -44.1088     11.206     -3.936      0.000     -66.396     -21.821
EXP.L0        -0.5739      0.046    -12.419      0.000      -0.666      -0.482
EXP.L1         0.6428      0.046     14.023      0.000       0.552       0.734
==============================================================================
```

In 1970 the statisticians George Box and Gwilym Jenkins proposed Box-Jenkins Method[3] to fit any kind of time series model. They simplified the formal procedure for model selection which involves three primary steps (1) Identification where we have to identify the ARMA models by looking at ACF/PACF plots and statistical tests, (2) Estimation where we need to estimate the parameters of the model and finally (3) Diagnostic Checking where we check the residuals to ensure the model fits the data well and does not leave out important patterns.

We already have the GDP series. We will focus on this series for ARMA modeling. Some initial observations can be made looking at the line plot shown below. The GDP consistently increased from 2010 to 2023, showing overall economic growth.

[3] Box–Jenkins method - Wikipedia.

**Table 22** Sanity check (original vs fitted GDP) visualization

```
predict = ardl_model.predict(start=len(data), end=len(data) + 4, exog_oos=data[['CPI', 'EXP']])
print("Prediction GDP Values:")
print(predict)

data['Fitted'] = ardl_model.fittedvalues
data[['GDP', 'Fitted']].plot(figsize=(10, 4), title="Actual vs Predicted GDP")
plt.grid()
plt.show()
```

```
Prediction GDP Values:
2024-01-01    27772.258134
2024-04-01    29070.498992
2024-07-01    29707.214610
2024-10-01    31651.038432
2025-01-01    32242.901114
Freq: 3MS, dtype: float64
```

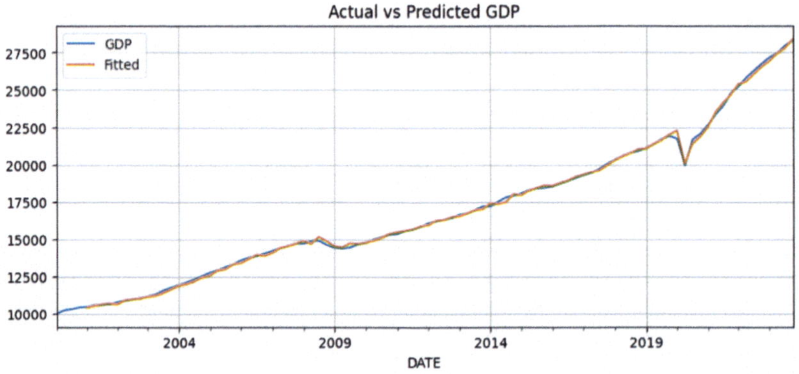


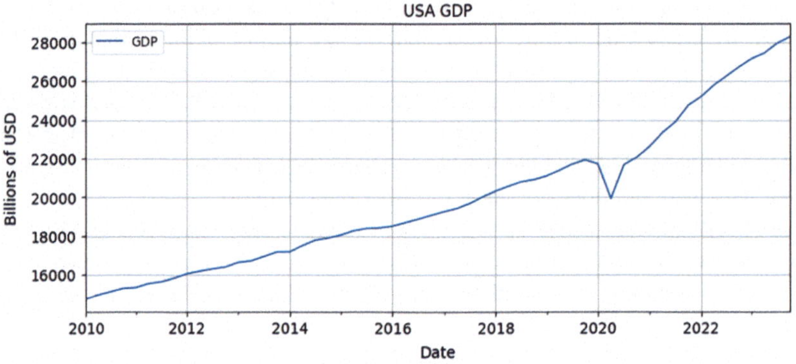


This upward trend reflects long-term economic expansion. A sharp decline is visible around 2020, corresponding to the COVID-19 pandemic, which led to global economic disruptions. The drop suggests a significant contraction in economic activity during that period. Following the sharp decline, there is a strong recovery and growth in GDP starting from 2021. This rebound signifies that the economy recovered relatively quickly after the initial shock of the pandemic. From 2021 onwards, GDP growth appears to accelerate, with a steep upward slope compared to earlier years. This shows post-pandemic economic recovery measures,

**Table 23** Forecast future GDP values

```
predict_df = pd.DataFrame(predict, columns=['Predicted_GDP'])
predict_df.index = pd.to_datetime(predict_df.index)

combined_data = pd.concat([data[['GDP', 'Fitted']], predict_df], axis=0)
combined_data = combined_data.rename(columns={'GDP': 'Actual_GDP'})

plt.figure(figsize=(10, 4))
plt.plot(combined_data.index, combined_data['Actual_GDP'], label='Actual GDP')
plt.plot(combined_data.index, combined_data['Predicted_GDP'], label='Predicted GDP', linestyle='--',
color='red')
plt.xlabel('Date')
plt.ylabel('GDP')
plt.title('Actual vs Predicted vs Fitted GDP')
plt.legend()
plt.grid(True)
plt.xticks(rotation=45)
plt.tight_layout()
plt.show()
```

such as increased government spending, stimulus packages, and a resurgence in economic activities. By the latest point in the graph (2023), the GDP reaches its highest recorded value, around 28,000 billion USD.

Table 24 displays the auto correlation plot where we can see that the autocorrelation starts close to 1 at lag 0, which is expected since a variable is perfectly correlated with itself at lag 0. As the lag increases, the autocorrelation gradually decreases. The autocorrelation declines slowly, indicating a strong persistence or dependency in the time series data. This suggests that the series may have a trend component or is not yet stationary. The autocorrelation values eventually drop below the confidence bands (dashed lines), which indicates that the relationship between observations weakens as the lag increases. There is no noticeable repeating pattern (cyclic ups and downs) in the autocorrelation values, which suggests no strong seasonal component in the data.

The slow decay of autocorrelation suggests the series may not be stationary and could require transformations such as differencing or detrending to stabilize the mean. The gradual decline implies that an AR($p$) model (Autoregressive) could be suitable, where $p$ depends on the significant lags in the plot.

**Table 24** Autocorrelation plot

```
autocorrelation_plot(gdp)
plt.show()
```

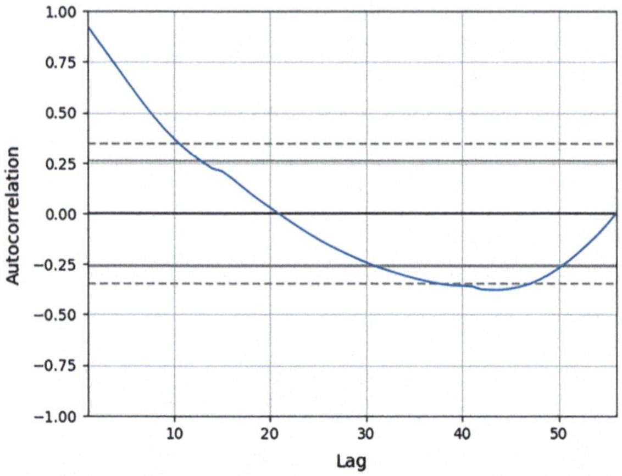


We perform a stationarity check as usual. The series shows a strong upward trend with no clear signs of seasonality. The increase is exponential-like, as the slope appears to steepen over time. So, we will Log transformation to stabilize variance in the time series. After log transformation, we will apply differencing to remove the trend.

Table 25 displays the process, and the results table provides a clear summary of the stationarity analysis.

**Table 25** Stationarize data

```
gdp_diff = np.log(gdp).diff().dropna()
adf_result = adfuller(gdp_diff)

table_data = []
stationary = 'Yes' if adf_result[1] <= 0.05 else 'No'
table_data.append([
    'gdp_diff',
    adf_result[0],
    adf_result[1],
    stationary])

headers = ['Variable', 'ADF Statistic', 'p-value', 'Stationary']
table = tabulate(table_data, headers=headers, tablefmt='fancy_grid')
print(table)
```

| Variable | ADF Statistic | p-value | Stationary |
|---|---|---|---|
| gdp_diff | -7.95465 | 3.06031e-12 | Yes |

We know now that we must find optimal $p$ and $q$ parameters for ARMA model. These parameters determine the structure of the ARMA model and how it captures the patterns in the time series data. Manually searching for the optimal order can be time-consuming and tedious. auto_arima automates this process by searching through a range of possible parameter values and selecting the combination that minimizes an information criterion. This automation helps streamline the model-building process and ensures that a well-performing ARIMA model is selected. Table 26 displays the auto-ARIMA procedure to find the optimal AR and MA values.

ARIMA(0,1,0) shows that the data was modeled as a random walk with a constant drift (intercept). There is no AR or MA component. The model determined that the best way to forecast GDP was to simply use the most recent differenced value, without considering older values or errors.

To find the optimal parameters, one approach is trial and optimization, while another is to employ Auto-ARIMA as shown above. It effectively does the heavy lifting and adjusts the hyperparameters. We should not forget that the explainability of the parameters will be something we must deal with while working on Auto-ARIMA, and ensure that it does not become a BlackBox, as forecasting models must go through governance before deployment.

Let us proceed with the ARMA model fit and view the forecast plot to confirm the aforesaid observations. Table 27 displays the ARMA model.

**Table 26** Auto-ARIMA to identify optimal parameters ($p$ & $q$)

```
auto_model = auto_arima(
  gdp,
  start_p=0, start_q=0,
  # max_p=5, max_q=5,
  seasonal=True,
  m=4,
  stepwise=True,
  suppress_warnings=True,
  trace=True)

print(f"Optimal ARIMA Order: {auto_model.order}")
```

```
Performing stepwise search to minimize aic
 ARIMA(0,1,0)(1,0,1)[4] intercept   : AIC=inf, Time=0.40 sec
 ARIMA(0,1,0)(0,0,0)[4] intercept   : AIC=815.285, Time=0.02 sec
 ARIMA(1,1,0)(1,0,0)[4] intercept   : AIC=818.868, Time=0.11 sec
 ARIMA(0,1,1)(0,0,1)[4] intercept   : AIC=818.903, Time=0.60 sec
 ARIMA(0,1,0)(0,0,0)[4]             : AIC=832.021, Time=0.04 sec
 ARIMA(0,1,0)(1,0,0)[4] intercept   : AIC=817.269, Time=0.26 sec
 ARIMA(0,1,0)(0,0,1)[4] intercept   : AIC=817.262, Time=0.07 sec
 ARIMA(1,1,0)(0,0,0)[4] intercept   : AIC=816.877, Time=0.03 sec
 ARIMA(0,1,1)(0,0,0)[4] intercept   : AIC=816.910, Time=0.07 sec
 ARIMA(1,1,1)(0,0,0)[4] intercept   : AIC=818.918, Time=0.13 sec

Best model:  ARIMA(0,1,0)(0,0,0)[4] intercept
Total fit time: 1.841 seconds
Optimal ARIMA Order: (0, 1, 0)
```

**Table 27** Fitting an ARIMA(0, 0, 0) model to differenced GDP data

```
arma_model = ARIMA(gdp_diff, order=(0, 0, 0))
arma_results = arma_model.fit()
print(arma_results.summary())
```

```
                               SARIMAX Results
==============================================================================
Dep. Variable:                    GDP   No. Observations:                   55
Model:                 ARIMA(1, 0, 1)   Log Likelihood                 144.149
Date:                Wed, 18 Dec 2024   AIC                           -280.299
Time:                        15:26:02   BIC                           -272.269
Sample:                    04-01-2010   HQIC                          -277.194
                         - 10-01-2023
Covariance Type:                  opg
==============================================================================
                 coef    std err          z      P>|z|      [0.025      0.975]
------------------------------------------------------------------------------
const          0.0118      0.003      3.435      0.001       0.005       0.019
ar.L1         -0.1033      0.747     -0.138      0.890      -1.568       1.361
ma.L1         -0.0826      0.726     -0.114      0.909      -1.506       1.341
sigma2         0.0003   2.57e-05     12.062      0.000       0.000       0.000
===================================================================================
Ljung-Box (L1) (Q):                   0.00   Jarque-Bera (JB):               927.61
Prob(Q):                              0.98   Prob(JB):                         0.00
Heteroskedasticity (H):              36.77   Skew:                            -2.91
Prob(H) (two-sided):                  0.00   Kurtosis:                        22.26
===================================================================================

Warnings:
[1] Covariance matrix calculated using the outer product of gradients (complex-step)
```

Now we go ahead to the residual diagnostics. First let us have a quick check looking at the residual plots. Table 28 displays the residual estimation and subsequently visualization.

Residuals are not perfectly normally distributed, indicating that the ARMA model may not fully capture the underlying structure of the data. Long tails suggest the presence of extreme values or outliers that the model struggles to explain. Statistical tests can provide more rigorous evidence for or against white noise. So, we perform Ljung–Box test and Box–Pierce test to ensure that residuals are white noise. Table 29 displays Ljung-Box test for residuals autocorrelation.

The null hypothesis of the Ljung-Box test is that there is no autocorrelation in the residuals (i.e., the residuals are white noise). The lb_pvalue column shows the *p*-values for the test at different lags (from 1 to 10 in this case). If the *p*-value $< 0.05$, we reject the null hypothesis. Here, all the *p*-values (lb_pvalue) are $> 0.05$. This means we do not reject the null hypothesis for all lags. The test does not find any patterns or relationships between the residuals at different time points. This is what we expect to see if the residuals are truly random and unpredictable, which is a characteristic of white noise.

Like the Ljung-Box test, the null hypothesis for the Box-Pierce test is that there is no autocorrelation in the residuals (i.e., the residuals are white noise). All the *p*-values (bp_pvalue) $> 0.05$. This means we do not reject the null hypothesis for all lags. The Box-Pierce test also provides no significant evidence of autocorrelation

**Table 28** Residuals diagnostics through visualization

```
arma_residuals = arma_results.resid

fig, axes = plt.subplots(1, 2, figsize=(10, 4))

# Residuals plot
axes[0].plot(arma_residuals)
axes[0].set_title('Residuals of ARMA Model')
axes[0].grid()

# Histogram
sns.histplot(arma_residuals, kde=True, ax=axes[1])
axes[1].set_title('Distribution of ARMA Model Residuals')
axes[1].set_xlabel('Residuals')
axes[1].set_ylabel('Frequency')
axes[1].grid(True)

plt.tight_layout()
plt.show()
```

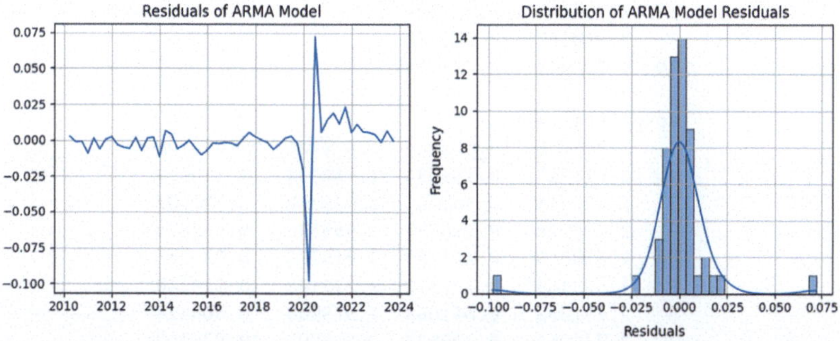


in the residuals of the model. Thus, we can statistically confirm that the model has likely captured the essential patterns in the data, and the remaining residuals are random and unpredictable.

While both the tests lead to the same conclusion in this case, however, the Ljung-Box test is generally considered to be more powerful and is often preferred, especially for smaller sample sizes.

Table 30 displays out-of-sample forecast procedure. Here, we must inverse the differenced data to ensure that the forecasted values are meaningful and directly comparable to your original GDP data. The first line forecast_diff.cumsum() calculates the cumulative sum of the forecasted differences (forecast_diff). Since differencing involves subtracting consecutive values, the cumulative sum helps us undo this step and partially reconstruct the original series. np.log(gdp['GDP'].iloc[−1]) adds the log of the last observed GDP value from your original data to the cumulative sum. This is essential because differencing loses information about the starting level of the series. By adding back, the log of the last observed value, we anchor the forecast to the correct starting point on the log-transformed scale. Finally, np.exp() is the exponential function (the inverse of the log) to forecast_log. Since we initially applied a log transformation to the data, using the exponential function

**Table 29** Ljung-Box and Box-Pierce tests for residuals

```
print('Ljungbox_test')
ljungbox_test = acorr_ljungbox(arma_residuals.dropna(), return_df=True)
print(ljungbox_test)
print('--------------------------------')
print('Boxpierce test')
boxpierce_test = acorr_ljungbox(arma_residuals.dropna(), boxpierce=True, return_df=True)
print(boxpierce_test)
```

```
Ljungbox_test
    lb_stat  lb_pvalue
1   2.016147   0.155634
2   2.032436   0.361961
3   2.076226   0.556737
4   2.130348   0.711799
5   2.425168   0.787720
6   2.731958   0.841658
7   2.731965   0.908642
8   2.951018   0.937394
9   3.040142   0.962682
10  3.127462   0.978263
--------------------------------
Boxpierce test
    lb_stat  lb_pvalue   bp_stat  bp_pvalue
1   2.016147   0.155634 1.910034   0.166959
2   2.032436   0.361961 1.925180   0.381902
3   2.076226   0.556737 1.965129   0.579676
4   2.130348   0.711799 2.013553   0.733266
5   2.425168   0.787720 2.272168   0.810346
6   2.731958   0.841658 2.535900   0.864428
7   2.731965   0.908642 2.535905   0.924369
8   2.951018   0.937394 2.716528   0.950869
9   3.040142   0.962682 2.788453   0.972095
10  3.127462   0.978263 2.857390   0.984584
```

reverses this transformation and brings the forecast back to the original scale of GDP values.

## 4 Auto Regressive Integrated Moving Average (ARIMA)

We have known from Chapter 3 that ARIMA introduces a differencing step (the "Integrated" part) to transform non-stationary data into stationary data, enabling ARMA-like models to work effectively. Differentiating is used to make a time series stationary, meaning it does not show any trend or seasonality. It usually involves deducting one observation from the previous one. Therefore, along with the $p$ and $q$, another difference ($d$) component is involved here which is the integrated component here. Therefore, along with $p$ and $q$, we require $d$ component here.

**Table 30** Forecast out of sample 10 steps ahead

```
n = 10
forecast_diff = results.forecast(steps=n)
forecast_index = pd.date_range(start=gdp.index[-1], periods=n + 1, freq='QE')[1:]

forecast_log = forecast_diff.cumsum() + np.log(gdp['GDP'].iloc[-1])
# Reverse the log transformation (exponential)
forecast = np.exp(forecast_log)

plt.figure(figsize=(10, 4))
plt.plot(gdp.index, gdp['GDP'], label='Original Data')
plt.plot(forecast_index, forecast, label='Forecast', color='red')
plt.xlabel('Date')
plt.ylabel('GDP (Billions of USD)')
plt.title('ARMA Forecast of GDP')
plt.legend()
plt.grid(True)
plt.show()
```

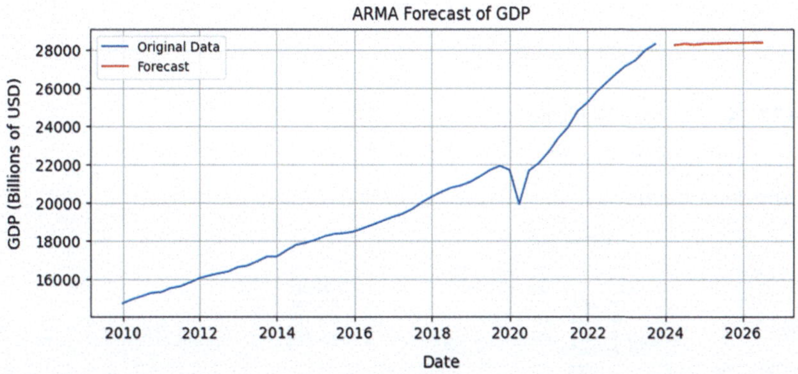


- *p* is the lag order means the number of lag observations (AR terms) incorporated in the model.
- *q* is the number of MA terms which is the size of the MA window.
- *d* is the degree of differencing which is the number of times series undergo differencing.

Here, we will opt for manual grid search to determine optimal parameter values. We have discussed about the black-box approach using Auto-ARIMA which may raise compliance issue. In the grid search approach, we have explicit control over the range of (*p*, *d*, *q*) values to be tested. This makes the process more transparent and allows for a deeper understanding of the model selection process. We can easily modify the search space or add constraints based on your domain knowledge or specific requirements. Table 31 displays the procedure to obtain the optimal order of *p*, *d*, and *q*.

We get the ARIMA order: (1, 1, 1), AIC: 819.301045456819. Now we fit the model with the best order. Table 32 displays the ARIMA model fit with the optimal values of *p*, *d*, and *q*.

**Table 31** Manual grid search for optimal (*p*, *d*, *q*) values

```
p_values = range(0, 3)
d_values = [1]
q_values = range(0, 3)

best_aic = float('inf')
best_order = None

for p, d, q in itertools.product(p_values, d_values, q_values):
    try:
        model = ARIMA(gdp['GDP'], order = (p, d, q))
        results = model.fit()
        if results.aic < best_aic:
            best_aic = results.aic
            best_order = (p, d, q)
    except:
        continue

print(f"Best ARIMA order: {best_order}, AIC: {best_aic}")
```

**Table 32** ARIMA model with the best order of *p*, *q*, *d*

```
model = ARIMA(gdp['GDP'], order = best_order)
results = model.fit()
print(results.summary())
```

```
                               SARIMAX Results
==============================================================================
Dep. Variable:                    GDP   No. Observations:                   56
Model:                 ARIMA(1, 1, 1)   Log Likelihood                -406.651
Date:                Sat, 14 Dec 2024   AIC                            819.301
Time:                        06:45:23   BIC                            825.323
Sample:                    01-01-2010   HQIC                           821.630
                         - 10-01-2023
Covariance Type:                  opg
==============================================================================
                 coef    std err          z      P>|z|      [0.025      0.975]
------------------------------------------------------------------------------
ar.L1          1.0000      0.002    519.109      0.000       0.996       1.004
ma.L1         -0.9971      0.072    -13.943      0.000      -1.137      -0.857
sigma2      1.516e+05   4.84e-07   3.13e+11      0.000    1.52e+05    1.52e+05
===================================================================================
Ljung-Box (L1) (Q):                   0.84   Jarque-Bera (JB):               592.77
Prob(Q):                              0.36   Prob(JB):                         0.00
Heteroskedasticity (H):              60.67   Skew:                            -1.37
Prob(H) (two-sided):                  0.00   Kurtosis:                        18.85
===================================================================================

Warnings:
[1] Covariance matrix calculated using the outer product of gradients (complex-step).
[2] Covariance matrix is singular or near-singular, with condition number 2.27e+26. Standard errors may be unstable.
```

Here we are using the original data, the ARIMA model handles the differencing internally based on the d value in the order. Explicit differencing might be needed in specific scenarios. This warning indicates that the method used to estimate the covariance matrix of the model parameters is based on numerical approximations. It is not necessarily a major concern, but it suggests that the estimates might not be as precise as with other methods.

Similar line ARMA, diagnostics plots can be obtained to ensure the assumption about residuals are met. Once, we are sure that model met all necessary statistical assumptions, we may proceed to forecasting step as shown in Table 33 and the next plot.

**Table 33** ARIMA forecast technique

```
n = 10
forecast = results.get_forecast(steps=n)
forecast_values = forecast.predicted_mean


forecast_index = pd.date_range(start=gdp.index[-1], periods=n + 1, freq='M')[1:]
plt.plot(gdp.index, gdp['GDP'], label='Original Data')
plt.plot(forecast_index, forecast_values, label='Forecast', color='red')
plt.fill_between(forecast_index, forecast_conf_int.iloc[:, 0], forecast_conf_int.iloc[:, 1], color='k',
alpha=0.3, label='Confidence Interval')
plt.xlabel('Date')
plt.ylabel('GDP')
plt.title('ARIMA Forecast of GDP')
plt.legend()
plt.grid(True)
plt.show()
```

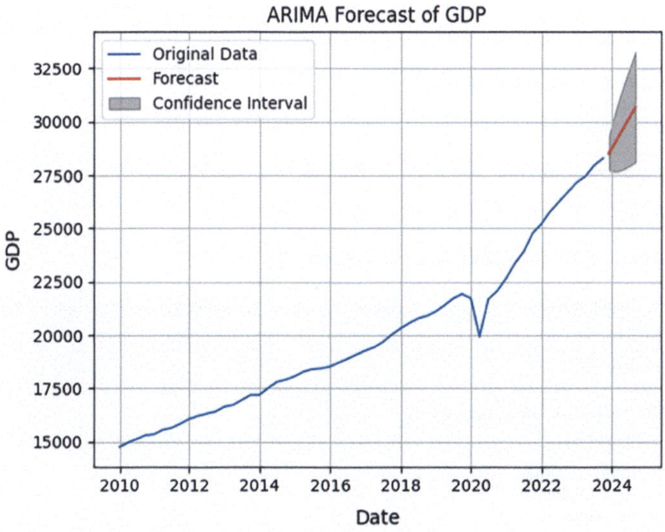


## 4.1 Rolling Forecast

A rolling forecast is often needed when working with time series data because of the reliance on previous observations. Business environments are dynamic where rolling forecasts allow for continuous adjustments based on the latest data and trends, making them better and relevant than static forecasts.

One way to do this is to recreate the model after each observation. We will maintain a history list which starts with training data and gets updated with new observations in every iteration. Table 34 displays the complete implementation of rolling forecast using Henry Hub (Natural Gas) spot price.

**Table 34** Rolling forecast implementation on Henry Hub natural gas data

```
# Natural gas series
start_date = '2010-01-01'
end_date = '2023-12-31'
henryhub_data = web.DataReader('DHHNGSP', 'fred', start_date, end_date)
henryhub_data.reset_index(inplace=True)
henryhub_data.columns = ['Date', 'Price']
henryhub_data.set_index('Date', inplace=True)

# train/test split
split_index = int(len(henryhub_data) * 0.9)
test = henryhub_data[split_index:]

# grid search for best p,d,q
p_values = range(0, 3)
d_values = [1]
q_values = range(0, 3)

best_aic = float('inf')
best_order = None

for p, d, q in itertools.product(p_values, d_values, q_values):
  try:
    model = ARIMA(train, order = (p, d, q))
    results = model.fit()
    if results.aic < best_aic:
      best_aic = results.aic
      best_order = (p, d, q)
  except:
    continue

print(f"Best ARIMA order: {best_order}, AIC: {best_aic}")

history = train['Price'].tolist()
predictions = list()

for i in range(1, len(test)):
  # predict
  model = ARIMA(history, order=best_order)
  model_fit = model.fit()

 yhat = model_fit.forecast()[0]
 # invert transformed prediction
 predictions.append(yhat)
 # Append the actual observation to the history for the next iteration
 history.append(test['Price'].iloc[i])

 print(f"Iteration: {i + 1}, Original: {test['Price'].iloc[i]}, Predicted: {yhat}")
```

(continued)

**Table 34** (continued)

```
mse = mean_squared_error(test['Price'], predictions)
mae = mean_absolute_error(test['Price'], predictions)
rmse = math.sqrt(mse)
print('MSE:', mse)
print('MAE:', mae)

plt.figure(figsize=(10, 5))
plt.plot(train.index, train['Price'], label='Train series')
plt.plot(test.index, test['Price'], label='Actual Price')
plt.plot(test.index, predictions, label='Predicted Price')
plt.title('Henry Hub Natural Gas Price Prediction')
plt.xlabel('Time')
plt.ylabel('Henry Hub Natural Gas Price')
plt.legend()
plt.grid(True)
plt.show()
```

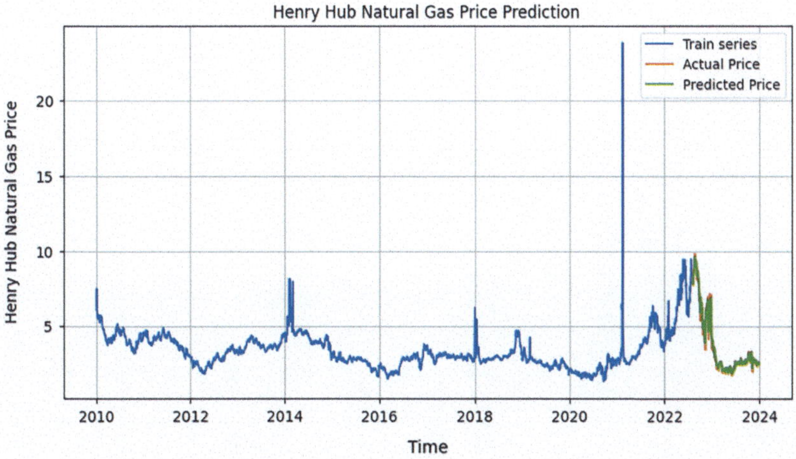


## 5 Key Takeaways

The chapter introduced different dynamic models and their applicability in dynamic business environment. It started with Two-Stage Least Squares (2SLS) estimation and delved into Auto Regressive (AR) models. AR models are fundamental for time series analysis and forecasting due to their ability to capture and use the dependence between consecutive data points. In the end, this chapter implemented Auto Regressive Integrated Moving Average (ARIMA) model. ARIMA models are specifically designed for time series data, which is data collected over time. They excel at capturing the underlying patterns and dependencies within this type of data. One of the primary applications of ARIMA models is forecasting. By understanding past patterns, these models can make predictions about future values of the time series. This chapter also introduced rolling forecast technique which is an important tool for dynamic business environments.

## Reference

Johansen, S., & Juselius, K. (1990). Maximum likelihood estimation and inference on cointegration—With applications to the demand for money. *Oxford Bulletin of Economics and Statistics, 52*(2), 169–210.

# Vector Auto Regression and Vector Error Correction Model

# 7

This chapter introduces Vector Auto Regression (VAR) and Vector Error Correction (VEC) model. Both VAR and ARIMA are valuable tools for time series analysis; however, VAR models are considered superior in situations where we deal with multiple time series that influence each other. This is a significant advantage over ARIMA, which is primarily designed for univariate analysis. VAR models explicitly model the interdependencies between multiple time series. They can capture how changes in one variable affect other variables in the system, providing a more comprehensive understanding of the dynamics between them. When forecasting with multiple related time series, VAR models leverage the interactions between them to produce potentially better predictions. This can be crucial in economics, where variables like GDP, inflation, and interest rates are interconnected. All source code[1] for this chapter can be found at footnote.

## 1 Vector Auto Regression (VAR) Model Implementation

We already know from Chapter 3 that a VAR model combines several Auto Regressive (AR) models. A vector representation of the variables influencing one another is produced by these models. The VAR model explains how observations on a given variable at one point in time relate to its own observations on the same variables at other points in time as well as to observations on other variables at prior times.

[1] PracticalGuideEconometrics/Chapter_7.ipynb at main · saritmaitra/PracticalGuideEconometrics.



S. Maitra, *A Practical Guide to Static and Dynamic Econometric Modelling*,
Contributions to Economics, https://doi.org/10.1007/978-3-031-86862-7_7

In principle, the estimation of multivariate time series models is the same as the univariate time series model. Below we have expanded the steps we have seen earlier and added more granularity to perform VAR analysis.

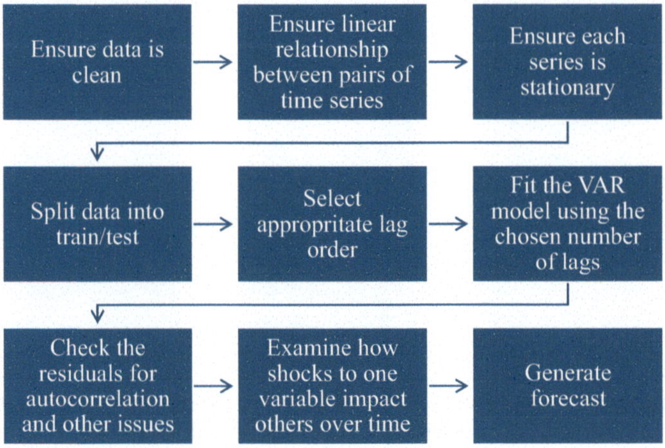


Now let us assume that we want to use a VAR model to study the effect of a government stimulus package on real GDP growth and inflation. By analyzing the impulse responses and FEVD, we can assess the magnitude and duration of the policy's impact on these key economic variables.

Impact of government spending on economic growth and inflation. We want to understand how changes in government spending affect real GDP growth and CPI.

Following are the data sources:

- Real GDP Growth Rate: FRED (e.g., GDPC1)
- CPI: FRED (e.g., CPIAUCSL)
- Government Spending: FRED (e.g., FGEXPND) or national statistical agencies.

This use case provides an example of how VAR can be used for Econometric modeling to understand important relationships and inform policy decisions. Feel free to ask any further questions about this use case or any other aspects of your VAR analysis (Table 1).

We perform a quick linearity check to ensure the dataset with all the variables is linearly connected with each other (Table 2).

The variables at levels are not stationary. We know here that for time series analysis, stationarity is a critical requirement when working with VAR models. So, we apply logarithmic differentiation (https://en.wikipedia.org/wiki/Logarithmic_differentiation) log(data).diff() to stationarize the dataset as displayed in Table 3.

Now that we have the stationary dataset with all three variables (Real GDP Growth Rate, CPI, and Government Spending), we can proceed with the VAR

**Table 1** Data ingestion and ensure clean data

```
start = datetime.datetime(1970, 1, 1)

end = datetime.datetime(2024, 1, 1)


gdp_growth = web.DataReader('GDPC1', 'fred', start, end)
cpi = web.DataReader('CPIAUCSL', 'fred', start, end)
govt_spending = web.DataReader('FGEXPND', 'fred', start, end)


data = pd.concat([gdp_growth, cpi, govt_spending], axis=1)
data.columns = ['Real GDP Growth Rate', 'CPI', 'Government Spending']
data.dropna(inplace=True)
data.plot(figsize=(10, 5))
plt.grid()
plt.show()
```

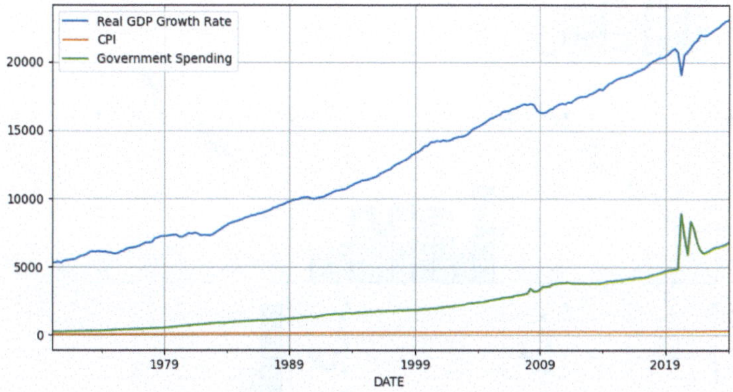


analysis. The first step is the lag order selection. Using information criteria AIC (Akaike Information Criterion), BIC (Bayesian Information Criterion), or HQIC (Hannan-Quinn Information Criterion), we will obtain the optimal number of lags to include in the model. Table 4 shows information criteria-based order selection.

Here the lag order as per AIC is 4. To derive the Vector Auto Regression (VAR) equations for the given variables (Real GDP Growth Rate, CPI, and Government Spending) with 4 lags, let us write the equations in their standard form $Y_t = c + \beta_1 Y_{t-1} + \beta_2 Y_{t-1} + \beta_3 Y_{t-3} + \beta_4 Y_{t-4} + \varepsilon_t$, where $Y_t$ is the vector of variables at time $t$ [$\text{RealGDPGrowthRate}_t$, $\text{CPI}_t$, $\text{GovernmentSpending}_t$], $c$ is a vector of constants , $A_i (i = 1, 2, 3, )$ are the coefficient matrices for the lag terms, and $\varepsilon_t$ is the vector of error terms at time $t$.

**Table 2** Linearity check: ensure linear relationship between pairs of the series

```
sns.pairplot(data)
plt.show()

correlation_matrix = data.corr()
mask = np.triu(np.ones_like(correlation_matrix, dtype=bool))
plt.figure(figsize=(10, 6))
sns.heatmap(correlation_matrix, mask=mask, annot=True, fmt='.2f',
        vmin=-1, vmax=1, center=0, linewidths=0.5)

plt.title('Correlation Matrix (Lower Triangle)')
plt.show()
```

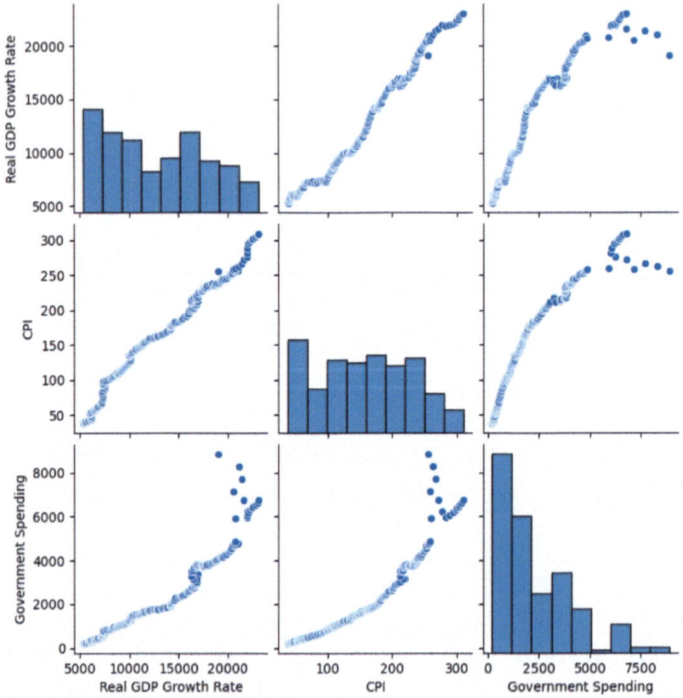


Now each variable is regressed on the lags of all variables in the system. So, with 4 lags, the equations are as follows:

$$Y_{1,t} = c_1 + \sum_{i=1}^{4} \beta_{11}^{(i)} Y_{1,t-i} + \sum_{i=1}^{4} \beta_{12}^{(i)} Y_{2,t-i} + \sum_{i=1}^{4} \beta_{13}^{(i)} Y_{3,t-i} + \varepsilon_{1,t}$$

$$Y_{2,t} = c_2 + \sum_{i=1}^{4} \beta_{21}^{(i)} Y_{1,t-i} + \sum_{i=1}^{4} \beta_{22}^{(i)} Y_{2,t-i} + \sum_{i=1}^{4} \beta_{23}^{(i)} Y_{3,t-i} + \varepsilon_{2,t}$$

**Table 3** Data stationarize and ADF test to ensure stationarity

```
data = np.log(data).diff().dropna()

def adf_test(data_df):
    test_stat, p_val = [], []
    cv_1pct, cv_5pct, cv_10pct = [], [], []
    for c in data_df.columns:
        adf_res = adfuller(data_df[c].dropna())
        test_stat.append(adf_res[0])
        p_val.append(adf_res[1])
        cv_1pct.append(adf_res[4]['1%'])
        cv_5pct.append(adf_res[4]['5%'])
        cv_10pct.append(adf_res[4]['10%'])
    adf_res_df = pd.DataFrame({'Test statistic': test_stat,
                    'p-value': p_val,
                    'Critical value - 1%': cv_1pct,
                    'Critical value - 5%': cv_5pct,
                    'Critical value - 10%': cv_10pct},
                   index=data_df.columns).T

    adf_res_df = adf_res_df.round(4)
    table = tabulate(adf_res_df, headers='keys', tablefmt='fancy_grid')
    return table

table_output = adf_test(data)
print(table_output)
```

| | Real GDP Growth Rate | CPI | Government Spending |
|---|---|---|---|
| Test statistic | -14.7186 | -3.4626 | -6.459 |
| p-value | 0 | 0.009 | 0 |
| Critical value - 1% | -3.4611 | -3.4614 | -3.4622 |
| Critical value - 5% | -2.8751 | -2.8752 | -2.8755 |
| Critical value - 10% | -2.574 | -2.5741 | -2.5742 |

$$Y_{3,t} = c_3 + \sum_{i=1}^{4} \beta_{31}^{(i)} Y_{1,t-i} + \sum_{i=1}^{4} \beta_{32}^{(i)} Y_{2,t-i} + \sum_{i=1}^{4} \beta_{33}^{(i)} Y_{3,t-i} + \varepsilon_{3,t}$$

The vectorized form:

$$\begin{pmatrix} Y_{1,t} \\ Y_{2,t} \\ Y_{3,t} \end{pmatrix} = \begin{pmatrix} c_1 \\ c_2 \\ c_3 \end{pmatrix} + \sum_{i=1}^{4} \begin{pmatrix} \beta_{11}^{(i)} & \beta_{12}^{(i)} & \beta_{13}^{(i)} \\ \beta_{21}^{(i)} & \beta_{22}^{(i)} & \beta_{23}^{(i)} \\ \beta_{31}^{(i)} & \beta_{32}^{(i)} & \beta_{33}^{(i)} \end{pmatrix} \begin{pmatrix} Y_{1,t-i} \\ Y_{2,t-i} \\ Y_{3,t-i} \end{pmatrix} + \begin{pmatrix} \varepsilon_{1,t} \\ \varepsilon_{2,t} \\ \varepsilon_{3,t} \end{pmatrix}$$

Here, to estimate these equations, we would fit a VAR model. Before modeling let us explore the cointegration. Cointegration helps to find out the statistical connection between two or more time series. When two or more time series are

**Table 4** Information criteria-based lag order selection

```
model = VAR(data)
lag_order = model.select_order(maxlags=12)

print(lag_order.summary())
```

```
VAR Order Selection (* highlights the minimums)
==================================================
      AIC         BIC         FPE         HQIC
--------------------------------------------------
0     -24.69      -24.64      1.902e-11   -24.67
1     -25.39      -25.20      9.373e-12   -25.31
2     -25.64      -25.30      7.305e-12   -25.50
3     -25.86      -25.37*     5.862e-12   -25.67*
4     -25.87*     -25.24      5.797e-12*  -25.62
5     -25.83      -25.05      6.058e-12   -25.51
6     -25.82      -24.89      6.152e-12   -25.44
7     -25.80      -24.72      6.271e-12   -25.36
8     -25.81      -24.59      6.202e-12   -25.32
9     -25.76      -24.39      6.527e-12   -25.21
10    -25.73      -24.21      6.773e-12   -25.11
11    -25.71      -24.05      6.884e-12   -25.04
12    -25.64      -23.83      7.433e-12   -24.91
--------------------------------------------------
```

cointegrated, they have a long run, statistically significant relationship. Table 5 displays the Johansen cointegration test.

The hypothesis here is $H_0$ (null hypothesis) → There are '*r*' or fewer cointegrating relationships and $H_1$ (alternative hypothesis) → There are more than '*r*' cointegrating relationships.

The first row with $r = 0$ shows the trace statistic (87.2715) > the critical values at all significance levels (90%, 95%, 99%). We reject the null hypothesis ($H_0$: $r =$

**Table 5** Johansen cointegration test

```
johansen_test = coint_johansen(data, det_order=0, k_ar_diff=1)
results_df = pd.DataFrame({
    'Trace Statistic': johansen_test.lr1,
    'Critical Value (90%)': johansen_test.cvt[:, 0],
    'Critical Value (95%)': johansen_test.cvt[:, 1],
    'Critical Value (99%)': johansen_test.cvt[:, 2]
}, index=['r = 0', 'r = 1', 'r = 2'])

print(tabulate(results_df, headers='keys', tablefmt='fancy_grid'))
```

| | Trace Statistic | Critical Value (90%) | Critical Value (95%) | Critical Value (99%) |
|---|---|---|---|---|
| r = 0 | 87.2715 | 27.0669 | 29.7961 | 35.4628 |
| r = 1 | 42.4414 | 13.4294 | 15.4943 | 19.9349 |
| r = 2 | 7.0491 | 2.7055 | 3.8415 | 6.6349 |

**Table 6** VAR model

```
model = VAR(data).fit(lag_order.aic)
print(model.summary())
```

```
Correlation matrix of residuals
                         Real GDP Growth Rate       CPI  Government Spending
Real GDP Growth Rate                 1.000000  0.127277            -0.567028
CPI                                  0.127277  1.000000            -0.143104
Government Spending                 -0.567028 -0.143104             1.000000
```

0). This means there is at least one cointegrating relationship, indicating that the variables are not all independently moving. The second row with $r = 1$, the trace statistic (42.4414) > the critical values at all significant levels. We reject the null hypothesis ($H_0$: $r = 1$). This means there are at least two cointegrating relationships. The third row with $r = 2$, the trace statistic (7.0491) > the critical values at all significance levels. While there is some evidence to suggest the presence of a third cointegrating relationship, it is not as strong as the evidence for the first two. In such cases, it is advisable to consider the economic context and theory behind the variables to assess the plausibility of a third cointegrating relationship.

Based on the trace statistics and critical values, there is statistically strong evidence to suggest the presence of at least two cointegrating relationships among the variables in the data. This implies a long-term equilibrium relationship between them.

Now we can directly put the data in the VAR module for modeling purposes as displayed in Table 6.

The correlation matrix of residuals offers valuable information about the relationships between variables that the VAR model might not fully explain. It is important to consider these correlations when interpreting the results and to explore and enhance the model's adequacy and economic interpretation.

In the study's context, the Real GDP Growth Rate and CPI show positive correlation which suggests a potential shock or omitted variable influencing both. This could be related to aggregate demand, supply-side factors, or other macroeconomic forces. The Real GDP Growth Rate and Government Spending show strong negative correlation which is likely reflecting counter-cyclical fiscal policy. This is an important economic relationship that the model should ideally capture accurately. CPI and Government Spending show a weak negative correlation which might suggest a subtle interplay between inflation and government spending.

```
model.plot()
plt.show()
```

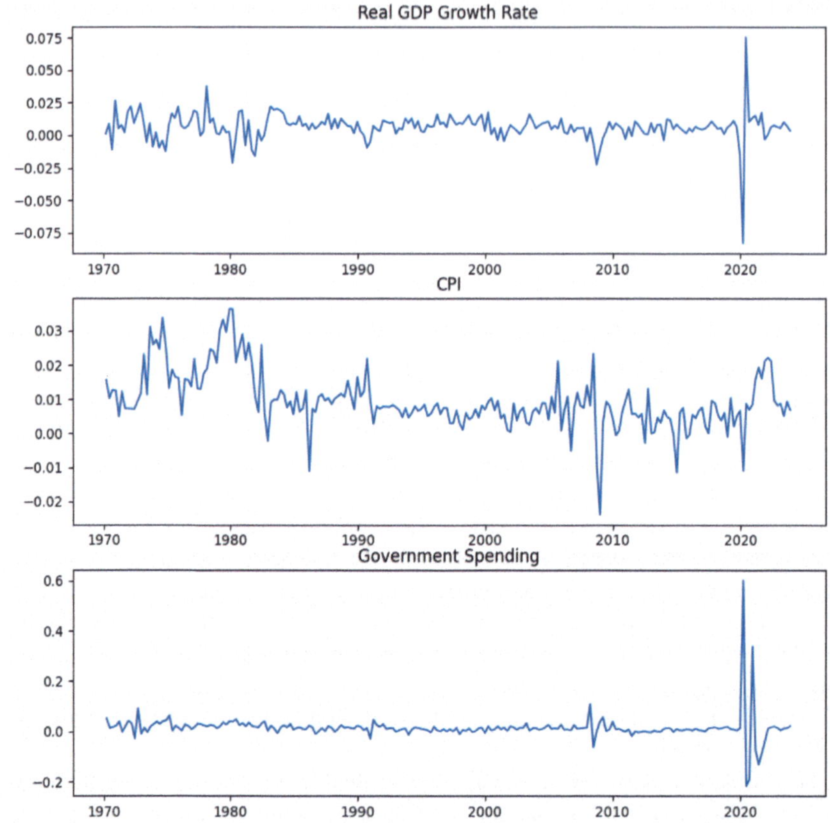


Residuals are also available for analysis. Table 7 displays the ACF of the residuals. We can examine these plots in the cross-correlation matrix.

Dashed lines are the confidence interval bounds, typically at a 95% confidence level ($\pm 2\sqrt{T}$, where $T$ is the sample size). The plots along the diagonal are the individual ACFs for each model's residuals. We also see the cross-correlation plots of each set of residuals. Ideally, these would also resemble white noise at every lag, including lag 0; however, we do see remaining cross-correlations. If most bars (autocorrelation coefficients) fall within the bounds, this suggests that the residuals are approximately white noise, meaning that they have no significant autocorrelation and are random. If any bars are significantly outside the bounds (which is the case here), it implies that there is still autocorrelation in the residuals, which violates the assumption of white noise. Here, we can see that the model is not fully capturing the dynamics of the data.

We can also plot the forecasted values by the model as displayed in Table 8.

**Table 7** Residuals analysis

```
model.plot_acorr()
plt.show()
```

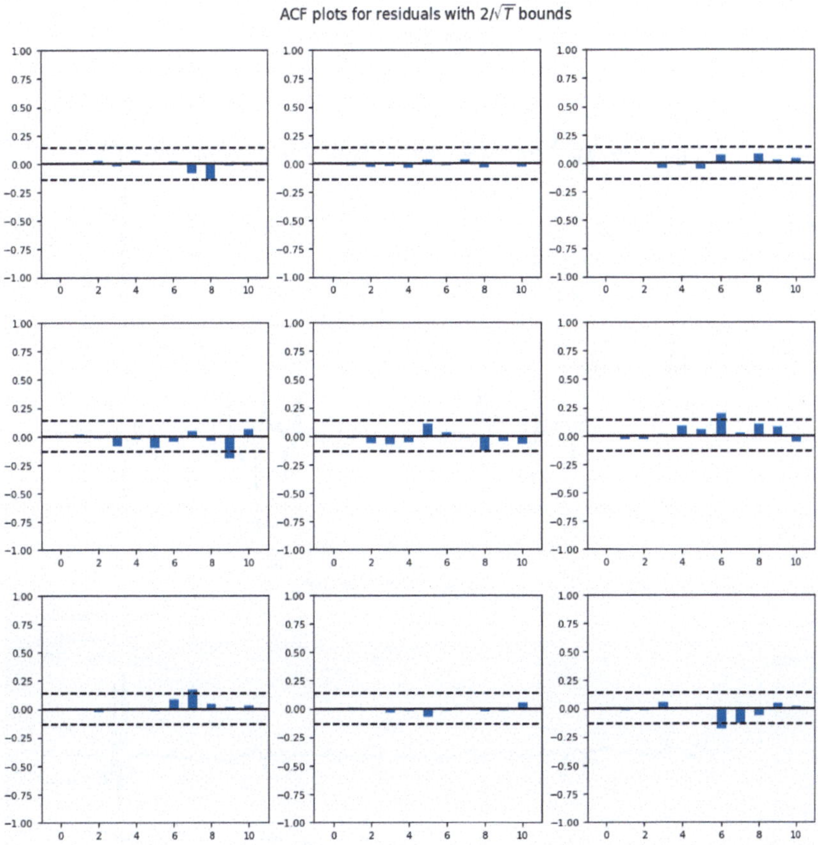


Here, the model's output is displayed for each variable. We can see that the lags we have determined are good and the lines for the predicted values for the next 12 steps are moving in a steady manner (Table 9).

CPI → Real GDP Growth Rate ($p = 0.0022 < 0.05$), so CPI Granger-causes Real GDP Growth Rate. This suggests that past values of CPI have predictive power for future changes in GDP growth. Government Spending → Real GDP Growth Rate ($p = 0.0000 < 0.05$), so Government Spending Granger-causes Real GDP Growth Rate. Government spending has strong predictive power for future GDP growth. Real GDP Growth Rate → CPI ($p = 0.0571 > 0.05$), so we do not reject the null hypothesis. Real GDP Growth Rate does not Granger-cause CPI at a 5% significance level. There is no significant predictive relationship from GDP growth to CPI in this case. Government Spending → CPI ($p = 0.0653 > 0.05$), so

**Table 8** Forecasted values

```
model.plot_forecast(12)
plt.show()
print(model.forecast(data.values[-lag_order:], 5))
```

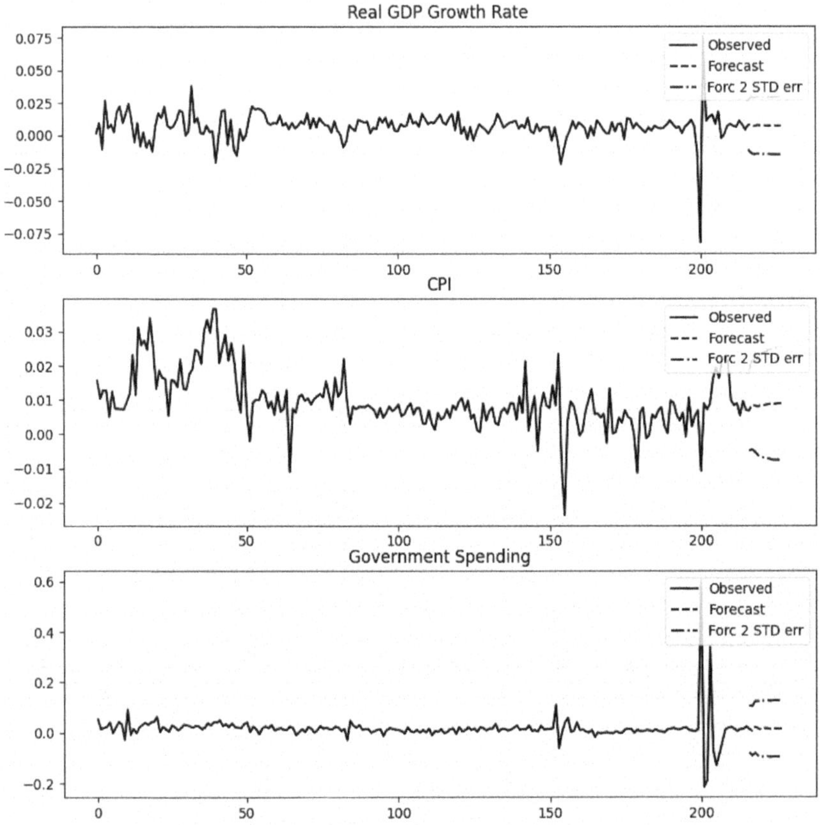


```
[[0.00747993 0.00668422 0.01344105]
 [0.00770168 0.00832798 0.00634206]
 [0.00664256 0.00816319 0.02104117]
 [0.00725709 0.00788354 0.01534075]
 [0.00715148 0.00833039 0.00992566]]
```

Government Spending does not Granger-cause CPI at a 5% level. The relationship might be weak, but it is not statistically significant.

Real GDP Growth Rate → Government Spending ($p = 0.0000 < 0.05$), so Real GDP Growth Rate Granger-causes Government Spending. Past values of GDP growth can predict future changes in government spending. CPI → Government Spending ($p = 0.1134 > 0.05$), so CPI does not Granger-cause Government

**Table 9** Granger causality analysis

```
p = lag_order
def granger_causation_matrix(train, variables, p, test = 'ssr_chi2test', verbose=False):

    df = pd.DataFrame(np.zeros((len(variables), len(variables))), columns=variables, index=variables)
    for c in df.columns:
        for r in df.index:
            test_result = grangercausalitytests(train[[r, c]], p)
            p_values = [round(test_result[i+1][0][test][1],4) for i in range(p)]
            if verbose: print(f'Y = {r}, X = {c}, P Values = {p_values}')
            min_p_value = np.min(p_values)
            df.loc[r, c] = min_p_value
    df.columns = [var + '_x' for var in variables]
    df.index = [var + '_y' for var in variables]
    return df

granger_causation_matrix(data, data.columns, p)
```

| | Real GDP Growth Rate_x | CPI_x | Government Spending_x |
|---|---|---|---|
| **Real GDP Growth Rate_y** | 1.0000 | 0.0022 | 0.0000 |
| **CPI_y** | 0.0571 | 1.0000 | 0.0653 |
| **Government Spending_y** | 0.0000 | 0.1134 | 1.0000 |

Spending. No significant predictive relationship is found from CPI to government spending.

The relationships suggest a feedback loop where government spending influences GDP growth, which in turn influences government spending. CPI also plays a role in predicting GDP growth, reflecting potential inflationary dynamics. However, there is no statistical evidence that GDP growth or government spending significantly predicts CPI, possibly indicating other determinants of inflation.

Point to be noted here that Granger causality does not imply true causality. It only suggests a predictive relationship. These results are based on the specific lag order we used in the test. Changing the lag order might affect the results. We must interpret the results in the context of economic theory and the research question.

Further to the above details, a covariance matrix of the residuals offers valuable insights into the relationships between the errors. By examining the covariance matrix, you can assess the quality of your VAR model. High variances or unexpected covariances might suggest potential issues with the model's assumptions or specification.

| | Real GDP Growth Rate | CPI | Government Spending |
|---|---|---|---|
| **Real GDP Growth Rate** | 0.000087 | 0.000007 | -0.000244 |
| **CPI** | 0.000007 | 0.000033 | -0.000038 |
| **Government Spending** | -0.000244 | -0.000038 | 0.002130 |

Considering the variances of the diagonal elements in the matrix where Real GDP Growth Rate has a variance of 0.000087. This shows that the model's errors in predicting real GDP growth rate have a relatively small spread. The CPI has a variance of 0.000033, suggesting a smaller spread of errors compared to real GDP growth rate. The Government Spending has a variance of 0.002130, which is significantly larger than the variances of the other two variables. This implies that the model's predictions for government spending are less precise and have a wider range of errors.

Considering the off-diagonal elements, the Real GDP Growth Rate and CPI have a small positive covariance (0.000007) which suggests a weak positive relationship between the errors in predicting these two variables. When the model overestimates Real GDP Growth Rate, it might slightly overestimate CPI as well and vice versa. The Real GDP Growth Rate and Government Spending have a negative covariance (−0.000244) which writes down a negative relationship between the errors in predicting these variables. When the model overestimates Real GDP Growth Rate, it tends to underestimate government spending and vice versa. The CPI & Government Spending has a negative covariance (−0.000038) which suggests a negative relationship between the errors in predicting these variables, like the relationship between Real GDP Growth Rate and Government Spending.

Overall, we can infer that from this matrix that the model's predictions For Government Spending have the largest variance, indicating less precision in this area. There are also weak relationships between the errors in predicting the different variables, with negative covariances suggesting that overestimating one variable might lead to underestimating another.

## 1.1 Structural VAR Analysis

This structural analysis is widely used in macroeconomics to evaluate economic theories and investigate how macroeconomic shocks (such as financial and monetary shocks) are transmitted. The causal impacts of unanticipated shocks (perturbations) to a particular variable on the many variables in the model are summarized, and assumptions are made about the causal structure of the dataset. Two popular techniques for calculating the effects of these causal impacts are Forecast Error Variance Decompositions (FEVD) and Impulse Response Functions (IRF).

### 1.1.1 Impulse Response Functions (IRFs)

The coefficients of a VAR model are often difficult to interpret. Individual coefficient estimates only offer a limited amount of information on how the system will respond to a shock because every variable in a VAR model depends on every other variable. Impulse responses are used to better understand the dynamic behavior of the model. The covariance matrix is used in impulse response analysis to estimate the impact of a shock to one variable on other variables in the system.

Mathematically, $\Phi_i$ captures the response of endogenous variables to shocks over time. It offers a way to understand how unexpected changes (impulses) in one variable spread through the system, affecting other variables over subsequent periods.

$$\Phi_i = \sum_{j=1}^{i} \Phi_{i-j} A_j, \quad i = 1, 2, \ldots$$

where

- $\Phi_0 = I_K$ represents the immediate (impact) response of each variable to a unit shock, which is untransformed initially.
- $A_j = 0$ for $j > p$: Beyond the lag order $p$, matrices $A_j$ are zero, meaning that responses do not depend on periods further than $p$ lags back. Responses are calculated only up to the maximum lag order, meaning that after $p$ periods, the effect of the shock will gradually decay if the model is stable.
- $i$ represents the period after the shock (i.e., $i = 1$ is the immediate period after the shock, $i = 2$ is two periods after, and so on). For each period $i$, $\Phi_i$ is calculated as a weighted sum of previous responses, where the weight is given by the lag coefficient matrices $A_j$.

We must know here that Impulse Responses cannot assess contemporaneous (same period) reactions because they rely solely on lagged coefficient matrices ($A_j$) from the model. To address contemporaneous effects, we can consider a Structural VAR (SVAR) model, where constraints can be placed on contemporaneous relationships among variables using identification restrictions.

Going back to Impulse Responses, they are computed using the MA($\infty$) representation of the VAR($p$) process. We apply orthogonal impulse responses to separate these shocks to observe the isolated effect of each variable on the others. The basic idea is to decompose the variance–covariance matrix and for this the orthogonalization is done using the Cholesky decomposition of the estimated error covariance matrix ($\widehat{\Sigma}_\epsilon$) and hence interpretations may change depending on variable ordering. IRFs trace out the time path of the effects of an exogenous shock to one (or more) of the endogenous variables on some or all the other variables in a VAR system.

Considering $Y_{1,t}, Y_{2,t}, Y_{3,t}$ are the time series corresponding to Real GDP Growth Rate, Government Spend and Consumer price index, respectively. The moving average representation of the system is:

$$\begin{bmatrix} Y_{1,t} \\ Y_{2,t} \\ Y_{3,t} \end{bmatrix} = \begin{bmatrix} \alpha_1 \\ \alpha_2 \\ \alpha_3 \end{bmatrix} + \sum_{i=0}^{\infty} \begin{bmatrix} \beta_{1,1} & \beta_{1,2} & \beta_{1,3} \\ \beta_{2,1} & \beta_{2,2} & \beta_{2,3} \\ \beta_{3,1} & \beta_{3,2} & \beta_{3,3} \end{bmatrix} \begin{bmatrix} \alpha_{1,t-i} \\ \alpha_{2,t-i} \\ \alpha_{3,t-i} \end{bmatrix}$$

Suppose $\alpha_1$ increases by a value of one standard deviation. This shock not only will change $Y_1$ in the current as well as the future periods, will also have an impact on $Y_2$ and $Y_3$. Likewise, if $\alpha_2$ equation increases by a value of one standard deviation, the shock will change $Y_2$ in the current as well as the future periods and will also have an impact on $Y_1$ and $Y_3$ and so on.

The VAR model captures complex interdependencies between the variables. To visualize the impact of changes in one variable on the others at different horizons, we obtain the impulse responses for the estimated model displayed in Table 10. This time we select a VAR model with one lag of each variable and arbitrarily select to 12. By default, it is orthogonalization false. Non-orthogonalized IRFs reflect the real-world interdependencies between variables, where shocks may simultaneously affect multiple variables. This provides a more realistic scenario for cumulative effects; however, the interpretation is not straightforward due to contemporaneous correlations.

A shock to "Real GDP Growth Rate" has a strong initial effect that gradually diminishes. "CPI" and "Government Spending" shocks also decay but at different rates. The off-diagonal plots illustrate how a shock to one variable affects another. A shock to "Government Spending" has noticeable effects on "Real GDP Growth Rate" and "CPI". The "Real GDP Growth Rate" affects the CPI more strongly in the initial periods than later.

Shocks to "Real GDP Growth Rate" appear to have transitory effects on itself and other variables. "CPI" seems to have persistent responses when shocked, but its impact on other variables diminishes quickly. "Government Spending" has a more immediate and pronounced impact on both "Real GDP Growth Rate" and "CPI". The responses generally decay to zero, showing that the system is stable, and shocks do not have permanent effects.

Table 11 displays orthogonalized IRFs which provide insights into the dynamic relationships between Real GDP Growth, CPI, and Government Spending. The interpretation of these responses often depends on economic theory and the specific context of the analysis. The order in which we list the variables in the VAR model matters for orthogonalized IRFs. The earlier a variable appears in the order, the more it is assumed to influence the variables that come after it but less likely to be influenced by them.

Real GDP Growth Rate→ Real GDP Growth Rate where a positive shock to GDP growth initially leads to a significant increase in GDP growth, which diminishes over time. The initial response is strong, showing persistence in the growth dynamics, with some oscillations before stabilizing.

**Table 10** IRFs—Unit shocks to the non-orthogonalized residuals plot

```
irf = model.irf(10)
irf.plot()
plt.show()
```

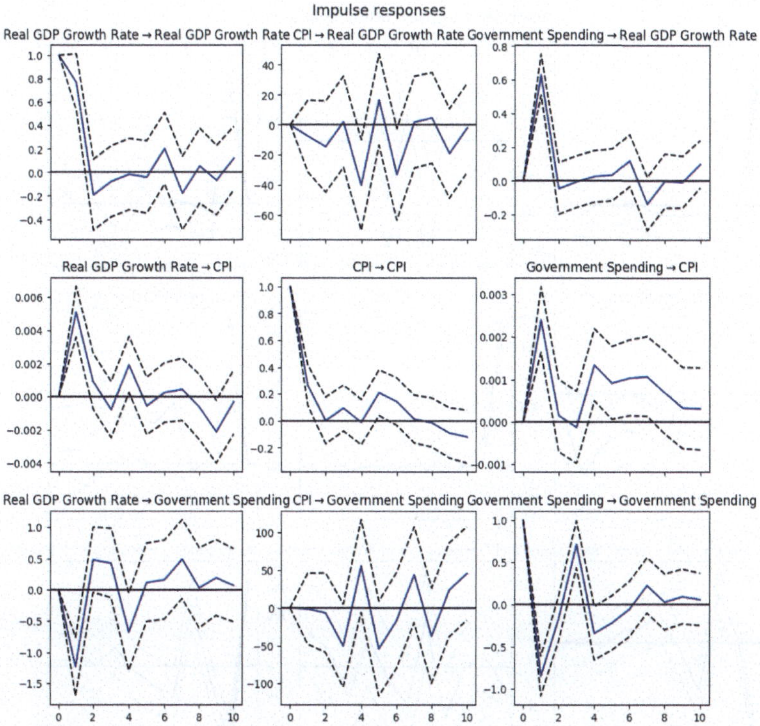


CPI → CPI where CPI (Consumer Price Index) shows a strong immediate response to its own shocks. The response decays relatively quickly, suggesting that CPI shocks are transitory in nature.

Government Spending → Real GDP Growth Rate where government spending positively affects GDP growth initially. The response stabilizes after a few periods, suggesting short-term benefits from fiscal stimulus.

Real GDP Growth Rate → CPI where the GDP growth shocks seem to lower CPI initially, potentially showing a supply-side response where higher growth mitigates inflationary pressures. However, the effect diminishes over time.

Government Spending → CPI (Right subplot in the second row) where the shocks to government spending slightly increase CPI initially, likely due to demand-side inflationary pressures. The effect decays over time, showing temporary inflationary effects.

CPI → Government Spending where CPI shocks appear to reduce government spending initially, possibly reflecting policy adjustments to inflation. This relationship stabilizes after a few periods.

**Table 11** Unit shocks to the orthogonalized residuals

```
irf.plot(orth = True)
plt.show()
```

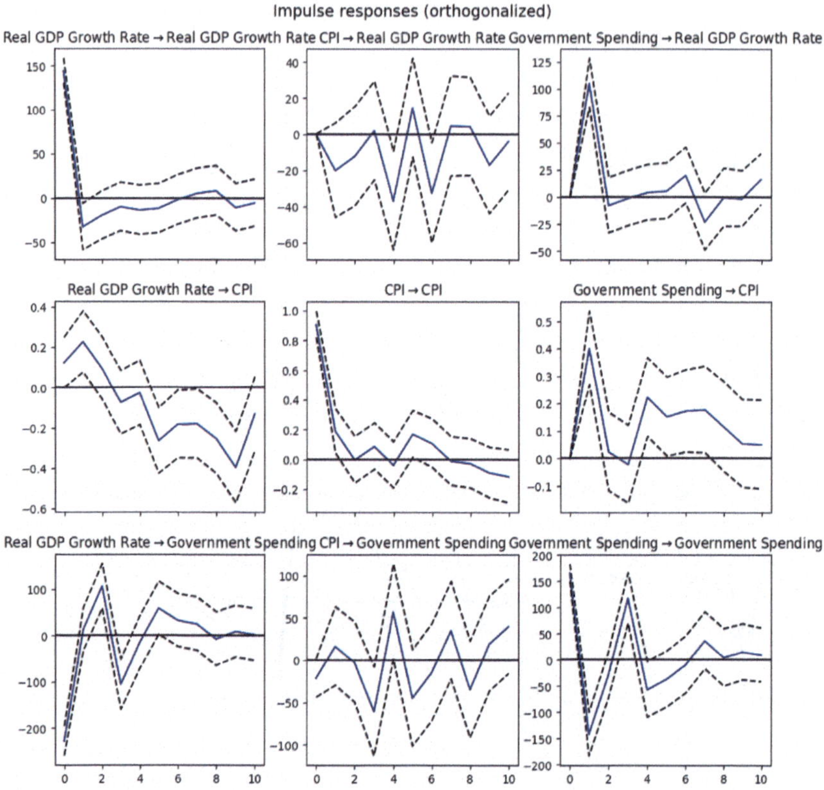


Government Spending → Government Spending where the shocks to government spending have a persistent self-effect with oscillations, reflecting cyclical fiscal patterns.

Wide confidence intervals show higher uncertainty in the responses, especially in off-diagonal subplots (e.g., CPI → Government Spending or Real GDP Growth Rate → CPI). Responses crossing the zero line within the confidence intervals may not be statistically significant.

### 1.1.2 Forecast Error Variance Decomposition (FEVD)

FEVD indicates the amount of information each variable contributes to the other variables in the autoregression. While IRF trace the effects of a shock to one endogenous variable on to the other variables, variance decomposition separates the variation in an endogenous variable into the component shocks. This can reveal how much of a variable's forecast error variance is due to shocks in other variables.

Table 12 illustrates the FEVD for three economic indicators: Real GDP Growth Rate, CPI, and Government Spending, over a 10-period horizon.

The black portion (Real GDP Growth Rate) dominates throughout the 12-period horizon, showing that its own shocks explain most of its variance. Contributions from CPI (dark gray) and Government Spending (light gray) slightly increase but remain relatively small over time. Initially, most of the variance in CPI is explained by itself (dark gray). Over time, the contributions of Real GDP Growth Rate (black) and Government Spending (light gray) gradually increase, suggesting that these factors have a growing influence on CPI fluctuations. The variance in Government Spending is largely self-explanatory (light gray) at all horizons.

**Table 12** FEVD estimation

```
fevd = model.fevd(12)
fevd.plot()
fevd.summary()
```

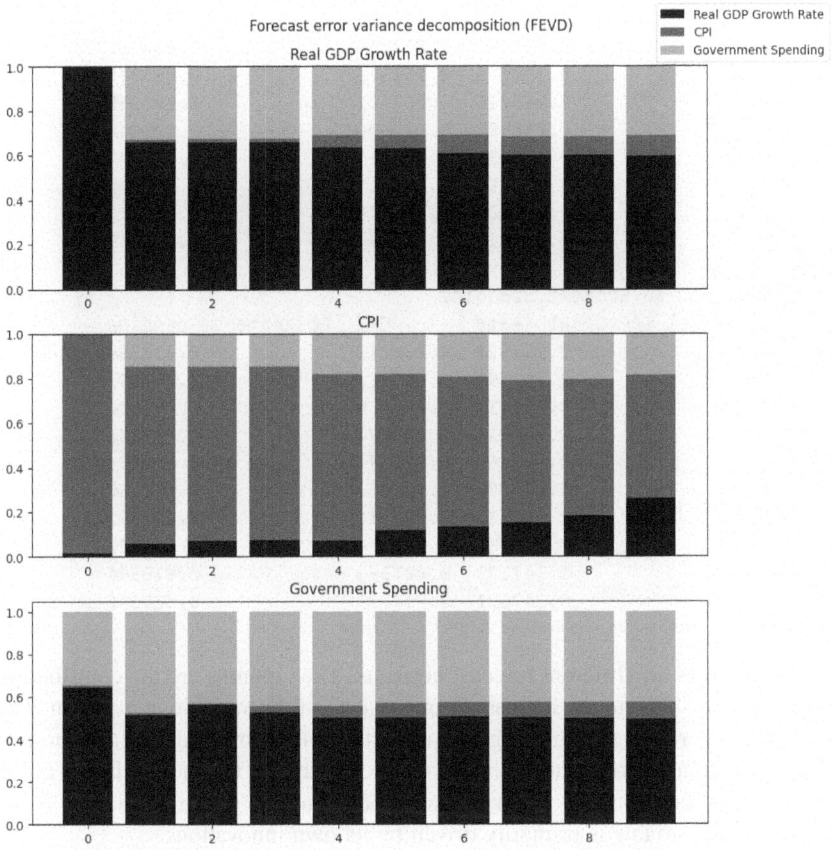

Contributions from Real GDP Growth Rate (black) and CPI (dark gray) remain relatively small but appear stable over the forecast horizon.

```
FEVD for Real GDP Growth Rate
     Real GDP Growth Rate         CPI  Government Spending
0                1.000000  0.000000             0.000000
1                0.759553  0.027591             0.212856
2                0.756597  0.030633             0.212770
3                0.749131  0.034393             0.216476
4                0.740508  0.045260             0.214231
5                0.740724  0.045326             0.213950
6                0.740392  0.045915             0.213693
7                0.739664  0.046522             0.213814
8                0.738937  0.046594             0.214469
9                0.738695  0.046656             0.214648

FEVD for CPI
     Real GDP Growth Rate         CPI  Government Spending
0                0.016200  0.983800             0.000000
1                0.028424  0.916090             0.055487
2                0.037447  0.897866             0.064687
3                0.034648  0.901378             0.063975
4                0.049615  0.852131             0.098255
5                0.050981  0.827406             0.121614
6                0.057898  0.818856             0.123247
7                0.057452  0.801317             0.141231
8                0.057004  0.793370             0.149626
9                0.058816  0.789344             0.151839

FEVD for Government Spending
     Real GDP Growth Rate         CPI  Government Spending
0                0.321521  0.005115             0.673364
1                0.291559  0.005438             0.703003
2                0.330439  0.006435             0.663126
3                0.347038  0.007074             0.645888
4                0.342162  0.022174             0.635664
5                0.347272  0.022771             0.629957
6                0.346512  0.022996             0.630492
7                0.346466  0.026514             0.627021
8                0.347103  0.027393             0.625504
9                0.347291  0.027373             0.625336
```

Here the rows are different forecast horizons. The columns are the contribution of each type of shock to the forecast error variance of the variable in question. The values are in percentages, showing the proportion of the movements in a variable that can be explained by its own shocks versus the shocks to other variables in the model. A high percentage consistently where the variable's own shocks are listed shows that the variable is primarily driven by its own innovations.

FEVD for RealGDPGrowthRate where at period 0, all the forecast error variance of RealGDPGrowthRate is due to its own shocks. As we move to subsequent periods (1, 2, 3, …), the forecast error variance for RealGDPGrowthRate is mostly explained by its own shocks (as shown by the high percentages in the RealGDPGrowthRate column), but the influence of shocks to CPI gradually reduces while GovernmentSpending gradually increases.

FEVD for CPI where at period 0, all the forecast error variance of CPI is due to its own shocks. In the following periods, the variance of CPI is predominantly explained by its own shocks (high percentages in the CPI column). However, the effect of shocks to RealGDPGrowthRate reduces while GovernmentSpending increases over time but remains relatively small compared to the shocks to CPI itself.

Likewise, FEVD for GovernmentSpending at period 0, all the forecast error variance of GovernmentSpending is due to its own shocks. Shocks to GovernmentSpending account for most of the forecast error variance of GovernmentSpending throughout all periods. The influence of shocks to RealGDPGrowthRate and CPI increases where RealGDPGrowthRate is quite large.

If we change the ordering of the variables, it influences the impulse responses and variance decompositions, and therefore when the theory does not suggest an obvious ordering of the series, some sensitivity analysis should be undertaken. Table 13 shows how to test the sensitivity by ordering the variables to a different way.

So, we see here that IRF is a powerful mechanism for interpreting the dynamic interactions within a VAR framework. It allows researchers and policymakers to derive meaningful insights from complex time series relationships. By carefully considering the implications of orthogonalization and variable ordering, practitioners can utilize IRFs to enhance their understanding of economic and financial systems. Because of the sensitivity to ordering, it is advisable to test different orderings in the Cholesky decomposition to understand how robust the results are. If the impulse responses change significantly with different orderings, it suggests that the contemporaneous relationships between variables are not fully captured by the chosen ordering. In such cases, further structural analysis may be necessary.

To this end, the choice of ordering in the Cholesky decomposition affects the interpretation of orthogonal impulse responses, and it is best to explore multiple orderings to ensure that the analysis remains stable and interpretable across different setups.

Finally, we can go for forecast depends on the requirement as displayed in Table 14.

## 2 Error Correction Model (ECM)

For VECM, the series should be used in their levels, not after differencing, as the VECM is designed for variables that are cointegrated and non-stationary (typically integrated of order 1, or I(1).

**Table 13** FEVD with reverse order variables

```
model = VAR(data[['Government Spending', 'CPI', 'Real GDP Growth Rate']]).fit(maxlags=lag_order)
fevd = model.fevd(12)
fevd.plot()
plt.show()
```

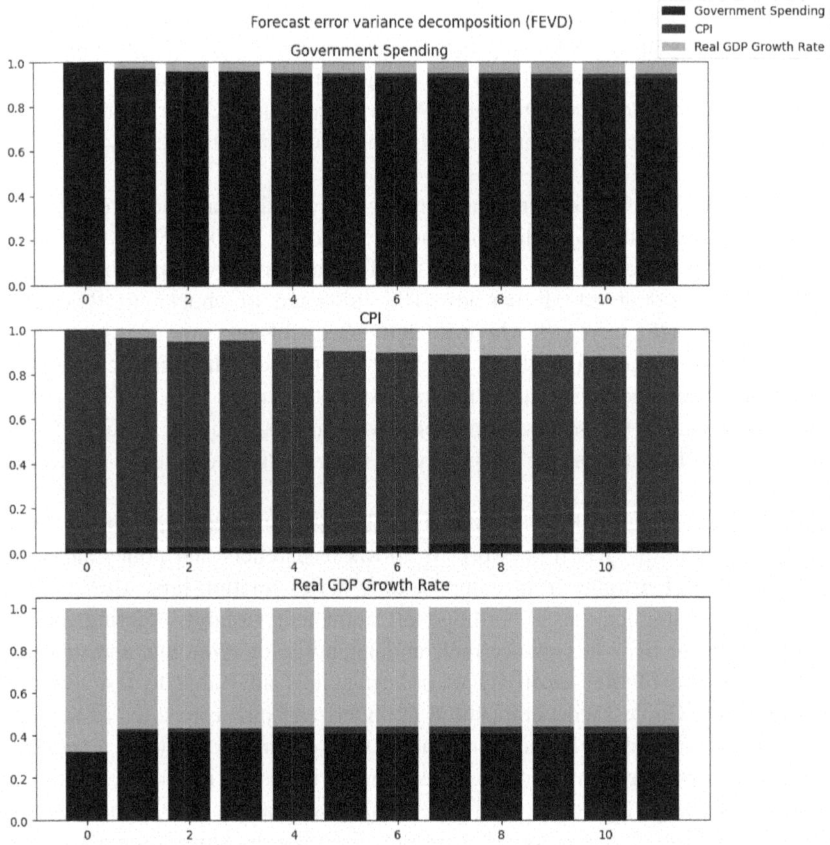


1. First, test if the non-stationary series are cointegrated. If cointegration exists, it means there is a long-term relationship among the variables despite them being individually non-stationary.
2. Apply VECM which incorporates both the long-term equilibrium relationship (cointegration term) and short-term dynamics. The model works by including an error correction term, which brings the variables back to equilibrium after short-term deviations.

**Table 14** Forecast and inverse logdiff() back to the original shape

```
forecast_values = model.forecast(data_diff.values[-lag_order.aic:], 5)
last_observed_values = data.values[-1]
inversed_forecast = np.zeros_like(forecast_values)

for i in range(forecast_values.shape[1]):
    cumulative_sum = np.cumsum(forecast_values[:, i])
    inversed_log_values = np.log(last_observed_values[i]) + cumulative_sum
    inversed_forecast[:, i] = np.exp(inversed_log_values)

forecast_df = pd.DataFrame(inversed_forecast, columns=data.columns)
print(forecast_df)
```

```
   Real GDP Growth Rate         CPI  Government Spending
0          23226.630403  311.761936          6864.475429
1          23406.205004  314.369125          6908.148689
2          23562.199576  316.945883          7055.044223
3          23733.814596  319.454413          7164.108313
4          23904.154892  322.126708          7235.570880
```

3. While we do not difference the variables prior to applying the VECM, the model itself accounts for short-term adjustments by using differenced terms of the variables in the equations, allowing it to capture both the short-term dynamics and the long-term equilibrium relationship.

Table 15 implements ECM. Here we have used Consumer Price Index (CPI), Personal Consumption Expenditure (PCE), and Disposable Personal Income (DPI) datasets. The use case can be written as:

> We deal with economic variables like CPI (Consumer Price Index), PCE (Personal Consumption Expenditures), and DPI (Disposable Personal Income). We have found evidence of cointegration among these variables, showing a long-run equilibrium relationship. The primary use case for VECM in this scenario is to model and analyze the dynamic relationship between these cointegrated variables, considering both their short-term fluctuations and the long-run equilibrium.

We perform Pearson's linear correlation test to ensure all the series are correlated. Table 16 displays the visual inspection as part of Step 2 to check the correlation among the series. We can see that all the series are moving together in the same direction, showing linear and positive correlation.

We can see all the series are highly correlated, which makes this an ideal case scenario for VAR estimation. Now we move on to check the stationarity using the ADF test. Table 17 implements the unit root test.

All the series have $p$-values > 0.05, and their ADF test statistics are above the critical values at the 5% level. This shows that we do not reject the null hypothesis of a unit root, showing that all series are non-stationary.

Table 18 displays the Autocorrelation Function (ACF) which checks the correlation between time series with a lagged version of itself. The correlation between the observation at the current time and the observations at previous time. The ACF

**Table 15** Data ingestion for error correction model

```
start = datetime.datetime(1990, 1, 1)
end = datetime.datetime(2024, 1, 1)

def get_data(symbol, start, end):
    data = web.DataReader(symbol, 'fred', start, end)
    return data.resample('QE').mean()

cpi = get_data('CPIAUCNS', start, end)
pce = get_data('PCE', start, end)
dpi= get_data('DPI', start, end)

data = pd.concat([cpi, pce, dpi], axis=1)
data.columns = ['CPI', 'PCE', 'DPI']
data = data.dropna()
data.plot()
plt.grid()
plt.show()
```

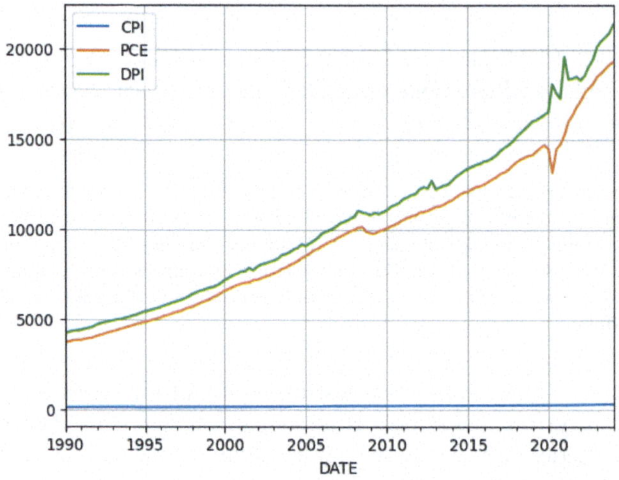


starts a lag 0, which is the correlation of the time series with itself and therefore results in a correlation of 1.

The blue-shaded area in the plot depicts the 95% confidence interval and is an indicator for the significance threshold. We can see that several autocorrelations in the series are non-zero, showing a persistent pattern or structure in the data, meaning that past values have a significant influence on future values.

**Table 16** Series plots to check correlation

```
correlation_matrix = data.corr(method = 'pearson')
print(correlation_matrix)
mask = np.triu(np.ones_like(correlation_matrix, dtype = bool))
plt.figure(figsize = (10, 6))
sns.heatmap(correlation_matrix, mask = mask, annot = True, fmt = '.2f',
        vmin = -1, vmax = 1, center = 0, linewidths = 0.5)
plt.title('Correlation Matrix (Lower Triangle)')
plt.show()
```

```
          CPI       PCE       DPI
CPI  1.000000  0.993804  0.984578
PCE  0.993804  1.000000  0.988981
DPI  0.984578  0.988981  1.000000
```

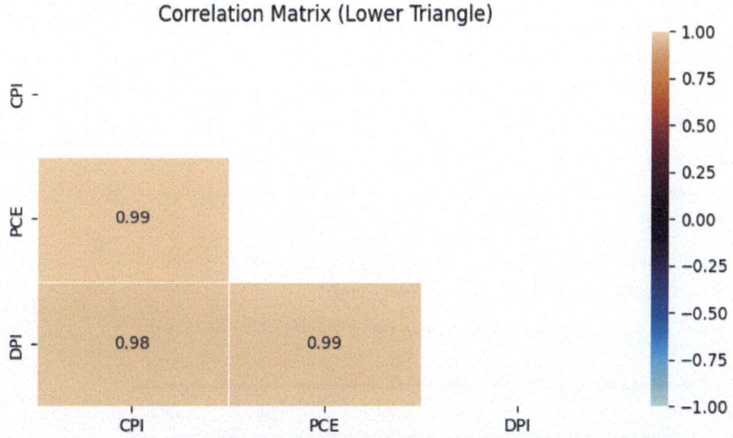


Table 19 performs the Johansen cointegration checks among the series. It tests the null hypothesis that there are at most $r$ cointegrating vectors ($r$ is the rank) against the alternative that there are more.

The first two test scores have $p$-values > 0.05, which means we do not reject the null hypothesis of no cointegration at the 5% significance level. The third test score has a $p$-value < 0.05, which shows we can reject the null hypothesis of no cointegration at the 5% significance level. Thus, based on the third score, there is evidence of cointegration among the variables in the data, meaning that there is a long-term equilibrium relationship between them.

For the first row in the table, the first value (72.26) > critical value at all significance levels (1%, 5%, 10%). Therefore, we reject the null hypothesis of zero cointegration vectors which suggests that there is at least one cointegrating relationship. The second value (32.56) > critical values at all levels. This means we reject the null hypothesis that there is only 1 cointegrating relationship. This further suggests there are at least two cointegrating relationships. The third value

**Table 17** Stationarity check

```
def adf_test(data_df):
    test_stat, p_val = [], []
    cv_1pct, cv_5pct, cv_10pct = [], [], []
    for c in data_df.columns:
        adf_res = adfuller(data_df[c].dropna())
        test_stat.append(adf_res[0])
        p_val.append(adf_res[1])
        cv_1pct.append(adf_res[4]['1%'])
        cv_5pct.append(adf_res[4]['5%'])
        cv_10pct.append(adf_res[4]['10%'])
    adf_res_df = pd.DataFrame({'Test statistic': test_stat,
                               'p-value': p_val,
                               'Critical value - 1%': cv_1pct,
                               'Critical value - 5%': cv_5pct,
                               'Critical value - 10%': cv_10pct},
                              index=data_df.columns).T
    adf_res_df = adf_res_df.round(4)
    return adf_res_df

adf_results = adf_test(data)
table = tabulate(adf_results, headers='keys', tablefmt='fancy_grid')
print(table)
```

| | CPI | PCE | DPI |
|---|---|---|---|
| Test statistic | 1.584 | 3.1915 | 4.8606 |
| p-value | 0.9978 | 1 | 1 |
| Critical value - 1% | -3.4838 | -3.4794 | -3.4821 |
| Critical value - 5% | -2.885 | -2.883 | -2.8842 |
| Critical value - 10% | -2.5793 | -2.5782 | -2.5789 |

($r = 2$) the trace statistic (9.15) > critical value. This means we reject the null hypothesis that there are only 2 cointegrating relationships.

Cointegration indicates a long-term equilibrium relationship between the variables, meaning that they move together in the long run despite short-term fluctuations. Since there are likely two or more cointegrating relationships, a Vector Error Correction Model (VECM) would be proper for modeling.

Here point to be noted is that the cointegration test should be done on the original series. When we differentiate the series, we are removing any potential

**Table 18** Autocorrelation plot

```
num_plots = len(data.columns)
num_rows = (num_plots + 1) // 2
fig, axes = plt.subplots(num_rows, 2, figsize=(15, num_rows * 5))
axes = axes.flatten()

for idx, column in enumerate(data.columns):
  plot_acf(data[column], lags=10, ax=axes[idx])
  axes[idx].set_title(f'ACF of {column}')
axes[idx].set_xlabel('Lags')
  axes[idx].set_ylabel('ACF')

  axes[idx].tick_params(axis='both', which='major')
for ax in axes[num_plots:]:
  ax.set_visible(False)
plt.tight_layout()
plt.show()
```

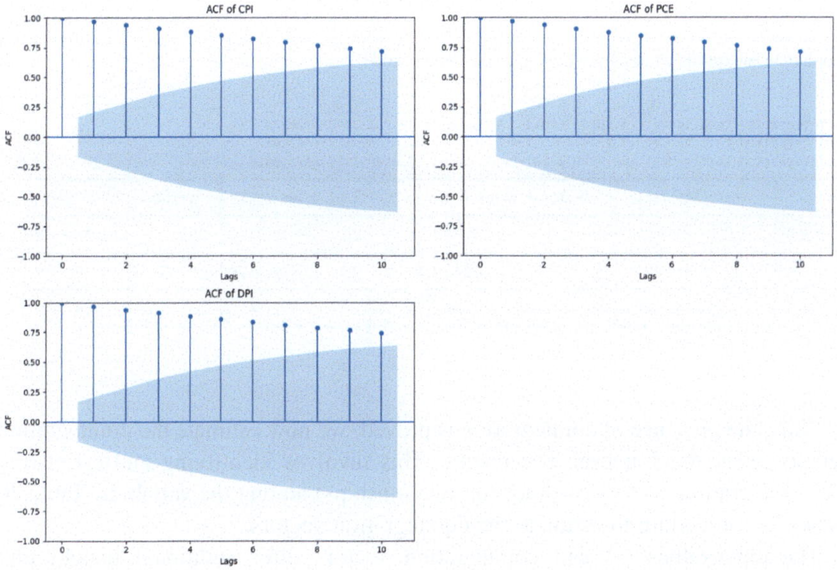


long-term trend, which is precisely what cointegration aims to capture. Table 19 provides trace statistics and critical values for testing the null hypothesis of a specific number of cointegration vectors. This approach gives a formal test result showing how many cointegration relationships are present. Let us check the eigenvalues and cointegration vectors directly, which can be used to understand the nature and strength of these relationships.

**Table 19** Cointegration checks

```
def test_cointegration(series1, series2):
    score, p_value, _ = coint(series1, series2)
    print(f'Cointegration test score: {score}, p-value: {p_value}')

for i in range(len(data.columns)):
    for j in range(i+1, len(data.columns)):
        test_cointegration(data.iloc[:, i], data.iloc[:, j])

johansen_test = coint_johansen(data, det_order=0, k_ar_diff=1)

# Create a DataFrame for the results
results_df = pd.DataFrame({
    'Trace Statistic': johansen_test.lr1,
    'Critical Value (90%)': johansen_test.cvt[:, 0],
    'Critical Value (95%)': johansen_test.cvt[:, 1],
    'Critical Value (99%)': johansen_test.cvt[:, 2]
}, index=['r = 0', 'r = 1', 'r = 2'])

print(tabulate(results_df, headers='keys', tablefmt='fancy_grid'))
```

```
Cointegration test score: -1.522815508125729, p-value: 0.7523397070726376
Cointegration test score: -2.112445090519480 5, p-value: 0.4698635574421082
Cointegration test score: -4.59300207081588, p-value: 0.0008578319888068618
```

| | Trace Statistic | Critical Value (90%) | Critical Value (95%) | Critical Value (99%) |
|---|---|---|---|---|
| r = 0 | 72.2629 | 27.0669 | 29.7961 | 35.4628 |
| r = 1 | 32.5624 | 13.4294 | 15.4943 | 19.9349 |
| r = 2 | 9.15057 | 2.7055 | 3.8415 | 6.6349 |

Since the presence of cointegration is proved, we now estimate the cointegration vectors using the Johansen test results. This involves identifying and estimating the cointegration vectors (or long-run relationships) among the variables. Table 20 shows the procedure to estimate the cointegration vectors.

The eigenvalues ($\lambda$) and cointegration vectors offer additional insight into the long-term relationships among the variables. Eigenvalues are the strength of the cointegrating relationship for each vector. Larger eigenvalues correspond to stronger cointegration. Here, the first eigenvalue (0.254781) shows the strongest cointegration relationship, followed by the second (0.159217) and the third (0.0655358). Cointegration vectors are the coefficients of the linear combination of the variables that form the stationary (cointegrated) series. Each vector corresponds to a cointegrating relationship.

This vector can be interpreted as a long-run equilibrium relationship between CPI, PCE, and DPI. The relationship can be represented as $0.145874 * \text{CPI} +$

**Table 20** Cointegration vectors

```
results_df = pd.DataFrame({
  'Eigenvalues': johansen_test.eig,
  'Cointegration Vector 1': johansen_test.evec[:, 0],
  'Cointegration Vector 2': johansen_test.evec[:, 1],
  'Cointegration Vector 3': johansen_test.evec[:, 2] })
print(tabulate(results_df, headers='keys', tablefmt='fancy_grid'))
```

| | Eigenvalues | Cointegration Vector 1 | Cointegration Vector 2 | Cointegration Vector 3 |
|---|---|---|---|---|
| 0 | 0.254781 | 0.145874 | 0.0990585 | 0.186951 |
| 1 | 0.159217 | -0.00193226 | -0.00347324 | -0.000798268 |
| 2 | 0.0655358 | 2.49454e-05 | 0.00218374 | -0.00109478 |

0.0990585∗ PCE+0.186951∗DPI = stationary series. If we normalize by the coefficient of CPI, we get CPI + 0.678994 ∗ PCE + 1.28125 ∗ DPI = stationary series. This normalized equation shows that a 1 unit increase in CPI is associated with a 0.678994 unit increase in PCE and a 1.28125 unit increase in DPI in the long run, to maintain the equilibrium relationship.

The positive coefficients for CPI, PCE, and DPI suggest that these variables tend to move together in the long run. An increase in one variable is associated with increases in the others and vice versa.

Based on the eigenvalues, there appear to be three potential cointegrating relationships. The cointegrated relationships can be decided in the following way too. Let us find the lag order as shown in Table 21.

In the framework of this example, we follow the AIC and select a lag length of eight. Once the lag order is decided based on AIC (*) in above, we can use the function select_coint_rank which helps us choose the cointegration rank. The rank attribute of the resulting CointRankResults gives us the information about cointegration rank shown in Table 22.

The *r*_0 and *r*_1 columns are the number of cointegration relationships being tested. *r*_0 tests if there are 0 cointegration relationships, *r*_1 test if there is 1 cointegration relationship. The test statistic (45.36) > critical value (29.80), so we reject null hypothesis that there are no cointegration relationships. This suggests that there is evidence for at least one cointegration relationship. The test statistic (22.16) > critical value (15.49), so we reject null hypothesis that there is only one cointegration relationship. This suggests that there is evidence for more than one cointegration relationship. The test statistic (4.59) > critical value (3.84), so we reject null hypothesis. Based on these results, we should fit an ECM with 2 cointegration relationships to capture both short-term dynamics and long-term equilibrium among the variables.

In above we employed $\lambda_{trace}$ statistic; however, we can also employ an alternative the maximum-eigenvalue statistic ($\lambda_{max}$). In contrast to the trace statistic, the

**Table 21** Lag-order selection

```
data.index = pd.to_datetime(data.index)
data = data.asfreq('QE')
lag_order = select_order(data=data, maxlags=10)
print(lag_order.summary())
print(lag_order)
```

```
VECM Order Selection (* highlights the minimums)
==================================================
       AIC         BIC           FPE         HQIC
--------------------------------------------------
0        22.09       22.36     3.922e+09       22.20
1        21.90       22.37     3.248e+09       22.09
2        21.39       22.07     1.958e+09       21.67
3        20.48      21.36*     7.877e+08       20.84
4        20.38       21.46     7.094e+08      20.81*
5        20.36       21.64     6.992e+08       20.88
6        20.37       21.85     7.066e+08       20.97
7        20.28       21.97     6.507e+08       20.96
8       20.23*       22.12    6.235e+08*       21.00
9        20.32       22.41     6.857e+08       21.17
10       20.25       22.54     6.461e+08       21.18
--------------------------------------------------
```

**Table 22** Johansen cointegration rank test

```
rank_test = select_coint_rank(data, det_order = 0, k_ar_diff = lag_order.aic, method = "trace", signif = 0.05)
print(rank_test.rank)
print(rank_test.summary())
```

```
3
Johansen cointegration test using trace test statistic with 5% significance level
=====================================
r_0 r_1 test statistic critical value
-------------------------------------
  0   3          45.36          29.80
  1   3          22.16          15.49
  2   3          4.596          3.841
-------------------------------------
```

maximum-eigenvalue statistic assumes a given number of $r$ cointegrating relations under the null hypothesis and tests this against the alternative that there is $r + 1$ cointegrating equations.

```
rank2 = select_coint_rank(data, det_order = 0, k_ar_diff = lag_order.aic, method = 'maxeig', signif=0.05)
print(rank2.summary())
```

```
Johansen cointegration test using maximum eigenvalue test statistic with 5% significance level
=====================================
r_0 r_1 test statistic critical value
-------------------------------------
  0   1          23.19          21.13
  1   2          17.57          14.26
  2   3          4.596          3.841
-------------------------------------
```

The test statistic (23.19) > the critical value (21.13), suggesting that the null hypothesis of no cointegration ($r\_0 = 0$) can be rejected in favor of the alternative hypothesis that there is at least one cointegration vector. The test statistic (17.57) > the critical value (14.26), so the null hypothesis of having one cointegration vector ($r\_1 = 1$) can be rejected in favor of the alternative hypothesis that there are two cointegration vectors.

These results guide us in finding the number of cointegrating vectors to include in an ECM. The trace test suggests three cointegrating relationships. Table 23 displays the model fitting using VECM.

We have fitted a VECM model and now let us analyze the use case we discussed earlier: understanding long-run relationships, $\beta$ and $\alpha$ coefficients to understand the long-run equilibrium relationship between the variables.

The $\beta$ matrix is the cointegration vectors, which define the long-run equilibrium relationship between the variables (CPI, PCE, and DPI). This is essentially an identity matrix which suggests a weak or potentially non-existent long-run relationship between CPI, PCE, and DPI as captured by the model.

The $\alpha$ matrix is the adjustment coefficients, which show the speed at which the variables adjust back to equilibrium after a shock. In the row 1, CPI adjusts

**Table 23** VECM model fitting

```
model = VECM(data, k_ar_diff = lag_order.aic, coint_rank = rank_test.rank).fit()
print('beta')
print(model.beta)
print('_______________________________')
print('alpha')
print(model.alpha)
```

```
beta
[[ 1.00000000e+00  2.93048144e-15  2.06368193e-15]
 [ 1.55895685e-16  1.00000000e+00  1.46382161e-15]
 [-8.39083727e-17  5.10748131e-16  1.00000000e+00]]
_______________________________
alpha
[[ 0.00241328 -0.00087055  0.00071    ]
 [ 0.57364815 -0.26414727  0.2278808 ]
 [-0.07848754 -0.02589927  0.04074233]]
```

**Table 24** Ljung-Box test of residuals

```
residuals = model.resid.flatten()
ljungbox_test = acorr_ljungbox(residuals, return_df=True)
print(ljungbox_test)
```

```
      lb_stat    lb_pvalue
1   36.189241  1.790564e-09
2   36.220603  1.363943e-08
3   36.226275  6.707236e-08
4   36.231484  2.593130e-07
5   36.262009  8.418075e-07
6   36.268864  2.444004e-06
7   36.322803  6.300065e-06
8   36.402222  1.481928e-05
9   36.572547  3.136496e-05
10  36.581451  6.684548e-05
```

slightly to deviations from its own equilibrium (0.00241328) and weakly to deviations in PCE (−0.00087055) and DPI (0.00071). In row 2, PCE adjusts strongly to deviations from its own equilibrium (0.57364815), negatively to deviations in CPI (−0.26414727), and positively to deviations in DPI (0.2278808). In row 3, DPI adjusts negatively to deviations from its own equilibrium (−0.07848754) and weakly to deviations in CPI (−0.02589927) and DPI (0.04074233). The adjustment coefficients suggest that PCE is the most responsive to deviations from equilibrium, while CPI and DPI are relatively less responsive. PCE seems to be more influenced by short-term dynamics than long-run equilibrium relationships with the other variables.

Here, instead of visualization, here we opt for numerical measure to check the residuals using Ljung-Box test as displayed in Table 24.

The Ljung-Box test results show significant autocorrelations for all lags from 1 to 10. The *p*-values are small, suggesting that the null hypothesis of no autocorrelation can be rejected at these lags. The goal is to achieve a model where residuals are white noise, meaning no significant autocorrelation should be present. This significant autocorrelation implies that there may be patterns or dependencies in the data that have not been captured by the model, which could suggest the need for further model adjustments or the inclusion of additional terms to address this autocorrelation.

## 3 Key Takeaways

This chapter puts the complex dynamic models into practice by implementing Auto Regressive Vector Auto Regression (VAR) and Vector Error Correction Model (VECM). VAR and VECM are widely used in Econometrics for analyzing multivariate time series data, particularly when there are interdependencies and potential long-run relationships between the variables. They offer several advantages over traditional single-equation models. VAR models allow for the analysis of interdependencies between multiple variables by treating all variables as endogenous (determined within the system). This is crucial in economics, where many variables are interconnected and influence each other. VECM extends VAR by incorporating the cointegration relationship, which is the long-run equilibrium between the variables. This provides a more comprehensive understanding of the dynamic interactions between variables.

The manufacturer's authorised representative in the EU is Springer Nature Customer Service Centre GmbH, Europaplatz 3, 69115 Heidelberg, Germany. If you have any concerns regarding our products, please contact ProductSafety@springernature.com

Printed and bound by CPI Group (UK) Ltd, Croydon, CR0 4YY
01/10/2026
02225852-0013